DID YOU KNOW . . .

(1) That the Federal Reserve Act was concocted by a group of bankers and politicians at a secret meeting on Jekyll Island in 1911?

(2) That it established a government-sponsored but private banking system which controls interest and credit, issues our money, and therefore controls our economy?

(3) That in passing this Act, Congress surrendered one of its most vital constitutional mandates to a consortium of private financiers and thereby created an all-powerful fourth division in the federal government?

(4) That Woodrow Wilson was financed by the very financiers against whom he conducted a public crusade during his campaign for the presidency in 1912?

(5) That the Fed was "sold" to the American people as a permanent safeguard against depressions, panics, inflation, and deflation; but that Charles A. Lindbergh, father of the Lone Eagle, correctly foretold that the Fed would create panics and depressions "scientifically"?

(6) That both world wars — which made hundreds of billions for the financiers — could not have been financed without the Fed?

(7) That the Fed caused the panic of 1920-21, the stock market explosion of 1926-29, and the great collapse of 1929?

(8) That it caused the terrible depression to continue for ten years in order to liquidate the people and condition them for war?

(9) That the Fed can cause the stock market to go up or down by rigging interest rates and by buying bonds through its Open Market Committee?

(10) That the member banks of the Fed obtain government bonds for nothing and use them to lend up to ten times their value at high interest on good collateral?

(11) That foreign bankers now own about 18,000 tons of formerly American gold which, purchased at $35.00 an ounce, will yield them a profit of perhaps $100 billion, all tax-free?

(12) That the fiat money now being issued by the Fed is unconstitutional and could become as worthless as the continentals?

The Federal Reserve
and our
Manipulated Dollar

OTHER BOOKS BY MARTIN A. LARSON

MILTON AND SERVETUS
THE THEORY OF LOGICAL EXPRESSION
THE MODERNITY OF MILTON
THE PLASTER SAINT
THE RELIGION OF THE OCCIDENT
WANTON SINNER
CHURCH WEALTH AND BUSINESS INCOME
THE ESSENE HERITAGE
THE GREAT TAX FRAUD
THE CHURCHES: THEIR RICHES, REVENUES,
AND IMMUNITIES
PRAISE THE LORD FOR TAX EXEMPTION
WHEN PAROCHIAL SCHOOLS CLOSE
TAX REVOLT: U.S.A.!
TAX REBELLION, U.S.A.

The Federal Reserve and our Manipulated Dollar

With Comments
on the Causes
of Wars, Depressions,
Inflation and Poverty

BY

MARTIN A. LARSON

THE DEVIN-ADAIR COMPANY
OLD GREENWICH, CONN.

Library of Congress Catalog Card Number: 75-13346
ISBN: 0-8159-5513-8 (cloth)
0-8159-5514-6 (paper)

Printed in the United States of America

AUTHOR'S NOTE

An Emergency National Monetary Conference representing various patriotic groups, convened by Liberty Lobby, met in Los Angeles on March 17, 1973, and passed the following resolution, introduced by Mr. Willis A. Carto:

"Resolved that this body establish a Committee with Dr. Martin A. Larson as chairman, with authority to appoint his own members, to report back to this body . . . a concrete proposal . . . to deal with banking and money problems in a constructive way . . . when the recommendations of Dr. Larson and his Committee can be considered. . . ."

Pursuant to this resolution, a committee was established, seminars were conducted, monetary experts consulted, and various proposals were considered and debated; but there was no complete consensus concerning a solution for the monetary problem.

However, as the research continued, it evolved into something much more ambitious than a mere monetary proposal or even an attempt to influence legislation.

This book, which is the result, attempts to do what, so far as we know, has never been done before: namely (1) to give a complete, critical, but objective history of the Federal Reserve System; (2) present an analysis in depth of the monetary problems involved with fiat currency, the gold standard, inflation, deflation, depressions, and panics, and (3) summarize the solutions offered by the best-known authorities to meet and solve the impending American monetary crisis.

Our purpose is to produce an accurate portrayal of the forces which created and fostered the Federal Reserve System, who understood and who was deceived by it in the beginning, what were its esoteric provisions, and how it was sold to the American Congress and public.

An extensive literature consisting of pamphlets, books and articles dealing with monetary questions has been published; most of these, however, lack balance and objectivity, because they are passionately committed to a single point of view: either for or against redeemable currency. In this study, we present the most persuasive and convincing arguments available, pro and con, dealing with fiat currency on the one hand, and the gold or specie standard on the other. In summarizing the two positions, we have striven to reproduce with faithful objectivity the arguments of the various authors.

We have also attempted to explain the monetary problem in terms which the layman can readily understand. We hope that we have made an abstruse, complex, and controversial theme comprehensible, interesting, and fascinating, but even more to the point, that we may have aided the reader in arriving at conclusions of his own concerning these all-important questions.

Martin A. Larson

CONTENTS

INTRODUCTION

When our federal government passed the Federal Reserve Act and foisted the Sixteenth Amendment upon us in 1913, it forged the most subtle and efficient instruments for exploitation ever known in the United States. Since our Founding Fathers were well aware that it is the nature of every, and especially of a central, government to become a tyranny, they devised a strictly limited system, and enumerated the only powers it might exercise and the only functions for which it could spend money under the Constitution. For generations, clever men sought to overturn these strictures; but not until Woodrow Wilson prepared the way and Franklin Delano Roosevelt opened wide the floodgates, were they successful in creating the chains which now bind us in a modern species of servitude.

In creating the Fed, Congress conferred upon a consortium of private bankers a life-and-death power over our economy—which it has used and continues to employ to the infinite detriment of the American people. Between 1960 and 1972 it sold many billions of our gold to foreign central banks at $35 an ounce, even when its true value was 300% greater; and when it ceased such redemption of our currency in 1973, it laid the basis for the world-wide inflation which ensued. To make matters worse, it reduced the reserve requirements for the creation of checkbook money for most banks from 17 to 10 on November 9, 1972, which enabled them to increase their loans by almost 80%. This caused prices to rise everywhere, and unions obtained huge increases, which have now become frozen into all living costs. Then, in order to "cool" the economy, the Fed reversed itself and increased reserve requirements in April 1974 to 18, meaning that loans and checkbook money had to be reduced by more than

44%, a total of several hundred billion dollars. The result was the tightest money since the Thirties, accompanied by a fast deepening depression, for which, under existing conditions, no remedy was apparent, except lower interest rates and a flood of new printing-press money and expanded credit, which must result in a new and greater surge of inflation. The end result points toward economic chaos and national ruin, in which all of the so-called free world will be involved.

The Fed has placed the American nation under astronomical public and private debt, which has enabled the bankers to reap enormous profit by manipulating the dollar; and unless drastic reforms in our monetary system are instituted before it is too late, the ultimate result will be the tragedy that befell the Roman Empire after Diocletian and the horrors of the French and the Russian revolutions.

For all the tragedies which have befallen us and loom ahead, Congress must be held responsible; for it has created the bureaucracy which has grown in cost from $350 million in 1925 to more than $60 billion in 1975—or one-half of the money collected from the personal federal income tax. This levy purports to be progressive, but makes it possible for a person with an income of $100 million a year to pay less than does a day laborer. It has enacted a tax code that violates the Constitution in many of its sections; which is replete with loopholes for the rich and the favored; but which contains innumerable traps and snares which can be and are used to destroy individuals who, by their own efforts, seem likely to succeed. This tax extorts more than $160 billion, which causes all prices for goods and services to increase by at least 30%, with the result that our useful citizens pay this fantastic sum *three* times—first as producers and then, because the tax pyramids, doubly again as consumers.

The Internal Revenue Service is the one and only efficient federal agency, for it has developed a high degree of expertise in the fine art of picking the flesh from the bones of little taxpayers, and especially of small businessmen.

This same Congress has given us a ridiculous Social

Security System from which more than one-third of those who contribute to it will never receive anything; and even those who live long enough to retire are lucky if they ever enjoy an annuity equal to one-third of what a private pension fund would provide *for all contributors* at the same cost.

Our spendthrift Congress has paid $6 or $8 billion to hospitals with the result that their charges have increased 1,000%. It distributes $14 billion or more a year to education, with the result that per-student college costs have risen from $800 to $4,000. It disburses $20 billion a year for the support of children, most of them illegitimate, a charge so heavy upon self-supporting citizens, that they can scarcely afford children of their own. Since 1960, it has increased annual allocations for health and scientific research from nothing to about $6 billion—with no apparent benefit to the public—with the result that medical fees have increased about 2,000%. The Department of Agriculture spent $11.6 billion in fiscal 1972, which was more than half of what all the farmers in America earned. It makes deals with the Soviet Union and others—from which private manipulators, who are paid at once by the Treasury, make huge fortunes—for the sale of our wheat and other raw materials at extremely low prices, and for these the taxpayers may never be reimbursed at all.

Congress passed a war emergency rent-control law in 1942, which continued for eight years after the war ended and caused the confiscation of the properties owned by some seven million small investors, while bankers and war profiteers became rich beyond their wildest dreams. It has embroiled us in one completely unnecessary war after another since 1914, costing hundreds of thousands of lives and trillions of dollars. It has given away hundreds of billions of dollars to foreign nations, who repay us with hatred and contempt.

At least 50% and probably not less than 70% of the national budget should and could be deleted at once, because only a fraction of federal expenditures are for purposes enumerated and therefore permissible under ARTICLE I, Section 8, of the Constitution, which spells out the only functions that Congress may exercise; and ARTICLES IX and X of the Bill of Rights state categorically that all others reside in the people, or may be exercised only by the states.

How long will decent, self-supporting people continue to work when they must surrender the major portion of their earnings to bankers and to government for the support of parasites who live in idleness far better than those who support them? In 1972, according to the official figures published in the 1973 *Statistical Abstract,* all levels of government spent $369.4 billion; the private debt was $1,667 billion which, at 10%, required interest payments totalling $166 billion. Since the overall national income was $934.7 billion, we find that 57.2% of this went for taxes and interest—and in 1974–75 this ratio has risen to about 63%. In 1972, the net income of all farmers was $20.3 billion, an average of $7,089 per farm. At the same time, the average salary of all federal employees was $11,600, and the cost of his maintenance—including overhead—about $23,000.

The operation of our federal government, at least since 1913, calls to mind a great and happy warrior, a man of incisive wit, Henry L. Mencken, who, with George Jean Nathan, founded the *American Mercury* in 1924, and who often pilloried the Rooseveltian bureaucrats with his flashing sarcasm and irony. In an article published in this periodical in March, 1936, Mencken wrote: "On one point only did the Roosevelt bureaucrats and brain trusters appear to agree, and that was on the point that any man who worked hard at some useful task, husbanded his money prudently, and tried to provide some security for his old age and some heritage for his children, was a low and unmitigated scoundrel. . . . The one characteristic that really shines forth from all of them is . . . their implacable hatred of every man who is able to earn an honest and decent living in the world, and has industry enough in his bones to want to do it, and beyond that asks only to be left alone. This man has been the special target of their piratical forays and objurgations ever since Dr. Roosevelt dragged them out of their natural obscurity and set them in places of power. . . . One and all, these are shabby fellows, toters of inferiority complexes, natural zeroes, and one and all they hate their betters. . . ."

Again and again in this work, we return to Thomas Jefferson, whose genius remains forever a reliable guiding light. Had it been obeyed, this nation would today be solvent and powerful beyond comparison; it would have been without debt, and our people would be by far the most prosperous and independent in the world. Jefferson spoke often of the necessity for maintaining a frugal and limited general government, an ideal which he set forth succinctly in a letter to Albert Gallatin, dated June 17, 1812: "Our tenet ever was . . . that Congress had not unlimited power to provide for the general welfare, but were restrained to those specifically enumerated; and that, as it was never meant that they should provide for the welfare but by the exercise of enumerated powers, so it would not have been meant that they should raise money for purposes which the enumeration did not place under their action; consequently, that the specification of powers is a limitation of the purposes for which they may raise money."

Oh, for some Jeffersonian statesmanship today!

Among the more reprehensible acts committed by our central government was and remains the establishment of the Federal Reserve System—which is the subject of the present study and which has taken so many billions from our people that the finite mind simply cannot comprehend the swindle; one who understands it fully is likely to become inarticulate with rage, since no vocabulary contains expletives of sufficient force to describe its operations in terms at once adequate and comprehensible.

Any person with an elementary understanding of monetary economics must know that the basic causes of inflation are government deficit spending and the issuance of huge quantities of fiat money by the Federal Reserve System. Yet Congress can see no remedy except higher spending, greater deficits, and more fiat money. It also permits the Fed to increase interest rates, which create inflation and depression at once; and it seems intent on increasing taxes, which will divert buying power from producers to parasites and therefore create more inflation.

If Congress really wanted to stop inflation, it would start by cutting the federal budget by at least $100 billion and getting rid of not less than one million bureaucrats.

We believe the Fed in 1974 drove interest rates to dizzy heights not merely to provide enormous profits for the bankers, but also to depress stock prices to the lowest level—based on earning power—in history. Securities that paid 3 or 4 percent in the early Sixties sold at prices which produced from 12 to 15 percent in 1974. This enabled foreign corporations, governments, and central banks which held billions of our currency, but no longer could buy American gold at $35 an ounce, to purchase controlling interest in American corporations at ridiculously low prices; and on their income from such investments, they will be exempt from both taxation and disclosure under sections 892 and 895 of the Internal Revenue Code.

This should tell us who really is in control of the United States.

And so we observe here a phenomenon reminding us of George Orwell's *Animal Farm,* where the horses (the taxpayers) are worked into exhaustion, the swine (the parasites) live in idleness and luxury, and the wolf dogs (the government and the exploiters) exercise their despotic tyranny. For the great majority—those who produce the wealth and support all the profligate activities of the state—there is only persecution and extortion; for bureaucracts, for foreign governments, for every conceivable kind of waste, for the rich who are virtually exempt from taxation, and for a myriad of unconstitutional expenditures, there is such lavish generosity that it staggers the imagination. It seems as if the federal government is consumed with hatred for the people who support it, and afire with tender love for those who do nothing but consume and destroy.

The day foreseen by Jefferson has arrived in which those who pay the taxes are so overwhelmed with burdens that they are unable to bring their mismanagers to account and are therefore happy to sell themselves into the service of the tyrants in order to bind the chains of slavery securely upon their fellow men.

What else can we expect when our people spend their leisure time watching the boob-tube and listening to the babble of a thousand contradictory and irrational voices?

Sometimes we are asked whether this country, in spite of everything, is nevertheless not better than most others; does it not confer more freedom and economic opportunity than is found elsewhere? The answer to this is Yes—and the reason is that our nation was founded upon the finest Constitution ever devised by the mind of man: but should we, therefore, seek to imitate the worst tyrannies in the world until we become wholly indistinguishable from them? Should we gradually or rapidly permit our heritage to be destroyed simply because some vestiges thereof still remain?

Yes, the United States is still better than most other countries; but much of what our Founding Fathers gave us has been lost and the termites are busy day and night trying to eradicate what remains.

Eternal vigilance is the price of liberty, and never was this more true than it is today.

A Free Market in Gold At Last!

After more than forty years, it is possible that a return to the gold standard in the United States may not be as far distant as most people believe. For years, leading monetary experts—von Mises, Hazlitt, Bakewell, Groseclose, Sennholz, Browne, The American Institute for Economic Research, and many others—have advocated an American free market in gold as the first step necessary for such restoration.

On August 13, 1974, President Gerald Ford signed a bill which allocated $1.5 billion to the International Development Association and included an amendment establishing a free gold market in the United States not later than December 31, 1974.

As a result of this, thousands of Americans will no doubt store smaller or larger quantities of the metal as a hedge against inflation, and since it will be available in bars, prepared by private dealers, and in the coins of various countries, we believe that these will come into wide use to effect exchanges between individuals. When this occurs, we will have a situation similar to what existed after 1865 when gold coins circulated side by side with greenbacks, but with a much higher purchasing power, until the latter were made fully redeemable in 1879 under the Resumption Act of 1875.

The gold bars or coins available in 1975 and afterward will, of course, not be legal tender; but their value will be universal and they will have a profound influence upon the monetary system operated by the Fed.

The actual value of Federal Reserve notes will thus be determined by their purchasing power in relation to gold.

The next step would be for the United States Treasury to mint legal tender coins containing a definite amount and quality of gold which, under its authority, Congress would declare to constitute our official unit of exchange that would then constitute the full gold standard. We consider such a development entirely possible in the foreseeable future.

PART ONE

AMERICAN MONETARY HISTORY

from
1775 to 1973

THE IMPORTANCE
OF SOUND MONEY

Baron Meyer Amschel Rothschild is said to have declared: "Permit me to control the money of a nation, and I care not who makes its laws." Sir Josiah Stamp, President of the Bank of England, is quoted as saying: "If you want to remain the slaves of the bankers, and pay the costs of your own slavery, let them continue to create money and control the nation's credit."

In 1920, eight or nine years before he became the leading proponent of monetary expansion by fiat, John Maynard Keynes, speaking then with prophetic insight, stated: "Lenin is said to have declared that the best way to destroy the capitalist system was to debauch the currency. . . . Lenin was certainly right. There is no subtler, no surer means of overturning the existing basis of society. . . . The process engages all the hidden forces of economic law on the side of destruction, and does it in a manner which not one man in a million can diagnose. . . . The governments of Europe . . . are fast rendering impossible a continuance of the social and economic order of the 19th century."[1]

CHAPTER I

Pre-Civil War Money and Banking

PRE-CONSTITUTIONAL CURRENCY

One of the principal causes of our colonial revolt was the fact that the English crown denied Americans the right to issue their own currency[2] which made free trade impossible and resulted in enormous economic losses.

However, during the Revolution and in some cases prior to it, the colonies issued their own currencies; those guaranteed by taxation and redeemable in specie suffered no diminution in value;[3] others depreciated rapidly and most of them, in time, became virtually worthless. By 1789, the issues of individual colonies totalled about $200 million.[4]

When the war started, the Colonial Congress began printing bills known as "continentals." Between June 23, 1775, and November 29, 1779, there were thirty-three such issues totalling $200 million. The first four, comprising $14 million, circulated at par for slightly more than a year; but, since the Congress had no power to tax, and since the currency was not redeemable in specie, it soon declined in value. With the fifth issue of $5 million on August 20, 1777, its descent began; 2 and

2/3rds of the new dollars were required to obtain one of silver. Thereafter they fell precipitously, and when an issue of $10,000,140 appeared in November, 1779, the rate of exchange was 38.5 to 1. The total exchange value of the continentals in terms of specie at the time of emission was $36,367,719.63.[5]

In March, 1780, the Congress offered to exchange all its currency for new bills redeemable in specie at the rate of 40 to 1—which would reduce the then outstanding debt to $5 million and constitute a repudiation of more than $31 million. However, since the people had very little confidence in the currency thus offered, few continentals were brought in, and they continued to circulate and to depreciate even more rapidly than before. By the end of 1780, the exchange rate was 75 to 1; soon it was 1,000 and finally 5,000 to 1.[6]

THE REDEMPTION OF THE CONTINENTALS

During the years immediately preceding 1788, when the new Constitution was ratified, there was great uncertainty concerning the fate of colonial money. Thomas Jefferson estimated that the currency issued by the individual colonies represented an original value of $38,300,000;[7] the total obligations that the new government might rightfully be called upon to assume, incuding that of the states, should, therefore, not exceed $75 million.[8]

Virtually all of this currency had originally been paid either to the soldiers or to those who furnished supplies to the colonial troops. By 1788, however, most of it had been purchased for almost nothing by speculators, including some who had confidential information that the new Constitution would provide redemption in specie. Neither Jefferson nor Alexander Hamilton, however, were among those so enriched.

HAMILTON, JEFFERSON, AND THE
FIRST UNITED STATES BANK

Soon after the first election, which occurred in 1788, President Washington appointed Hamilton to be Secretary of the

Treasury, whose plan it was to redeem all colonial currency at face value and thus create a national obligation of $400 million; which, as Jefferson pointed out, would be 30 guineas per capita and greater in proportion than the staggering public debt of Great Britain.[9] In the powerful position he occupied, Hamilton was successful in establishing the privately owned First United States Bank, with power to issue legal tender notes based on government bonds as collateral. It was also his plan, as Jefferson charged, to increase the debt progressively and to create an enormous federal bureaucracy.

To all this, Jefferson was unalterably opposed. He wanted only a minimum, honest debt which should be liquidated as quickly as possible. He was bitterly opposed to the establishment of a federally chartered, but privately owned and controlled, bank of issue. He placed his confidence, not in the rich, but in the people, who, he said, "are our dependence for continued freedom. And to preserve their independence, we must not let our rulers load us with perpetual debt."[10]

Although Washington was entirely loyal to his country, he was, as Jefferson noted, an aristocrat by instinct who had no "firm confidence in the durability of our government."[11] Hamilton, the clear-thinking New York banker, exercised great intellectual influence over the President; as Secretary of the Treasury, he was in charge of finances and perpetually in conflict with Jefferson, who was Secretary of State.[12]

On February 15, 1791, in an attempt to defeat Hamilton's machinations, Jefferson published an article entitled *Against the Constitutionality of a National Bank,*[13] in which he declared that it would form private subscribers into a corporation with power to issue currency and control federal finances. Such an institution, he declared, would be contrary to the Constitution because it would have "the sole and exclusive right of banking under the national authority"; because it would be given the power to make laws superior to those of the States; and because "The incorporation of a bank, and the powers assumed by this bill, have not . . . been delegated . . . by the Constitution." Jefferson was outraged because the bill provided also that the government would lend the bank "two millions, and then borrow them back, . . . which will be a payment [a gift], and not a loan, call it by what name you please."

In spite of Jefferson's opposition, the First United States Bank, with a 20-year charter, was established in 1791. In due course, he became so discouraged and frustrated with what was happening in Washington, that he resigned his post in 1793, denouncing his Federalist enemies as monocrats.[14] He retired to Monticello, where he devoted his energies to writing on agriculture and to the creation of a free press and the Jeffersonian clubs which, in time, were to create the climate which made possible the election of Jefferson to the presidency.

In the meantime, Hamilton led federal troops into Pennsylvania to crush the "Whiskey Rebellion"; he almost succeeded in fomenting a war with France through the notorious XYZ Papers; he attempted to raise an army to colonize South America; he instigated the passage of the Alien and Sedition Act, under which Jeffersonian presses were destroyed and the editors thrown into prison; and he was able to increase the national debt in peacetime from $75,463,000 to $83,038,000.

President James Madison—who agreed entirely with Jefferson—permitted the First United States Bank to die when its charter expired in 1811.

When the establishment of the Second United States Bank was under consideration in 1815, Jefferson wrote to Gallatin that a continuation of the recent war would "have upset our government . . ." because "our money, the nerve of war . . ." was under the control of "our bitterest enemies. . . ."[15]

In 1816, Jefferson wrote to Sam Kercheval: "We must make our election between *economy and liberty, or profusion and servitude.* If we run into such debts as that we must be taxed in our meat and in our drink, in our necessities and our comforts, in our labors and our amusements, for our callings and our creeds . . . our people . . . must come to labor sixteen hours in the twenty-four, give our earnings of fifteen of these to the government . . . have no time to think, no means of calling our mis-managers to account; but be glad to obtain sustenance by hiring ourselves out to rivet their chains on the necks of our fellow-sufferers. . . . And this is the tendency of all human governments . . . till the bulk of society is reduced to be mere automatons of misery. . . . And the forehorse of this frightful team is public debt. Taxation follows that, and in its train wretchedness and oppression."[16]

During the same year, Jefferson wrote to John Taylor: "I believe that banking institutions are more dangerous to our liberties than standing armies. Already they have raised up a money aristocracy that has set the Government at defiance. The issuing power should be taken from the banks and restored to the Government, to whom it properly belongs."[17]

Jefferson emphasized repeatedly that no private bank—whether chartered by the federal or a state government—should *ever* be permitted to issue currency or control credit; for, once intrusted with such power, they become superior to the nation itself.

THE FIRST AMERICAN DOLLAR

Although Hamilton suggested a bimetallic currency in 1791, Congress rejected his proposal when it passed the Coinage Act of 1792, which established a dollar consisting of 371.25 grains of pure and 416 grains of standard silver. This continued to be the unit of currency—the dollar—until 1873, when it was replaced by one consisting of 25.8 grains of standard gold.

In 1791, when Hamilton reported that the value of gold was fifteen to one as compared to silver, Congress adopted this ratio and authorized coinage on that basis. However, it must be understood that gold coins did not at that time constitute official dollars or represent a legal standard of value.

What occurred between 1792 and 1834 demonstrates the impracticality of a bimetallic standard; for during this period, gold disappeared from the American scene, because the true ratio of value was not 15 but rather 16 to 1. The result was that American gold was exported to where it could be sold at a profit of about 6 percent.

JACKSON AND THE SECOND
UNITED STATES BANK

When the charter of the First United States Bank expired in 1811, Madison's refusal to renew it was based on his conviction that it was unconstitutional and that it was operated for the aggrandizement of private, predatory interests. However, the War of 1812–14 plunged the nation into heavy debt and created drastic inflation. For its bonds, totalling $80 million, floated between 1812 and 1816, the government received only $34 million of specie from those moneylenders, whom Jefferson condemned so bitterly. The Federal debt, therefore, increased from $45 to $127 million, all of which had to be repaid in hard money. In addition to interest, the money creators and lenders made a profit of almost 150 percent out of the war.

After the demise of the First United States Bank, the banking business passed wholly into the hands of state-chartered corporations, which increased in number from 58 to 246, and their note issues from $50 to $100 million in five years—an inflation so extreme that it compelled all but the strongest Eastern houses to suspend payments in specie.[18]

As a result, the establishment of the Second United States Bank was forced upon Madison and the Jeffersonian Republicans in 1816. This institution which, like the First United States Bank also had a 20-year charter, was not only controlled by private interests, but operated for their financial aggrandizement and the perpetuation of their political power.

When Andrew Jackson became president in 1828, he vowed that he would destroy this bank, which he did, in due course, partly by withdrawing government deposits from it and eventually in vetoing—shortly after his re-election in 1832—a bill passed by Congress to extend its life. Since its notes were legal tender throughout the nation, they drove the currency of the state-chartered institutions out of circulation, thus creating great losses to, and bitter hostility among, local bankers and their business allies.

Daniel Webster received large retainers from the Bank in

return for his political support; and the Bank contracted credit and called loans at will in order to destroy its political opponents. When Jackson mounted his fierce attack upon the Second United States Bank, he enjoyed the overwhelming support of the common people; and when he won re-election in 1832 by a landslide, he returned to the White House like a conquering Roman warrior.

Under Jackson, not only was the national debt completely liquidated: the federal government accumulated the only surplus it has ever had during its history. In fact, it was able to distribute more than $35 million among the states, which they used for the construction of a great variety of public works.

THE COINAGE ACT OF 1834

In 1834, Congress passed a coinage act designed to recover the gold that had fled this country and to encourage its domestic extraction; this provided for gold dollars with a ratio to silver of 16 to 1 and containing 25.8 grains of standard gold, nine-tenths fine, instead of the 27 which had constituted the gold dollar since 1791.

STATE-CHARTERED BANKS PRECEDING THE CIVIL WAR

After the Second United States Bank expired in 1836, there was no central bank of issue for almost eighty years. There were, indeed, serious difficulties under a monetary system which consisted entirely of state-chartered institutions—of which there were about 200 in 1816, but which proliferated after 1836 so rapidly that they numbered 1,600 in 1860, all of which emitted one or more kinds of circulating currency, totalling $202 million, based on specie reserves of about $87 million. With every recession or depression, many of these "wildcat banks" went out of business, with virtually total losses to their note holders and depositors alike: one with $580,000 of circulating notes had only $86.46 in specie on hand for redemption.[19]

Then, as now, bankers and politicians ignored or sidestepped ARTICLE I, Section 8, Paragraph 5 of the Constitution, which states that Congress [only] shall have power "To coin Money, regulate the value thereof, and of foreign Coin. . . ." as well as Section 10 of the same Article, which declares that "No State shall . . . make any Thing but gold and silver Coin a Tender in Payment of Debts. . . ."

No wonder, then, that millions of farmers, mechanics, tradesmen, small manufacturers, and businessmen in general, placed their trust only in coin of standard weight and fineness, stamped with the insignia of the United States Treasury. They feared a monopolistic private bank, even when its currency was redeemable in specie, for they knew it operated for the aggrandizement of rich owners and that it had the power to destroy small and independent enterprise almost at will. Yet they were no less suspicious of a multitude of state-chartered banks of issue because of their instability, their manipulations, their sheer and outright fraud. Finally, they had no confidence in any kind of fiat currency issued by the government, for they had no faith in the promises of politicians: they knew only too well what had happened to the continentals and the French assignats.

The schemes of devious men to dispossess the people of their savings and their property were then, as now, wonderful for their variety and ingenuity; for even though the Constitution forbade the states from issuing money or emitting bills of credit designed to circulate as currency, various attempts, some partially successful, were made to circumvent even this basic law.[20]

IN SEARCH OF A SOUND MONETARY SYSTEM

The two United States Banks had proved quite conclusively that Jefferson was correct in his opposition to such privately owned monopolies; nevertheless, the American monetary experience between 1836 and 1860 demonstrated with equal conclusiveness that it is not in the public interest to permit a large number of small, private banks to issue their own currency; for, during this period, there were in circulation no less than 7,000 different kinds of such paper, not to mention 5,000 others which were completely fraudulent.[21]

If history has any one lesson of greater significance than any other in the field of monetary policy, we think it is this: That we must have a central authority, operated by the federal government itself, which shall have the sole power to issue currency and regulate the value thereof. No other money can be in conformity with the Constitution and at the same time meet the complex needs of the American economy.

Citations

1. Keynes, *The Economic Consequences of the Peace* 235–37
2. Beard, *The Rise of American Civilization* Vol. I 201–2
3. *Basic Writings of Thomas Jefferson*, "Answers to Neusnier" 214
4. *Ib.* 224
5. *Ib.* 223
6. *Ib.* 215–16
7. *Ib.* 205
8. *Ib.* 224
9. *Ib.* 209
10. *Ib.* 749, Letter to Sam Kercheval, July 12, 1816
11. *Ib.* 724, Letter to Walter James, Jan. 2, 1814
12. *Ib.* 189–93, Letter to Destutt De Tracy, Jan. 26, 1811
13. *Ib.* 311–15
14. *Ib.* 652, Letter to Levi Lincoln, July 11, 1801
15. *The Writings of Thomas Jefferson*, Library Edition, Vol. XIV 356
16. *Basic Writings, op. cit.* 749–50
17. *The Writings of Thomas Jefferson*, Ford Edition, Vol. VI 208
18. Beard, *op. cit.* I 429–30
19. *Ib.* 684
20. *Ib.* 686 ff.
21. *Ib.* II 109

CHAPTER II

The Background of the Federal Reserve Act

THE LINCOLN GREENBACKS

After decades of monetary confusion, the Republicans came to political power in 1861; and, as it turned out, the Civil War, because of its financial strain, supplied not only the battleground to settle the political and economic issues which divided the North from the South, but also the monetary differences which arrayed the state-chartered banks and the federally established institutions against each other. Since the War required enormous expenditures, Lincoln persuaded Congress to authorize the issuance of a national currency known as "greenbacks," of which there were three issues in 1862 and 1863, each of $150,000,000. However, since these were not redeemable in specie and could not be used to pay duties, taxes, or the interest on the national debt, they declined rapidly in value: citizens were asked to receive as legal tender that which the issuing authority itself refused. By 1865, three greenback dollars exchanged for one of silver. In 1866, Congress enacted a bill under which $10 million of the greenbacks were retired at once and another $4 million each month until 1868, leaving $346,681,000 in circulation. In 1879, pursuant to the Resumption Act of 1875, they were made full legal tender, redeemable in gold. In the meantime, speculators who had obtained them for 40 cents or less on the dollar, made huge fortunes at the expense of those who had fought and died in combat or furnished supplies to the Union armies.

THE TRIUMPH OF THE BANKERS

The expenditure of the federal government during the five years 1862–66 inclusive, totalled $3,878,189,827;[1] and in spite of heavy taxation and the issuance of the fiat greenbacks, the debt rose to what was then an astronomical level. And this provided the powerful Eastern money men with precisely the situation they desired.

In order to obtain the support of the many hundreds of state-chartered banks, the Seaboard financiers prepared and circulated what was known as *The Hazard Circular* in 1862, which declared: "The great debt that capitalists will see to it is made out of the war, must be used as a means to control the volume of money. To accomplish this, the bonds must be used as a banking basis. We are now waiting for the Secretary of the Treasury to make this recommendation to Congress. It will not do to allow the greenback, as it is called, to circulate as money any length of time, as we cannot control that. But we can control the bonds and through them the bank issues."[2]

Propaganda of this kind, the monetary confusion which had existed so long, and the financial stress of the war combined to provide Salmon P. Chase, who became Secretary of the Treasury in 1861, with the impetus necessary to accomplish the objectives of those he represented. Like Wilson and Roosevelt of a later generation, he held the Jeffersonian Republicans in supreme contempt. Although he failed to establish a national banking system in 1861, he persuaded Congress to float interest-bearing bonds, which increased from $64,844,000 in 1861, to $2,755,764,000 in 1866.[3]

This, however, was not his principal achievement: for, with the powerful support of the banking fraternity, he was able to force through Congress the National Banking Act of 1863, which authorized the formation of local, private banking associations under federal authority, and empowered them to emit notes on the basis of United States bonds up to 90% of their par values. The banks, which purchased such government securities with 35-cent greenbacks valued at par, not only collected 7% interest upon them, but also used them for the issuance of currency and the placement of loans at heavy interest upon mortgaged property.

Having thus succeeded in their principal objective, the Party of Sound Money completed its program in 1865 by persuading Congress to enact a law which imposed a tax of 10% on all state bank notes, thus wiping them out of existence at a single stroke.[4]

The National Banking Act of 1863 thus concentrated national economic control in the hands of powerful Eastern bankers, who, acting in phalanx, as Jefferson had foreseen, now had unrestrained power to extend or contract credit; to induce inflation or deflation; create depression or prosperity; and promote either unemployment or a shortage of labor.

THE GOLD DOLLAR: EXPANSION AND PROSPERITY

As a whole, however, the thirty-five years following the Civil War saw constant expansion, based in large part upon a stable dollar, which continued officially as a coin of 371.25 grains of pure silver until 1873, when, after fierce debate, it was, as we have noted, replaced by a gold dollar of 25.8 grains of standard metal. However, since the greenbacks continued to circulate along with coin and national bank notes, the Treasury did not redeem other currency in gold until 1879, when the Resumption Act of 1875 became effective. From then until 1933, the country was on a full gold standard; currency could be exchanged at any bank for gold; the prices of all other commodities were measured by its value. The decline in the general price level between 1880 and 1895 was due primarily to more efficient methods of industrial production; the increase which occurred between 1895 and 1914 was due in part to the discovery of great amounts of new gold; in part, to improved methods of processing and refining, and in part to the overexpansion of credit by the banks.

PANICS AND CONFISCATION

However, there were recurring periods of very great distress. Since the National Banking Act had conferred upon the federally chartered associations of private banks the power to control the finances and the credit of the nation, they manipulated one devastating débacle after another, each calculated to confiscate the savings of farmers, tradesmen, individual manufacturers, and thrifty workers, who had pledged their property in return for bank-created credit. The worst of these catastrophes occurred in 1873, 1893, and 1907. Clever propagandists, however, not only deflected the blame for these from the financiers, but used them to further their own interests by demanding a more elastic and centralized monetary system, one controlled by a great central private bank of issue, which would arrogate to itself far greater powers and profits than were possible under the National Banking Act of 1863.

We should note, however, that the currency created by this Act became more and more restrictive with the passage of time because, as the national debt was reduced from $2.76 to $1.14 billion between 1866 and 1906,[5] the government bonds no longer constituted a sufficient reserve to supply the monetary needs of a rapidly expanding economy. When, therefore, a large number of depositors, fearing the solvency of the banks, demanded their money, the currency was not available and the banks simply closed their doors.

There were, as we have indicated, periods of inflation, caused, to a considerable extent at least, by the undue expansion of credit; these were terminated by panics, accompanied by the withdrawal of credit and the consequent foreclosures, unemployment, and temporary destruction of property values. During the periods of easy money, real estate prices rose, prosperity abounded, and every kind of business borrowed money to improve its facilities and cash in on the economic growth; during the subsequent deflation, the banks called their loans, money became scarce, property values declined, and those who owed money lost the possessions they had pledged.

THE PANIC OF 1893 AND THE INCOME TAX

After the terrible panic of 1893, a Democratic-Populist Congress passed the Income Tax Act of 1894. But, since this exempted incomes of less than $4,000, it was assailed as a socialist-communist conspiracy against property and the rewards of thrift. It did not take the Supreme Court long to declare it unconstitutional—which it undoubtedly was.

At the Democratic convention of 1896 in Chicago, William Jennings Bryan made his celebrated Cross-of-Gold speech, in which he condemned the Money Trust, proposed a bimetallic currency, and advocated the unlimited free coinage of silver at a ratio of 16 to 1.* "Congress," declared the platform which he dictated, "has the power to coin and issue money . . . we demand that all paper which is made legal tender . . . shall be issued by the government of the United States and shall be redeemable in coin"[6]—which in this case meant silver without restriction. The Republican answer to this was the Gold Standard Act of March 14, 1900, which prescribed a Treasury gold reserve of $150,000,000 for the redemption of other currency. Actually, the new and plentiful supplies of gold guaranteed a cheaper medium of exchange and blunted the arguments of the Free Silverites.

Following 1894, there was a prolonged period of prosperity, followed, in turn, by the panic of 1907, in which the bankers reaped another great harvest and because of which

---

*The bullion or commodity value of silver in the minted dollar in 1896 was 52.257 cents, or about 30 to 1 in terms of gold (1905 *SA* 564).

Congress was persuaded to pass the Aldrich-Vreeland Emergency Currency Act of May 30, 1908, which conferred upon private bankers even greater advantages than were given them by either the First or the Second United States Bank, or by the National Banking Act of 1863.

THE ALDRICH-VREELAND EMERGENCY CURRENCY ACT

Under the Aldrich-Vreeland Act, any ten national banks having equity funds of at least $5 million could organize themselves into an association with power of note issue, using as collateral state, municipal, or corporation bonds, as well as commercial paper. This privilege, however, was reserved for the largest banks only, which already had note issues secured by federal bonds at least equal to 40% of their capital. The amount of additional notes was limited to 75% of the cash value of commercial paper and to 90% of state and municipal bonds held as reserves. The Secretary of the Treasury could determine the conditions under which additional notes might be emitted. However, only twenty-one currency associations were formed between 1908 and 1913; and, because of a tax of 10% imposed on notes not based on federal bonds, no new currency was issued.[7]

Charles A. Lindbergh, Sr., describes the hectic events preceding the panic of 1907 and the enactment of the Aldrich-Vreeland Bill.* He states (1) that between 1896 and 1906, billions of watered stocks, bonds, and other securities had been issued by banks and other private interests; (2) that this had triggered an enormous inflation; (3) that the ensuing panic was

---

*Edward B. Vreeland was a congressman and banker from New York. It is interesting to note that Nelson Aldrich was a grandfather of the present generation of Rockefellers and the namesake of the Vice-President nominated for that position by President Gerald Ford. It is even more significant that the international consortium of financiers known as the Bilderbergers, which meet annually in profound secrecy to determine the destiny of the western world, is a creature of the Rockefeller-Rothschild alliance and that it held its third meeting on St. Simon's Island, only a short distance from Jekyll Island off the coast of Georgia.

engineered by the Money Trust for the purpose of destroying unaffiliated banks and to frighten the public into accepting the Aldrich-Vreeland Bill, and (4) that it conferred upon the "Money Trust the privilege of securing . . . government currency on their watered bonds and securities."[8]

Congressman Ollie M. James declared that the law gave the Secretary of the Treasury power to issue $500 million of federal notes for the benefit of the banks; that it provided for the creation of asset currency,* and that "under the Constitution . . . we have no more right to farm out to national banks . . . the right to issue money than we have to give them the power to levy taxes or declare war."[9]

Under the Aldrich-Vreeland Act, the government did indeed supply the private banks with currency free of charge; and, in addition, paid them interest on securities upon which their note circulation was based.[10] Lindbergh complained bitterly that "When the Aldrich-Vreeland Emergency Currency Bill was sprung upon the House . . . debate was limited to three hours . . ." and that members were permitted to see it only if they agreed in advance to support it.[11] As resentment against the "Money Trust" mounted in Congress during the succeeding period, a well-defined movement developed in support of legislation calling for government notes, similar to the Lincoln greenbacks.[12] And it soon became obvious that the Aldrich-Vreeland Act could not be extended beyond its 1914 date of expiration.

By 1907, the financial community no longer condemned income taxation as a Socialist conspiracy because it now understood that to accomplish its ultimate objective, it must have (1) a privately controlled bank of issue, which would regulate credit and the money supply; (2) a huge public debt, on which to base its currency, and (3) an unrestricted income tax to pay the interest on that debt.

Between 1894 and 1907, therefore, the political climate in

---

*That is, one based on private debts, securities, or trade acceptances (i.e., promissory notes from one businessman to another).

reference to a personal federal income tax underwent a radical transformation. Thus it was that in 1908, Congress passed the resolution to submit the Sixteenth Amendment to the states for ratification, which occurred in 1913. No limitations were imposed on the power to tax, since its promoters declared with pontifical solemnity that, except in time of war, rates would never exceed a range of from 1 to 6%; that only large, unearned incomes would be taxed at all; and that no portion of any income necessary to maintain a decent, contemporary living standard would ever be subject to levy. Naive liberals viewed the Amendment as a signal victory for the people, since it purported to be a progressive exaction upon the rich; we can, however, imagine how the latter were grinning and dancing in glee as their experts began devising the exemptions, exclusions, allowances, and deductions destined to place their incomes and their wealth in sacred places beyond the reach of the tax collector.

TABLE ONE demonstrates how the national debt and the federal income taxes have grown since 1916. (*see p. 28*)

THE DRIVE FOR A CENTRAL BANK OF ISSUE

With the ratification of the Sixteenth Amendment, the bankers had won their first great victory. The second, the Federal Reserve Act, was considerably more difficult.

Whether the Federal Reserve Act was the result of a long and carefully prepared conspiracy is quite irrelevant. What we do know is that the financiers yearned for a central bank of issue similar to the Bank of England or the Reichsbank of Germany, a federally established, but privately controlled, institution, whose notes would be legal tender and obligations of the government, with commercial paper or government securities as reserve-collateral, to be used for the creation of credit. Their conspiracy may be said to have consisted in advocating for the United States what was already in operation across the sea—a system which Jefferson and Jackson were determined should never exist on these shores. Since the Aldrich-Vreeland Act had

TABLE ONE
THE U. S. NATIONAL DEBT AND THE FEDERAL INCOME TAX[13]
(Debts and total taxes in millions of dollars)

(Note how the debt, the total personal income and average taxes have increased, especially since 1934 and particularly during the Second World War and after 1965, and how they are expected to increase.)

(Note that the federal government levies also a corporation income tax, which grew from $57 million in 1916 to $43 billion in 1974. Thus from personal and corporation income taxes, the federal government extorted about $161 billion. Note that collections from personal incomes more than tripled between 1960 and 1974.)

Year	Debt	Per Capita	Personal Tax	Average Tax	Av. Tax Per Taxable Return	Corp. Income Tax	Personal Per Capita Tax
1916	$1,225	$12.02	$175	$476		$57	$1.68
1919	25,482	242.54	1,270	468			12.10
1920	24,299	228.23	1,075	195			10.24
1925	20,516	177.12	735	294		916	6.50
1930	16,185	131.51	477	234		1,263	3.91
1935	28,701	225.55	657	311		577	517
1940	42,968	325.62	1,496	200		2,549	11.42
1945	258,682	1,852.74	17,225	403		10,795	122.12
1950	257,400	1,696.68	18,375	481		14,317	146.89
1955	274,400	1,660.38	29,614	512	$663	21,741	180.58
1960	286,300	1,585.00	39,464	651	822	21,806	221.72
1965	317,300	1,631.00	48,800	729	988	26,100	254.17
1970	370,900	1,803.00	90,400	1,134	1,593	35,000	445.32
1972	465,000	2,214.00	99,400	1,299	1,785	34,900	482.53
1974	486,400	2,316.20	118,000	1,475	1,903	43,000	561.91
1976	605,900,	2,858.00	108,300			47,700	501.40*
1978	656,900	3,055.35	173,500			55,300	806.98**

*Statistics for 1976 from *1976 Budget of U.S. Government*, 367
**Projection for 1978 from *1976 U.S. Budget in Brief*, 15-16

been consigned to oblivion, it was vitally important for Wall Street that an acceptable replacement be prepared.

THE NATIONAL MONETARY COMMISSION*

A provision of the Aldrich-Vreeland Act had created a National Monetary Commission to study government finances and banking.[14] Under the leadership of Senator Aldrich, this body, consisting of sixteen senators and representatives, toured Europe during 1909 and 1910 at a cost of $300,000 to the taxpayers, where they were wined and dined until they reached a consensus concerning the kind of banking system they would like for the United States.[15] Actually, very few members of the Commission knew anything at all about banking, and were invited to go on this sight-seeing vacation as window dressing for the financiers who had arranged it, and who intended to use them for their own ulterior purposes.

Although the Aldrich-Vreeland Act reflected the desires of the Wall Street financiers more fully than did the National Banking Act of 1863, it still did not satisfy their vaulting ambitions: in the first place, its monetary provisions were not sufficiently elastic; furthermore, it was due to expire in 1914, and the opposition to it in Congress was such that its renewal was admittedly impossible.

THE SAFARI TO JEKYLL ISLAND

Thus it was that on the 22nd of November, 1910, a group of bankers and their expert advisers, led by Senator Nelson Aldrich, boarded a private car at the railroad station in Hoboken, New Jersey, bound on a mission so secret that it was years before any of the facts concerning it were revealed. Among those shrouded within that coach were Shelton, Aldrich's private secretary, and A. Piatt Andrew, Assistant Secretary of the Treasury, who had acted as Special Assistant to the National

---

*It was generally recognized that without the panic of 1907 and the National Monetary Commission, there could have been no Federal Reserve Act—at least not in 1913. (Cf. *The Federal Reserve System,* by Henry Parker Willis, 1765 pp., The Ronald Press, New York, 1923, 89.)

Monetary Commission during its luxurious tour of Europe; Mr. Frank Vanderlip, who was president of the National City Bank of New York, which represented the Rockefeller interests as well as those of Kuhn, Loeb and Co., and who was accompanied by Henry P. Davison of J. P. Morgan and Co., and by Charles D. Norton of the First National Bank of New York—three men who, among them, through their interlocking directorates, controlled much of the nation's industry, commerce, and finance.

Following these came the German immigrant, Paul Moritz Warburg, who had grown up with the great Warburg banking interests in Germany and for whom Rothschild funds had purchased a partnership in Kuhn, Loeb; he was accompanied by Benjamin Strong, the Wall Street manipulator who had risen to power during the panic of 1907 as the servant of the J. P. Morgan interests—which, in alliance with other financial powers, had placed Teddy Roosevelt in the White House in 1904 so that this great and blatant Trustbuster might prevent any serious injury to the existing trusts.[16]

THE STORY OF JEKYLL ISLAND GRADUALLY UNVEILED

The first public reference to the Jekyll Island conference was in an article written by E. C. Forbes and published in *Frank Leslie's Magazine* in 1916. Although Warburg wrote a book entitled *The Federal Reserve System*,[17] which consists of two heavy volumes comprising almost 2,000 pages, he never mentions the Jekyll Island episode; nor do we find a word concerning it in Robert Latham Owen's *The Federal Reserve Act*[18] or in the *Adventures in Constructive Finance* by Carter Glass.[19] Nor is there any reference to it in *The Intimate Papers of Edward Mandell House*.[20] However, in 1933, James Laurence Laughlin, whose role in the passage of the Federal Reserve Act we shall discuss in due course, wrote in his informative book, *The Federal Reserve Act, Its Origin and Problems*,[21] that, following the passage of the Aldrich-Vreeland Act, "several banking schemes were proposed. Already the question of the enactment of a central bank like those in Europe had come up. The proponent of this plan was Mr. Paul M. Warburg of Kuhn, Loeb, and Co. He offered in March, 1910, a fairly well developed plan to be known as the Reserve Bank of the United States," which had eleven sections and was published in *The New York Times* on March 24, 1910.[22]

Laughlin continues that on November 12, 1910, a conference on the monetary problem was held at Columbia University,[23] and that in the following month,* "the group interested in the purposes of the National Monetary Commission headed by Senator Aldrich, met secretly at Jekyll Island, and, for about two weeks . . .** concentrated on the preparation of a bill to be presented to Congress by the National Monetary Commission. The men who were present at Jekyll Island were Senator Aldrich; Henry P. Davison, of J. P. Morgan and Co.; Paul M. Warburg of Kuhn, Loeb and Co.; Frank A. Vanderlip, of the National City Bank, and Charles D. Norton, of the First National Bank. There was much difference of opinion and discussion. No doubt the ablest banking mind in the group was that of Mr. Warburg, who had had a European banking training, and was familiar with the organization of the German Reichsbank and European practice. Senator Aldrich, of course, although the ablest politician in Congress, had no special training in banking. Mr. Vanderlip was ambitious and eager in pushing his own views, based on experience in the Treasury and as president of the National City Bank.

"Out of the discussion came a rough draft which Senator Aldrich used as a basis of the bill which he later recommended and which he finally laid before the National Advisory Commission."[24]

It is obvious from this and other information that the sixteen members of Congress who constituted the National

---

*We note that the date given by Laughlin for the Jekyll Island conference differs from that given by others; possibly his memory was slightly uncertain because of the long passage of time.
**To protect their incognitos, they even imported a different set of servants to wait on them and they used code names in addressing each other.

Advisory Commission and who travelled all over Europe, were no more than a rubber stamp for the bankers; except Aldrich, none of them were present on Jekyll Island or even consulted concerning the *Report* prepared there and later issued over their signatures.

In 1935, Frank Vanderlip wrote a rather full description of the Jekyll Island conclave in an article published in the *Saturday Evening Post.*[25]

In his *America's Sixty Families,* published in 1937,[26] Ferdinand Lundberg declares that "The Federal Reserve Act . . . was an offshoot of a bill originally presented . . . by the dubious Aldrich," chairman of a "monetary commission," the ideas of which "emanated from the fertile brains of a Wall Street clique, whose deputies worked out the details at the remote Jekyll Island Club* . . . off the Georgia coast, during an ostensible duck hunting expedition. Among those present were Paul M. Warburg, partner of Kuhn, Loeb and Co.; Frank Vanderlip, President of the National City Bank; Dr. Piatt Andrew, Special Assistant to the Senate Monetary Commission; and Benjamin Strong, Vice-President of the Bankers' Trust Company.

"The protracted Jekyll Island conference took place in the atmosphere of an elaborate conspiracy. The trip to Georgia was made in a private car chartered by Aldrich, and the travellers all used assumed names so that the train crew could not establish their identities. For a long time, there was no public knowledge that such a conclave had been held.

"The financiers wanted a central bank of the European model, to facilitate the large-scale manipulation of the national economy. An instrument was desired that would function as had the United States Bank, smashed by Andrew Jackson because it concentrated immense monetary power in private hands.

"But when Aldrich introduced the scenario produced by the Jekyll Island duck hunters, it was immediately hooted down

---

*This was owned by 200 of the wealthiest families in America, among whom bankers predominated (Lundberg, *op. cit.* 433).

as a nefarious Wall Street enterprise, and for the time being, came to naught.

"The task of the Wilson administration was to place essentially the Jekyll Island measure on the statute books, but in an eccentric disguise. The job of drawing up such a bill was given to Paul M. Warburg, one of the Jekyll Island plotters. Warburg collaborated with the big financiers, as his memoirs reveal, and when administration views were needed, he conferred with Colonel Edward M. House, Wilson's roving commissioner. . . .

"The Warburg-Wall Street draft, superficially revised by Wilson and Carter Glass of Virginia, was simply the Jekyll Island duck hunters' scheme for a central bank, dressed in fancy toggery. There was some opposition to it from uninformed Wall Street quarters, but it was significantly endorsed by the American Banking Association. . . .

"In practice, the Federal Reserve Bank of New York became the fountainhead of the system of twelve regional banks. . . . The other eleven were so many mausoleums created to salve the local pride and quell the Jacksonian fears of the hinterland."[27]

THE FED IN PREPARATION

Nelson Aldrich, who had sponsored the Aldrich-Vreeland Emergency Currency Act of 1908, had—as we have noted—headed the National Monetary Commission on its opulent tour of Europe. He had been a member of Congress for forty years—thirty-six of them in the Senate—and, although not a professional banker, considered himself the unquestioned leader and ultimate authority of the gathering. However, it was the astute Warburg, scion of European banking interests, who supplied the technical expertise and who, more than anyone else, understood what must be done to deceive the American people and to obtain congressional approval for any legislation proposed by the financiers.

Since Warburg foresaw that no law could be enacted which overtly gave the private institution he desired the power to issue the nation's currency, he opposed the term Central Bank and suggested that it be called the United States Federal Reserve Bank; and, since he was well aware of the opposition to Wall Street that existed in Congress and among the public, he opposed the use of Aldrich's name on any legislative proposal. On such issues, Aldrich, the eminent American, and Warburg, the clever foreigner, clashed continuously, and the latter's thick German accent grated doubly on the nerves of the venerable New Englander.

Aldrich was far too powerful, egotistical, and influential, however, to be diverted by the shrewd and cunning alien from what was dearest to his heart: he insisted on a far-reaching banking act which would not only give him and his fraternity complete control over the credit and finances of the nation, but which would also immortalize his name as its beneficent creator. When Warburg realized that he could not exclude provisions granting a private institution the same power of issue enjoyed by the central banks of Europe, and that he could not prevent the use of the Aldrich name in the proposed bill, he concentrated on polishing up some of its sections and incorporating the basic concepts of the German Reichsbank, a private corporation that exercised complete control over interest rates, as well as the expansion and contraction of credit, and whose notes were obligations of the German government.[28]

Warburg explains in his monumental *Federal Reserve System* that he moved from the Old World to New York in 1902, where he found bitter opposition to any form of central banking, because it "would inevitably result in one of two alternatives: either complete government control, which meant politics in banking, or control by 'Wall Street,' which meant banking politics. Abhorrence of both extremes had led to an almost fanatical conviction that the only hope of keeping the country's credit system independent was to be sought in complete decentralization of banking."[29]

To Warburg, the American banking system appeared "to do violence to almost every banking tenet held sacred in the Old World. In Europe, reserves were centralized, note issues elastic, and commercial paper permitting immediate sale formed the quickest assets of banks," while here, the note issues, based on government bonds, were inelastic. "Gold reserves," he complained, "were decentralized, investments in salable, single-name commercial paper were locking up the funds of the banks. . . ."[30]

He had, he declared, "developed a feeling of deep resentment" towards Aldrich, "because, whenever the question of banking was raised, one was told that so long as Aldrich was in power, there was no hope whatever of weaning the country from the mastery of bond-secured currency, to which he had so strongly committed his [Republican] Party."[31]

The whirligig of time was soon to bring on his revenge and thus demonstrate once and for all who was the more prescient—the stately Nelson Aldrich, or the keen and artful Paul Moritz Warburg.

Citations

1. *Historical Statistics of the United States,* U.S. Dept. of Commerce 300
2. Lindbergh, *Banking and Currency and the Money Trust* 102
3. *Historical Statistics, op. cit.* 306
4. Beard, *op. cit.* II 109
5. *Historical Statistics, op. cit.* 306–07
6. Laughlin, *The Federal Reserve Act, Its Origin and Problems* 97
7. Groseclose, *Fifty Years of Managed Money* 49, 95
8. Lindbergh, *op. cit.* 94–95
9. Willis, *The Federal Reserve System* 53
10. Lindbergh, *op. cit.* 295
11. *Ib.* 92–93
12. Willis, *op. cit.* 35
13. *Historical Statistics, op. cit.* 304, 305, 308; 1963 *SA* 401; 1973 *ib.* 394, 396, 401; 1974 *ib.* 221–222, 227.
14. Willis, *op. cit.* 67–69
15. *Ib.*
16. Mullins, *The Federal Reserve Conspiracy* 16
17. Warburg, *The Federal Reserve System,* 1930
18. Owen, *The Federal Reserve Act,* 1919

19. Glass, *Adventures in Constructive Finance*, 1927
20. House, *The Intimate Papers*, 1926
21. Laughlin, *op. cit.*
22. *Ib.* 9
23. *Ib.* 13
24. *Ib.* 15
25. Mullins, *op. cit.* 13
26. Lundberg, *America's Sixty Families*, 1937
27. *Ib., op. cit.* 121–22
28. *Ib.*
29. Warburg, *op. cit.* 12
30. *Ib.* 17
31. *Ib.* 31

CHAPTER III

An American Central Bank
at Last!

THE ALDRICH PLAN IS INTRODUCED

There is no doubt that the powerful Aldrich, who enjoyed the support of his party, and especially that of President William Howard Taft, felt assured that the so-called *Report* of the National Monetary Commission, also known as the Aldrich Plan, could be transformed into law. When the proposal was submitted to Congress on January 16, 1911, its members and the public were assured that its principal purpose was to prevent monopoly,* and that, after thorough study, it had been endorsed

*Willis, *op. cit.* 109 notes that he was retained by the House Banking and Currency Committee as "expert" consultant during 1912-13. He served as Secretary of the Federal Reserve Board from 1914 to 1918, after which he accepted a position as Professor of Banking at Columbia University. In 1923, he published his huge tome, which is extremely valuable as source material as a whole, and particularly because it includes the text of the various drafts of the Glass Bill. In this, he offers no adverse criticism of the Federal Reserve Act or the manner in which it originated and was enacted; he says nothing of the clandestine meeting on Jekyll Island; he minimizes Warburg's role in the legislation. He purports seriously to believe that this banker was opposed to the Act in its final

by all the bankers in the country;** by practically all the professors of political economy, and by many groups of business men.[1] The fact that virtually none of these had even seen the *Report* was ignored amidst the thunder of orchestrated propaganda.

THE GENIUS OF PAUL MORITZ WARBURG

However, as the battle over the proposal developed, Warburg's acumen became more and more apparent. It was soon obvious that what he had foreseen had already come to pass: since the *Report* reminded many members of Congress of the Aldrich-Vreeland Act, and since it reeked of the New York banking fraternity† it fell, in the words of Dr. Willis, "dead, upon a house wholly alienated."[2]

Professor Laughlin notes that at first the bankers supported the Aldrich Plan energetically;[3] however, when it became obvious even in "the spring of 1911 . . . that there would be opposition to the idea of a Central Bank in the Aldrich Bill . . ., the supporters of his plan, by giving it the name of the 'Reserve Association of America,' tried to avoid the idea of a central bank."[4] And he continues: "Ex-Secretary Leslie M. Shaw, of the Treasury, regarded as vicious Senator Aldrich's bank reform plan;"[5] and "with the change of political power to the Democrats in the House in June, 1911, the Republican Aldrich Bill ceased to be possible legislation."[6] Laughlin notes further that "Mr. Bryan gave the *coup de grâce* to . . . the Aldrich bill or . . . a central bank."[7]

---

form. Although Willis describes in detail the secrecy surrounding the Bill during its preparation, he denies the existence of any ulterior motive to anyone during this period. It is interesting to note, however, that within six years after the publication of this book, the author became one of the most severe and articulate critics of the Fed.

** The American Bankers Association did not endorse the Aldrich Plan until Nov. 21, 1911 (Warburg, *op. cit.* Vol. I, 74).

† Willis, *op. cit.* 77, states: "There can be no doubt that the Aldrich Bill was prepared under the general supervision of the larger bankers." And he adds, 83, that "it was . . . exclusively a banker's measure."

Before the general principles of the Aldrich Plan were presented to Congress as the Glass Bill, it was labelled as a Federal Reserve System and disguised as an operation of the government; all references to Aldrich or anything pertaining to Wall Street were meticulously deleted. In short, not only were Warburg's ideas incorporated into the bill, but his judgment and strategy were completely vindicated. The Federal Reserve Act as finally passed was his brainchild and a rough replica of the Reichsbank. Many years later, he wrote: "The Federal Reserve Act, with its structure of eight or twelve apparently autonomous regional banks, was politically by far the better, and in the long run the safer plan."[8] (Note the *apparently.*)

In Germany, Warburg's family was the principal stockholder in the Reichsbank; he came to the United States in 1902, joining the firm of Kuhn, Loeb and Co., where his annual salary soon rose to $500,000. In 1911, while continuing to enjoy this emolument, he emerged as the full-time apostle of an elastic currency and a central banking system. It was he, more than anyone else, who not merely created the Glass-Owen Bill, but who also made possible its enactment. In 1913, he accepted the Order of the Reich,[9] where his brother was head of the secret police.[10] In 1914, Wilson appointed Warburg to membership in the first Federal Reserve Board, and later he served for several years as Chairman of the Federal Advisory Council. He was not only the principal architect of the Fed, but continued also as its guiding spirit even during the years when we were at war with his motherland.

It has been stated on good authority that it was through the aid of Warburg's brother that Lenin was able to cross Germany to Russia in a sealed train in 1918.

CHARLES AUGUSTUS LINDBERGH, SR.

Outraged by the so-called *Report* of the National Advisory Commission, Lindbergh introduced into the House of Representatives a resolution calling for an investigation of the Money Trust; this was adopted April 22, 1912.[11] Woodrow

Wilson, then a possible candidate for the presidency, announced himself in favor of this investigation.[12] The hearings which followed revealed some bad practices and much concentration of control; but they were so cleverly manipulated by Chairman Arsene Pujo and the wealthy lawyer, Samuel Untermeyer, who conducted the interrogations, that no Money Trust was ever discovered.[13]

Lindbergh, however, was not deceived, and he declared on the floor of Congress: "The Aldrich Plan is the Wall Street Plan. It is a broad challenge to the Government by the champion of the Money Trust. It means another panic, if necessary, to intimidate the people. Aldrich, paid by the Government to represent the people, proposes a plan for the trusts instead. In 1907 . . . a panic entailed enormous losses upon us. Wall Street knew the American people were demanding a remedy against the recurrence of such a ridiculously unnatural condition. Most Senators and Representatives fell into the Wall Street trap and passed the Aldrich-Vreeland Emergency Currency Bill. But the real purpose was to get a monetary commission which would frame a proposition for amendments to our currency and banking laws that would suit the Money Trust. The interests are now busy everywhere educating the people in favor of the Aldrich Plan. It is reported that a large sum of money has been raised for this purpose. Wall Street speculation brought on the panic of 1907. The depositors' funds were loaned to gamblers and anybody the Money Trust wanted to favor. Then when the depositors wanted their money, the banks did not have it. That made the panic."[14]

PROPAGANDA UNLIMITED

The agency established by the Interests—to which Lindbergh referred—was the Chicago-based National Citizens' League which was created on May 11, 1911, to promote the gospel of an elastic currency and a great central bank. The propaganda machine was placed under the direction of Professor Laughlin, who describes its formation[15] and explains that since its New York promoters were well aware of the general hostility toward bankers, they based the organization in Chicago and tried to make it appear that it consisted of business men in general.[16] Laughlin states that $339,275 had been contributed to its support by June 16, 1911.[17]

Warburg also discusses the National Citizens' League; he states that it was fortunate in obtaining the services of Professor Laughlin, who for two years devoted himself exclusively to this work for which a half million dollars was contributed. "The first press statement of the League," he notes, "emphasized" its nonpartisanship and declared that its purpose was "to carry on an active campaign for monetary reform on the general principles of the Aldrich Plan without endorsing every detail of the National Reserve Association."[18]

At first the League supported the Aldrich Plan openly, now presented as the proposal of the Reserve Association of America, and, as such, introduced into Congress January 8, 1912; however, since this was merely the Aldrich Plan with a new name, the League soon began promoting the more subtle legislation being prepared by Dr. Willis under the veiled inspiration of Warburg and the overt tutelage of Carter Glass, who had replaced Arsene Pujo as Chairman of the House Banking and Currency Committee in November, 1911.

The National Citizens' League now flooded the country with its literature. "You insure your property against fire, your business against risks," it declared.* "We ask you to pay a single premium only for the insurance of your business against money panics . . . business collapse . . . and depression. . . . These are the benefits of banking and currency reform . . . assured if the businessmen will combine and lend it support. . . . Any subscription from $1 upward will constitute a membership in the League. . . ."[19] (Lindbergh pointed out that, since the League spent several times its subscription income for postage alone,** it could scarcely be without ulterior motivation.)[20]

---

* Willis states, *op. cit.* 1405, that "Nothing was more loudly declared at the inauguration of the System than that it would insure industrial stability."
** Representatives of the League were interrogated closely during the investigations of the Money Trust concerning the sources of their income and the total of their expenditures (Willis, *op. cit.* 135-36).

"The inauguration of the new banking and currency system," noted Elgin E. Groseclose, "was accompanied by exorbitant promises of the benefits that would flow from it, a typical statement being one issued by the Comptroller of the Currency, that . . . 'it supplies a circulating medium absolutely safe' and that 'under the operation of the law such financial and commercial crises or "panics" as the country experienced in 1873, 1893, and again in 1907, with their attendant misfortunes and prostrations, seem to be mathematically impossible.' "21

Since the great majority of the people, however, including most members of Congress, knew little or nothing about monetary intricacies, it is not surprising that many were deceived, and clever propagandists, pursuing time-honored methods, simply proclaimed as gospel the precise opposite of the truth.*

*That not only members of Congress are abysmally ignorant concerning monetary problems is reflected in an article published in the Philadelphia *Inquirer* on Aug. 8, 1974, which cites a conversation between Nixon and Haldeman which took place in the Oval Office on June 23, 1972, a few days after the Watergate break in. On the previous August 15, Nixon had severed the link between the dollar and gold, and in December the dollar was formally devalued at a meeting of the finance ministers of various nations. Then, in June, 1972, the agreement was threatened when the British withdrw their support of the pound, allowing it to drop well below the rate agreed upon in December.

The June 23, 1972 conversation ran as follows:

"Haldeman: Did you get the report that the British floated the pound?

"President: No, I don't think so.

"H: They did.

"P: That's devaluation?

"H: Yeah. Flannigan's got a report on it here.

"P: I don't care about it. Nothing we can do about it.

"H: You want a rundown?

"P: No, I don't.

"H: He argues it shows the wisdom of our refusal to consider convertibility until we get a new monetary system.

"P: Good. I think he's right. It's too complicated for me to get into *(unintelligible)*. I understand.

"H: Burns expects a 5-day percent devaluation against the dollar.

"P: Yeah. O.K. Fine.

"H: Burns is concerned about speculation about the lira.

"P: Well, I don't give a *(expletive deleted)* about the lira . . . *(unintelligible.)*

"H: That's the substance of that."

DR. HENRY PARKER WILLIS

To draw up the text of the desired legislation, Carter Glass engaged a protégé of Professor Laughlin, Dr. Henry Parker Willis, who, working for months in the utmost secrecy, prepared the first draft of the Glass Bill between June and October, 1912. Meanwhile, all members of Congress were kept in total darkness concerning the provisions of the proposed legislation; and when the Glass Committee held hearings, purportedly to sound out public opinion as to what kind of monetary legislation should be enacted,[22] Lindbergh charged that only bankers and their spokesmen were permitted to testify.[23] Since what was said at these hearings was printed in the newspapers, the public could only conclude that their testimony reflected the general desires of the people.

THE ELECTION OF WOODROW WILSON

As we have noted, there was intense and widespread distrust and hostility toward the financial interests, not only in Congress, but also among the general public. And since it was known that President Taft had endorsed the Aldrich Plan, no banking bill carrying his blessing could possibly be enacted. It was therefore mandatory that a reputed enemy of Wall Street replace him in the White House.

The endowments of Woodrow Wilson were precisely suited to accomplish the designs of the financiers. As president of Princeton University, he had attracted the favorable attention of Wall Street by his support of the Aldrich Plan when it was first announced, and this brought him the governorship of New Jersey. He was an orator of passionate fervency, and, because of his predilection for women—especially married ones—and an unfortunate habit of writing love letters to them, he was extremely vulnerable to blackmail.

Above and beyond all this, he was an outstanding adept in evangelistic proclamations advocating precisely the reverse of what he intended to do. He was, therefore, perfectly in character when, after having supported the Aldrich Plan in New Jersey, he mounted a national crusade against the very people who had prepared it and were conspiring to enact the Glass Bill.

The manner in which Taft was defeated in 1912 constitutes an instructive episode in practical politics; it has been described by various historians, including Ferdinand Lundberg.[24] After the financiers selected Wilson as their candidate, they also organized the Bull Moose Party under the leadership of Theodore Roosevelt, whose purpose it was to split the Republican vote and who, in this campaign, once again served the great interests as he had done so well in 1904.

And so it was that Wilson and Roosevelt, both lavishly financed by Wall Street, carried their flaming crusade to every corner of the nation, denouncing the moneyed interests in the most scathing terms. Among typical Wilsonian declarations, we may cite the following:* "The control of credit also has become dangerously centralized . . . the financial resources of the country are [controlled by] small groups of capitalists. . . . The great monopoly of this country is the monopoly of ·big credits. . . . A great industrial nation is controlled by its system of credit. Our system of credit is privately concentrated. The growth of our nation, therefore, and all our activities, are in the hands of a few men. . . . This Money Trust . . . is not a myth. . . ."[25]

For public consumption, Teddy Roosevelt had much the same line: the "issue of currency," he declared over and over, "should be lodged with the government and be protected from domination and manipulation by Wall Street, or by any special interests."[26] The Bull Moose platform adopted at its 1912 convention stated categorically: "We are opposed to the so-called Aldrich Currency Bill because its provisions would place our currency and credit system in private hands, not subject to effective public control." Warburg, however, had no reason to fear the redoubtable trust buster, for, as he noted in January,

*First published in the magazine, The New Freedom, and reprinted by Carter Glass in his book, Adventures in Constructive Finance.

1912, Teddy had been "fairly won over to a favorable consideration of the Aldrich Plan. . . ."[27]

Since the betrayed and brainwashed electorate had no means of learning the truth, we need not be surprised that Wilson garnered 6,286,214 votes; Roosevelt, 4,126,020; and Taft, no more than 3,483,922. Wilson had only 42.4% of the popular vote; but he obtained 435 electoral ballots out of a possible 524, a landslide victory of sorts. The Congress, which had been Republican, became overwhelmingly Democratic. However, since many of its members belonged to the Populist wing, led by William Jennings Bryan, all of whom were pledged to oppose all Wall Street machinations, it would not be an easy matter to enact any legislation endorsed by the New York Money Trust.

Nevertheless, now for the first time, the Federal Reserve Act had become politically possible;* for Warburg's genius would be guiding the man in the White House through Colonel Edward Mandell House, who was the President's mentor and *alter ego.***

WILSON AND THE GLASS BILL

While Wilson continued to affect an outward neutrality toward the banking legislation promoted by Wall Street, he was doing everything in his power to advance it.[28] Immediately after the election, Glass wrote him asking for an interview, which took place in Princeton on December 26.[29] When the draft of the new bill, which had been completed shortly before by Willis, was shown the President-elect, he was, we read, "deeply

---

* Willis states, *op. cit.* 134: "There was an informal agreement that in the event of the defeat of the Democratic Party in the autumn election, the task of further study of the banking and currency legislation might as well be laid aside, while in the event of [Democratic] success, the sooner the work was prosecuted, the better. Mr. Wilson, having been elected . . . with a Congress overwhelmingly of his own party, the outlook for legislation took on . . . an entirely new hue. . . ."

** Wilson wrote in a letter published in *The Intimate Papers of Colonel House,* Vol I, 114: "Mr. House is my second personality. He is my independent self. His thoughts and mine are one. If I were in his place, I would do just as he suggested. . . . If anyone thinks he is reflecting my opinion, by whatever action he takes, they are welcome to the conclusion."

interested. . . ." He also expressed "mild approval."[30] Thus encouraged, Glass returned, again accompanied by Willis, with a revised draft for a second interview on January 30, which took place in Trenton, New Jersey,[31] where there seems to have been complete understanding and agreement.[32]

Soon after Wilson took office, Colonel House asked Glass for a copy of the revised bill, of which Willis had prepared a digest;[33] it was given to House after Wilson personally directed that this be done.[34] House thereupon took it to *his* mentor, Paul Warburg, who delivered copies to the President and to Glass.[35]

THE ROLE OF WILLIAM JENNINGS BRYAN

On May 1st, Willis had completed still another revised draft[36] of the evolving Glass Bill. This was delivered to the President who, "satisfied at last that the measure was worthy of serious support, now necessarily faced the problem of obtaining . . . the all-important support of the Secretary of State, W. J. Bryan, the real leader of the powerful 'left wing' of the Democratic Party."[37] Without this, "it was clear that no progress could be made and that the Glass Bill . . . might as well be abandoned. . . ."[38] In the meantime, Bryan had been trying so desperately to obtain some information concerning the pending legislation that his importunities had become positively embarrassing.[39]

There is a curious passage in *The Intimate Papers of Colonel House* in regard to Bryan: "The Commoner's sense of loyalty had kept him from an attack upon the Federal Reserve Act, which, it would appear, he never entirely understood"; and he added: "with his influence in the Party, he could have destroyed the measure. . . ."[40] Professor Laughlin also has an interesting comment concerning Mr. Bryan, who "felt that his reputation depended on the insertion of government issues in the bill; and Senator Owen, the Chairman of the Senate Finance Committee, agreed with him . . . the attitude of Mr. Bryan did not depend on lack of security for the notes, but on the technical right to claim that they were government issues, which he had announced so often as pure Democratic doctrine."[41]

Since every version of the Bill, including that of June 6, provided for the creation of a purely private bank of issue to be controlled by a board of directors consisting of, and elected by, bankers only, it was necessary that Mr. Bryan, to preserve any appearance of integrity, demand a revision which would give the notes the aura and outward appearance of government issue.

When the Bill was finally printed early in June, it was still marked "Strictly Confidential." Bryan, however, obtained a copy; and lost no time in delivering his ultimatum, demanding

1. Revision of the section on notes so that these should appear to be Treasury currency, issued, payable, and guaranteed by the government;

2. Revision of the section setting up the Federal Reserve Board so that it would be a governmental body, selected by the President and confirmed by the Senate;

3. Modification of the sections relating to public deposits so as to insure full government control over public funds.[42]

Since these provisions were exactly what the more enlightened financiers knew to be the *sine qua non* for the passage of the legislation, Wilson hastened to accept them.

THE TECHNIQUE OF COMPROMISE

How this compromise was effected is explained by Carter Glass in his *Adventures in Constructive Finance.* When the conflicts with Bryan over the issuance of the Federal Reserve notes had reached a crisis, Wilson summoned Glass to the White House and stated that he would make the reserve notes "'obligations of the United States.' I was for an instant speechless!" wrote Glass. "I remonstrated. . . . The President was reminded of what was behind the federal reserve notes: the liability of the individual bank . . . the considerable gold cover with 100 percent commercial secondary reserves. . . .

"There is not any government obligation here, Mr.

President. . . . It would be pretense on its face. Was there ever a government note based on the property of a banking institution? Was there ever a government issue not one dollar of which could be put out except by demand of a bank? The suggested government obligation is so remote it could never be discovered. . . ."

"'Exactly so, Glass,' earnestly said the President. 'Every word you say is true; the government liability is a mere thought.* And so, if we can hold the substance of the thing and give the other fellow the shadow, why not do it and thereby save our bill?' "[43]

And thus one of the greatest political reversals and betrayals of all time was accomplished; and how the man who, for many years, had been declaring that only the government possesses the power under the Constitution to issue currency, could support the Glass Bill with such insubstantial revisions, must remain a mystery unless it is indeed true, as House surmised, that Bryan was simply loyal to his Party or did not understand the legislation.** Whether he was deceived, persuaded, bribed, or threatened, we cannot say; certain it is that without his blessing and the changes he instigated, there would have been no Federal Reserve Act—at least not in 1913.

---

* Warburg wrote, *op. cit.* Vol I, 409: "While technically and legally the Federal Reserve note is an obligation of the United States Government, in reality it is an obligation, the sole actual responsibility for which rests on the reserve banks. These notes are issued and redeemed in response to the rediscount and investment operations of the reserve banks; they are, in practical effect, Federal reserve circulation guaranteed by the United States. But the government could only be called upon to take them up after the reserve banks had failed."
** Cf. Willis, *op. cit.* 254. Aldrich pretended to believe that Bryan had succeeded in creating a system of government currency, similar to the Lincoln greenbacks: "The theory that the United States should issue currency in the form of promises to pay," he declared, "is a populistic doctrine. It had no standing as a Democratic party principle until the advent of Mr. Bryan as the nominee for the presidency in 1896. . . . If the House bill should be enacted into law, Mr. Bryan will have achieved the purpose for which he has been contending . . ." (*ib.* 429). Various bankers believed, or at least loudly declared, that the proposed Federal Reserve Act was nothing less than intolerable, since it removed the power to issue the nation's currency from the private bankers and opened the way for the emission of floods of purely fiat money by the Federal Treasury.

THE GREAT COMMONER
BLESSES THE BETRAYAL

On June 24, Bryan declared that in the proposed bill "The right of the government to issue money is not surrendered to the banks; the control over the money so issued is not relinquished by the government. . . ." And he added: "I am glad to endorse earnestly and unreservedly the currency bill as a much better measure than I supposed it possible to secure at this time. . . . Conflicting opinions have been reconciled with a success hardly to have been expected.

"The great advantage to the banks . . . is that it furnishes a currency which they can secure in time of need without having to put up bonds as security . . . under this bill when a bank can put up its good assets, it is able at all times, without sacrifice, to secure any additional circulation that the community may need. . . .

"The business interests will, I think, welcome this bill as an unalloyed blessing. It gives them, through their banks, a promise of relief in any time of stringency, and it gives the promise without putting in the hands of the banks a power which can be used against the public."[44] It is indeed interesting to note that Mr. Bryan was defending the Act, not against critics like Lindbergh, Shaw, and Ollie M. James, but against men like Aldrich and Warburg.

All copies of previous drafts—except those retained by Willis—were then destroyed, and still another revised version printed, incorporating the Bryan proposals; this was introduced into the House on June 16. Lindbergh, who seems to have been virtually the only member of Congress who fully understood the ultimate potentials of the legislation, immediately charged that the Glass Bill was nothing more nor less than the Aldrich Plan in disguise,* prepared by the Money Trust.[45]

---

* Willis states, *op. cit.* 85, that the Aldrich measure was the true predecessor of the Federal Reserve Act; and (*ib.* 428) that "there was no reason why anyone who believed in the principles underlying the Aldrich measure should not have regarded the Federal Reserve Act as a further development and broadening of

THE CONTROVERSY OVER THE ALDRICH PLAN AND THE FED

A significant clash of opinion concerning the relationship of the Aldrich Plan and the Federal Reserve Act broke out several years after its passage. Charles Seymour, who arranged and edited *The Intimate Papers of Colonel House,* declared that House was the unseen guardian angel of the Federal Reserve Bill, and that he was constantly assisting the Secretary of the Treasury as well as the chairmen of both the Senate and House committees who were handling the legislation.[46] He states that the Colonel was indefatigable in providing the President with the knowledge he sought and needed for his guidance in this matter.[47]

On November 25, 1911, House wrote Bryan that both he [Bryan] and Wilson were wrong in opposing the Aldrich Plan;[48] and on December 6, he wrote that J. P. Morgan, and most of the people in Chicago, were bitterly opposed to Wilson because of his virulent attacks upon Wall Street and the Money Trust.[49] On December 19, 1912, House wrote that he had conversed with Warburg concerning currency reform and told him what he had done to get the pending legislation in working order; he added that the members of Congress wanted to do what Wilson desired, and he concluded that he "knew the President-elect thought straight concerning the issue."[50] (A remarkable statement, indeed, concerning the man who had been attacking the Money Trust, especially coming from House, who was at that time a staunch supporter of the Aldrich Plan!)

On January 8, 1913, House wrote that the "Governor agreed to put me in touch with Glass . . . and I am to work at a measure which is to be submitted to him. He [Wilson] spoke of

---

those same principles." He declares also (*ib.* 526) that substantially all the principal elements of the Federal Reserve Act had appeared in the Aldrich-Vreeland Emergency Currency Act. Warburg and various others who were in a position to know agreed that the Aldrich Plan embodied the basic principles which finally appeared in the Federal Reserve Act.

his fear that Bryan would not approve such a bill as I had in mind."[51]

Glass, however, denied vehemently that either House or Warburg had anything whatever to do with the Federal Reserve Act; he maintained, on the contrary, that they were its constant and deadliest opponents. He branded the idea that House ever tutored Woodrow Wilson concerning this legislation as an "amazing suggestion."[52] He adds that during his first visit with the Governor on December 26, 1912, as well as during the second on January 30, following, "Wilson may be said to have already committed himself to every fundamental provision of the Federal Reserve Act—long before House could even have known anything about it. . . ." And when it was translated into shape so that it could be printed, "House was three thousand miles away."[53] The only technician who ever handled it, adds Glass, was Dr. Henry Parker Willis.[54]

House, who knew next to nothing about banking, explains Glass, accepted Warburg as his tutor and these two, who supported the Aldrich Plan and opposed the Glass-Owen Bill, claim to be the authors![55] However, the Aldrich Plan, a blatant attempt to ensnare Wilson into repudiating his Party platform, was never even considered by the Finance Committee of either chamber in the new Democratic Congress.[56]

Shortly thereafter, continues Glass, the President asked that a digest of the Bill be prepared, a task which Dr. Willis completed in a short time. When House obtained this, he instantly sent it to Mr. Warburg, who, as we have already noted, prepared an unsigned and hostile analysis demanding "radical alterations, which were not made, and advocating certain things which were not done. . . . And this is the way Colonel House 'whipped the Glass measure into final shape'!"[57]

In conclusion, Glass wrote: "Its paternity [the Federal Reserve Act] has curiously been ascribed to men who were savagely hostile to the Act; to men who never saw a sentence of the original draft; to men who could not write its title in a month's trial . . . the fact is that the master mind of the whole performance was Woodrow Wilson's. It was his infinite prescience and patience . . . courage and wisdom . . . patriotism and power . . . passion to serve mankind . . . that gave zest and inspiration to the battle for financial freedom."[58]

Although Glass, like Owen, expressed great repugnance toward the Aldrich Plan, he declared that "there was never a moment when the Committee could think it was not at liberty to appropriate any provision of the Aldrich Plan which might, to advantage, be woven into a regional bank scheme."[59]

That it did this and a good deal more becomes quite obvious when we read Warburg's massive *Federal Reserve System,* which established the fact that the Aldrich Plan was Warburg's brainchild; and when Glass engaged Dr. Willis to prepare a text that could be shown in due course to President-elect Wilson (who would agree to virtually anything), and later submitted to a suspicious Bryan and a sceptical Congress, he used the *Report* of the National Monetary Commission (i.e., the Aldrich Plan)* as the framework for his own version. Of this, there cannot be the slightest doubt, for we can compare this proposal, section by section, with the various versions of the Glass Bill, reproduced by Henry Parker Willis in his *Federal Reserve Act.* •

It is true that Warburg saw the Glass Bill—as prepared by Willis—for the first time in June, 1913;[60] but it is also true that he demonstrated its similarity to the Aldrich Plan by publishing both versions in juxtaposed columns in his book, where we see that the principal provisions of the two bills not only agree in their essentials, but that entire sections are sometimes identical even in their wording.[61]

Warburg declares: "For our part, we believe that evidence adduced from these comparisons will warrant the conclusion that there is a very distinct relationship between the two bills and that, instead of differing in 'principle, purpose, and processes'" (as Glass maintained), "they are surprisingly akin."[62] And again: "Brushing aside, then, the external differences affecting the

*Printed in full in Laughlin's *Federal Reserve Act* 325-40.

'shells,' we find the 'kernels' of the two systems very closely resembling and related to one another."[63]

THE GLASS BILL PASSES THE HOUSE

On September 18, with the blessings of Bryan, the Glass Bill passed the House by the margin of 287 to 85.[64] When this was sent to the Senate, a deluge of criticism, emanating from the National Citizens' League, from New York and Chicago bankers, and particularly from Paul Warburg* descended like a hurricane upon Congress, all of which affected a most strident opposition.** Such propaganda, calculated to convince the Populist Democrats that the law was contrary to the interests of the banking community, undoubtedly persuaded a considerable number of Congressmen, with little or no knowledge of banking, to favor the bill.

THE ROLE OF ROBERT LATHAM OWEN

When the Glass Bill reached the Senate, it became the duty of its Finance Committee, of which Senator Robert Owen was the chairman, to consider it. Here the legislation underwent some revision; and, in its amended form, became known as the Glass-Owen Bill. We can only conclude that this Senator, a country banker from Oklahoma, who after many years became a critic of the Fed, failed entirely at the time, like so many others, to understand what it would one day empower the bankers to do. In his foreword to a book written in 1934,[65] he declares that "In the Bill introduced in July, in which the Hon. Carter Glass joined me, I had inserted a provision *requiring* that the powers of the

---

*Warburg wrote that "the plan was practically impossible" (Willis, *op. cit.* 431, 385, 396, 433).
** That the bankers were chortling with glee is clear from a statement by Willis (*ib.* 439) in which he states that it was "well known during the spring of 1913" that they were already parcelling out the directorships and executive positions which would be at their disposal as soon as the Glass Bill became law.

Reserve System be employed in the service of commerce and to promote a *stable* price level. The meaning of this, of course, was to establish and maintain the stable value of money under mandate. This *mandatory* provision was stricken out in the House under the leadership of Hon. Carter Glass. I was unable to keep this mandatory provision in the bill because of the secret hostilities developed against it, the origin of which at that time I did not fully understand."[66]

When Owen declared many years later that there were provisions in the Bill he did not fully understand, we are quite ready to believe him; in fact, we do not believe he understood its essentials at all.

And whatever else may be true, it is certain that at the time the Federal Reserve Act was passed, and for years thereafter, he uttered nothing but praise concerning it. In his book, *The Federal Reserve Act,* published in 1919, there is not a word about his failure to retain the provision establishing a stable currency; on the contrary, he accuses Warburg and the Republicans of a conspiracy to make the Fed a private banking system; and he declares that the Democrats, led by Wilson, Glass, Bryan, and himself succeeded in fashioning the best of all possible monetary systems.[67] "The Federal Reserve Act," he rejoices, has now "completely demonstrated its value . . ." since it provides a quick, available supply of elastic currency issued and controlled by the government against adequate security and under an interest charge high enough to prevent inflation.[68] Owen had nothing but the highest praise for the Bank of England and its methods to avoid panics.[69] He states that since the Imperial Bank of Germany has the right to issue ample currency against commercial paper, even in excess amounts, "a panic in Germany is impossible. . . ."[70] He then lauds the Bank of France also to the skies and even praises the Aldrich-Vreeland Emergency Act.[71]

Owen declared his bitter opposition to the Aldrich Plan as a scheme fomented by Wall Street.[72] Woodrow Wilson, he states, was elected on a platform opposing a Central Bank and the

Money Trust.[73] The bill finally developed by Glass and himself, he explains, preserved the independence of the Treasury, thanks to the insistence of Wilson and Bryan.[74]

Owen represents Warburg as a determined opponent of the Glass Bill since he (Warburg) supported the Aldrich Plan and held that the reserve notes should be issued by a private bank.[75] Warburg, however, who had once argued with Owen for seven consecutive hours, was, according to the Senator, completely defeated in all his machinations; and the Reserve System was placed entirely under government control.[76] Owen declared further that the Federal Reserve Act gave "the United States the most gigantic and masterful [monetary] system of the world. . . . It assures them [the business men] absolutely against the danger of financial panics . . ."[77] He added that "Except for this Act, the United States could not adequately have financed the war. . . ."[78] And finally: "It is the best financial system the world has ever seen. It has made this nation and this government an impregnable financial force and the strongest the mind of man has ever devised. . . ." It was the Democrats, against the most determined opposition of the Republicans, who enacted this beneficent statute.[79]

THE FEDERAL RESERVE ACT IS PASSED

On December 19, the Senate approved the Glass-Owen Bill by a vote of 54 to 34.[80] This was reported to the House with a do-pass recommendation on December 22, where it passed by the generous majority of 282 to 60. Late in the evening of the next day, it passed the Senate 43 to 23, with 27 absent or abstaining.[81]

When the President—evidently fearing that the Bill was not exactly what Wall Street desired—was assured that all of its shortcomings would in time be corrected through remedial legislation, he signed it into law within an hour after it left the Senate floor. It seems that even he had been deceived by banker propaganda into thinking the Bill might not be precisely what his Wall Street masters had decreed!

And so Paul Moritz Warburg won his great and decisive victory over the American people, now bound hand and foot, heart and soul, by the invisible chains of the international financiers. He wrote Glass a jubilant letter expressing his satisfaction at the work done by him in regard to this legislation which, incidentally, completely demolishes the thesis put forward in Glass's *Adventures in Constructive Finance* concerning the role of Warburg in the preparation of the Glass-Owen Bill.*

The respected scholar, Elgin Earl Groseclose, has quite a different evaluation of the Federal Reserve Act from what we find in Owen, Glass, House and Warburg; he notes in a book written in 1962, that with its passage the "disintegration of the gold standard enacted in 1900 became a certainty. The guiding principle of the new system as stated by its most vocal proponent, Paul Warburg, was that of a flexible currency, the amount of which—and therefore the value—would fluctuate, not in accordance with the amount of gold, but with the amount of commercial bills in the market. . . . Needless to say, the prospect of ever-cheap money, which his proposals offered—the assurance that money would never be dear but always abundantly available—was highly appealing to a public nurtured on the spiced milk of speculative venture."[82]

---

*On Dec. 23, 1913, Warburg wrote Glass, congratulating him on his excellent work: "I rejoice at the many good features," he exulted, "that, after all, the law will contain. The fundamental thoughts for the victory of which some of us have worked for so many years, have won out." He intimated broadly that the purpose of his constant criticism had been merely to disarm the oppositon and perhaps to obtain a law even more heavily weighted in favor of the financiers; and, he added (as Wilson had also been assured) that if changes are needed in the future, "the country at large and its representatives at Washington will then be perfectly willing to amend the law." (The members of Congress were thus regarded as mere rubber stamps.) He closed by offering his most "sincere appreciation for having been permitted to counsel with you so frankly and so frequently" (Willis, *op. cit.* 543). In view of this letter, how could Glass have had the effrontery to declare, several years later, that Warburg had nothing to do with the Federal Reserve Act and that he was even opposed to it?

Citations

1. Willis, *op. cit.* 72
2. *Ib.* 78
3. Laughlin, *op. cit.* 20
4. *Ib.* 32
5. *Ib.* 38
6. *Ib.* 56
7. *Ib.* 83
8. Warburg, *op. cit.* Vol. I 409
9. Groseclose, *Fifty Years, op. cit.* 107
10. Mullins, *op. cit.* 43–46, 59
11. Willis, *op. cit.* 105
12. *Ib.* 107
13. *Ib.* 110–11
14. *The Congressional Record*, Dec. 16, 1911
15. Laughlin, *op. cit.*
16. *Ib.* 56
17. *Ib.* 65–67
18. Warburg, *op. cit.* 70–71
19. Lindbergh, *op. cit.* 114–15
20. *Ib.* 125
21. Groseclose, *op. cit.* 92
22. Willis, *op. cit.* 159–61
23. *Banking and Currency* 129
24. *America's Sixty Families* 110–12
25. Glass, *op. cit.* 77–79
26. *Documents of American History*, Henry S. Commager, F. A. Crofts, 1940, 77–79
27. Warburg, *op. cit.* 78
28. Willis, *op. cit.* 139
29. *Ib.* 141–3
30. *Ib.* 143–44; 151–52
31. *Ib.* 177; Glass, *op. cit.* 90
32. Willis, *op. cit.* 1531
33. *Ib.* 169–77
34. *Ib.* 169
35. *Ib.* 177–191
36. *Ib.* 1554–73
37. *Ib.* 210
38. *Ib.*
39. *Ib.* 245–46
40. House, *op. cit.* Vol I, 173
41. *The Federal Reserve Act, op. cit.* 152

42. Willis, *op. cit.* 247
43. Glass, *op. cit.* 123–25
44. *Ib.* 142–43
45. Willis, *op. cit.* 361, 364; Lindbergh, *op. cit.* 100
46. House, *op. cit.* 160
47. *Ib.*
48. *Ib.* 50
49. *Ib.* 51
50. *Ib.* 161
51. *Ib.*
52. Glass, *op. cit.* 8
53. *Ib.* 21
54. *Ib.* 22
55. *Ib.*
56. *Ib.* 29–30
57. *Ib.* 48–49
58. *Ib.* 59
59. *Ib.* 71
60. Warburg, *op. cit.* 98
61. *Ib.* 179–368
62. *Ib.* 408
63. *Ib.* 412
64. Willis, *op. cit.* 363
65. *Money Creators,* by Gertrude Coogan, 1935, republished by Omni
66. *Ib.* viii–ix
67. Owen, *op. cit.* 1
68. *Ib.* 2
69. *Ib.* 9
70. *Ib.* 12–13
71. *Ib.* 17–18; 21
72. *Ib.* 67–68; 71–73
73. *Ib.* 69
74. *Ib.* 77–78
75. *Ib.* 81–83
76. *Ib.* 81, 88–90
77. *Ib.* 88, 99
78. *Ib.* 102
79. *Ib.* 104
80. Willis, *op. cit.* 507
81. *Ib.* 516–17
82. *The Decay of Money,* The Institute of Monetary Research, 23

CHAPTER IV

Basic Provisions and Operation of the Fed

THE EVOLVING FEDERAL RESERVE ACT

Even after the Glass Bill was printed for the first time in June, 1913, it was, according to Senator Owen, amended 800 times.[1] Since becoming the Federal Reserve Act, it has undergone many additional alterations; yet its provisions remain basically intact or have been altered only, as Warburg foresaw, to confer upon the financiers greater powers and privileges.

PRINCIPAL PROVISIONS OF THE ACT*

Sections 1 and 2 provide for the establishment of not less than eight, or more than twelve, regional district banks to supply an elastic currency, rediscount commercial paper, establish a more effective supervision over banking, "and other purposes."

*All of the following material is taken from *The Federal Reserve Act,* published Dec., 1971 by the Board of Governors, 1–60, including all amendments through 1971. This has been compared in detail with the original version. Cf. Willis, *op. cit.* 1667–1696. Here are outlines of most of the thirty sections.

Section 4 provides that each regional bank shall have nine directors, divided into three classes, of whom three in Class A shall be elected by and represent the stockholding banks; three in Class B shall be elected by the same banks, but shall be persons actively engaged in their districts in agriculture, industry, or commerce; and three in Class C shall be appointed by the Board of Governors of the Fed. Thus two-thirds of the directors are elected by and represent the stockholders of the member banks, which means that the three appointed by the Board are mere supernumeraries.

Section 5 provides that member banks must subscribe stock equal to 3% of their capital and surplus; and that another 3% may be demanded later by the Board (which has never been done).

Section 7 provides that stockholders of the Reserve banks shall receive an annual dividend of 6% on their capital stock; and that this "stock and surplus thereon, and the income derived therefrom shall be exempt from Federal, State, and local taxation, except upon real estate."

In 1935, Section 10 was amended to provide for a Federal Reserve Board (renamed the Board of Governors) consisting of seven members appointed by the President to staggered 14-year terms.

Section 12 created the Federal Advisory Council, consisting of a representative from each of the regional banks.

Section 12-A—now one of the most important—was enacted in 1933 and amended in 1935 and 1942. This created the reconstituted Federal Open Market Committee, which consists of the seven members of the Board and the twelve presidents or vice-presidents of the regional banks, of whom only five of the latter may vote at any one time, although all of them attend and take part in the discussions.

Section 13 provides that every member bank "may discount notes, drafts, and bills of exchange arising out of actual commercial transactions" or "based on the importation or exportation of goods. . . ." It prohibits the use of bank credit for speculative purposes by limiting the security upon which loans may be made.

Section 14 provides that reserve banks may buy or sell gold coin or bullion, United States securities, or commercial paper. Until August 14, 1973, when Congress amended the Act, the reserve banks could buy and sell federal bonds, bills, etc., only in the open market; now, however, they are empowered to buy these from, or sell them to, the United States government directly.

Section 15 provides that government funds may be deposited in Federal Reserve banks, which shall act as the fiscal agent for the government.

On January 30 1934, Section 16 was altered to read: "Federal reserve notes, to be issued at the discretion of the Board of Governors . . . for the purpose of making advances to Federal Reserve banks through the Federal Reserve agent . . . are hereby authorized . . . said notes shall be obligations of the United States and shall be receivable by . . . banks for all taxes, customs, and other public dues."

Perhaps the most crucial provision of the law is the second paragraph of Section 16, which states that any member bank of the Federal Reserve System may obtain from its regional reserve bank such quantities of reserve notes as it may need by using discounted commercial paper or government securities as collateral. It provides further that the Comptroller of the Currency shall engrave notes bearing the imprint of the several district banks and supply them at cost of production to the Federal Reserve agents—this cost being charged against revenue received by the Reserve banks in the form of interest on government bonds purchased without funds of its own by writing checks against the United States Treasury.

Section 19 gives the Fed the power to establish reserve requirements which may vary from 10 to 22 under an amendment which became effective December 31, 1971.

The final section, No. 30, declares that "The right to amend, alter, or repeal this Act is hereby expressly reserved."

We find, therefore, (1) that all stock in the Fed is privately owned; (2) that the System is immune to income taxation; (3) that it obtains Federal Reserve notes for the cost of engraving and printing, and charges even this to the American taxpayers; (4) that it determines the reserve requirements of member banks; (5) that two-thirds of the directors in the regional Reserve banks are elected by the stockholders of member banks; and (6) that the Fed controls prices of government securities through the FOMC and is thus able, in effect, to set interest rates and determine the value of the national currency. We discover also, in due course, that it is immune to outside independent audit;* that it operates in complete freedom from government control; that member banks obtain government securities for nothing; and that it is, as a result, far more responsive to the interests and demands of the financial community than to the authority of Congress.

THE FRUITS OF AN ELASTIC CURRENCY

Paul M. Warburg passed into the silence of eternity in 1932; but his gospel of an elastic currency and a central banking system have now been fully established, with their long train of miseries, predicted by Lindbergh in 1913 and by Groseclose in 1962. When Americans were prohibited from retaining their own gold in 1934, the doors were flung wide open for international monetary manipulation of American gold at the expense of our citizens; and when our currency ceased to be redeemable in anything but itself, this nation entered upon the broad highway of unlimited inflation.

We noted that, under Section 16, member banks of the Fed may easily obtain such quantities of reserve notes as they may need, provided only that Federal Reserve agents approve. That the latter have been extremely generous in the distribution

---

* In June, 1974, the House of Representatives by an overwhelming vote passed a resolution to audit the Fed—but only its administrative expenditures—which means virtually nothing. What should be examined, in the manner that an IRS agent audits the accounts of a small businessman, is the international wheeling and dealing of the Fed, especially in its gold manipulations.

of fiat currency, especially since 1940, is obvious from the fact that such notes increased from $5,481,748,000 on that date to $68,160,683,000 in 1973.[2]

Since 1940, therefore, the Fed has increased its note circulation by nearly $63 billion, or 1,100 per cent; between 1970 and 1973 alone by nearly $18 billion.[3] Since this expansion of paper money has occurred against a constantly falling gold reserve, it is obvious that our Federal Reserve notes have been drastically diluted and thus reduced in value.

The Fed increased its portfolio of government securities from $27.4 billion in 1960 to $75.5 billion 1973[4]—which means that it put into circulation another $48 billion of spendable money and thus necessarily reduced the purchasing power of every dollar already issued.

THE OPERATION OF THE FED

As of December 31, 1973, the Fed member banks had purchased stock totalling $844,023,000, on which dividends for 1973 totalled $49,187,683. Each year the System allocates a certain amount to surplus: for 1973, this was $51,478,350, with an accumulated total of $794,845,050.[5]

The Fed is a public institution only in the sense that it was established by an act of Congress, which also has the power to abolish it at any time. Essentially, it is a private organization, since the member banks own all the stock, on which they receive tax-free dividends; it must pay postage, like any other private corporation; its employees are not on civil service; it may spend whatever it wishes; it always represents, and is responsive to the demands of, the banking fraternity; and its physical property, held under private deeds, is subject to local taxation. The stock, however, cannot be sold or hypothecated, nor does it confer a proprietary interest. In 1973, earnings totalled $5,016,769,930, derived almost entirely from interest on government securities; expenses were $526,685,898, and payments to the federal government totalled $4,340,680,483.[6]

Since the seven-member Board of Governors creates

policy, it should consist of persons with neutral or objective viewpoints; in practice, however, they reflect almost exclusively the thinking of the financial interests.

THE MAGIC OF FRACTIONAL RESERVE BANKING

Centuries ago, people used to leave their gold with a goldsmith, who charged a fee for its safekeeping. He found in time that he could lend this to others on good security and at a high rate of interest. He made the further interesting discovery that he could issue receipts or certificates in lieu of the gold itself and charge high interest on them; and since these were accepted as legal tender, they became "as good as gold." In time, he passed out receipts covering several times as much of the metal as he had in storage; and this was the origin of fractional reserve banking. When the rumor spread—according to legend—that a certain merchant in Amsterdam had issued certificates covering much more gold than had been deposited in his care, there was a "run" on his warehouse; when it was found empty, he was hanged by his furious depositors.

RESERVE NOTES AND CIRCULATING CURRENCY

The statistics in TABLE TWO show how the Federal Reserve notes and the money in circulation have increased and how the price index has risen with them; while the currency increased by 172%, prices did so by 167%.

THE CREATION OF FEDERAL RESERVE ASSETS

One of the first questions that intrigued this writer was precisely how the Fed could, without having any resources of its own, increase its holding in sixty years from virtually nothing to $106,164,462,000 in 1973.* The principal mechanism by which

---

* The principal liabilities of the Fed on Dec. 31, 1973, consisted of FR notes totalling $65,470,861,018—up from $54,955,741,000 just two years before; deposits of member banks, totalling $31,185,046,000; deferred cash items, $6,840,746,000; and capital accounts, $844,023,000 (*60th Annual Report* 273).

TABLE TWO
FEDERAL RESERVE NOTES,
MONEY IN CIRCULATION, AND PRICE INDEXES[7]

(Note that the price index of all consumer commodities fell from 60.9 in 1920 to 52.5 in 1925 and to 50 in 1930, in spite of the fact that the economy had been expanding throughout this period; that even though the price of gold was increased by 60% in 1934, prices remained virtually unchanged at depression levels throughout the Thirties; that the money in circulation increased from $26.7 to $72.5 billion between 1945 and 1973; and that, finally, the price-index increased from 53.9 to 144 between 1945 and 1974.)

Year	Federal Reserve Notes	Money in Circulation	Price[8] Index
1915		$3,148,684	35.4
1920	$3,164,700	5,467,589	60.9
1925	1,636,000	4,815,000	52.5
1929	1,692,700	4,746,300	51.3
1930	1,402,100	4,521,988	50.0
1932	2,780,200	5,695,200	40.0
1935	3,492,854	5,535,700	41.1
1940	5,481,778	7,847,501	42.0
1945	23,650,975	26,746,438	53.9
1950	23,602,680	27,156,290	72.1
1955	26,629,030	30,229,323	80.2
1960	28,495,000	32,065,000	88.7
1965	37,416,000	39,720,000	94.5
1970	50,507,000	54,351,000	116.3
1972	62,563,000	66,516,000	129.8
1973	68,160,683	72,497,000	133.1
1974	77,677,000	85,888,000	144.0

this has been accomplished is the reconstituted Federal Open Market Committee, created by legislation in 1933 and 1935, which operates entirely through the New York branch, and buys and sells government securities by using a checkbook provided by the United States Treasury. The FOMC has unlimited power to deal in federal bonds, bills, and notes—a business carried on through twenty-five dealers or brokers. Between December 31, 1971, and December 31, 1973, it increased its portfolio in such paper from $58,181,000,000 to $79,516,219,000—more than $20 billion.*

THE FEDERAL OPEN MARKET COMMITTEE

The FOMC has assumed powers so awesome and so contrary to the public interest that Congressman Patman, while Chairman of the House Banking-Currency Committee, repeatedly called for the transfer of its authority over the open market operations to the Federal Reserve Board.**

When the FOMC buys and sells federal securities in the open market at whatever price it may see fit to establish, it implements a *modus operandi* advocated by John Maynard Keynes; and it not only effectively sets interest rates for the entire economy, but dictates whatever extent of inflation or deflation it may desire. By this manipulation, it places huge amounts of currency in circulation; by diverting purchasing power from producers of goods and services—where it would result in prosperity and lower prices—to the government, it creates inflation and depression simultaneously, for reasons which we explain in detail elsewhere.

HOW THE FED CREATES MONEY AND PUTS IT INTO CIRCULATION

The Fed is not a commercial banking system; it is, as Wright Patman observes, "a total money-making machine." As

---

*Other assets consisted of Treasury gold reserves, totalling $11,460,399,000 in certificates; $9,533,218,000 in cash in process of collection; and miscellaneous items totalling $6,384,526,000 (*ib.* 272).
**H.R. 11 introduced by Wright Patman, Jan. 22, 1972. Cf. also *Open Market Operations,* by Paul Meek, 1969, published by the New York Federal Reserve Bank.

one of its principal functions, it has power to create currency out of nothing and virtually without limit via the printing press —especially since the gold standard was abolished completely; and through its member banks, it has total control over the expansion and contraction of credit by the creation or withdrawal of "checkbook money."

Let us see how this is done.

Through its Federal Open Market Committee, the Fed manufactures and puts into circulation annually billions of dollars in Federal Reserve notes which it uses to purchase government securities in the open market. In order to establish whatever interest rates it may desire, the FOMC will, for example, purchase $1 million (or $5 billion) of securities; the seller receives a check written against the United States Treasury; the recipient takes the check to his bank, where he may receive cash or deposit it to his account; then the bank returns the check to the Fed, where it increases the reserve account of the private bank or is cleared by the payment of Federal Reserve notes.*

In most instances, such checks are ultimately cleared by the payment of newly-printed currency, which the Bureau of Printing and Engraving can and must supply in whatever quantity ordered by the Fed.

Contemplate for a moment the significance of this

---

* Patman explains the operation thus: "Where does the Federal Reserve get the money with which to create bank reserves? Answer: It doesn't 'get' the money, it creates it. When the Federal Reserve writes a check for a government bond it does exactly what any bank does, it creates money. . . . It creates money purely and simply by writing a check. And if the recipient of the check wants cash, then the Federal Reserve can oblige him by printing the cash—Federal Reserve notes—which the check receiver's commercial bank can then hand over to him. The Federal Reserve, in short, is a total moneymaking machine. It can print money, if that is what is demanded, or issue checks. It never has any problem of making its checks 'good,' because, of course, it can itself print the $5 and $10 bills necessary to cover the check." (*A Primer on Money*, 34.)

"When the Federal Reserve buys Government securities, it pays for them by giving some bank or banks credit on their reserve accounts. The banks may take these credits in cash—that is, Federal Reserve notes—at any time they care to do so. The amount of Federal Reserve notes which the Federal Reserve has issued . . . is approximately equal to the amount of Government securities it owns." (*ib.* 47).

transaction. By purchasing government securities, the FOMC performs two extraordinary acts: (1) it liquidates a portion of the national debt by purchasing interest-bearing bonds, bills, or notes with noninterest-bearing Reserve currency; and (2) it contributes immediately and drastically to the existing inflationary pressures by releasing into circulation huge quantities of money which is certain to be spent at once.

Theoretically, at least, the Fed could print enough Reserve notes to liquidate the national debt. However, should it do so at once, it would certainly reduce the buying power of the dollar to about one-fifth of what it is now: in other words, all prices would rise by about 400 to 500 percent.

TABLE THREE demonstrates the relationship between the increase in Reserve notes issued by the Fed and its portfolio of government securities. In 1940, it had $2,184,000,000 in such

TABLE THREE
THE GROWTH OF THE FEDERAL RESERVE SYSTEM[9]
(In Thousands)

Year	Earnings	Assets	Gold	Government Securities	F.R. Notes
1916	$5,218	$1,210,968		$55,414	$1,246,761
1920	181,297	6,254,105		287,029	3,336,281
1930	36,424	5,200,648		591,000	1,746,501
1940	43,538	23,261,866	$21,995,000	2,184,100	5,930,977
1950	275,839	47,172,314	24,231,000	20,778,000	23,602,680
1960	1,103,385	52,984,000	19,322,000	26,500,000	28,495,000
1965	1,559,484	62,652,000	13,934,000	39,100,000	37,416,000
1970	3,877,218	85,913,000	11,157,000	57,700,000	50,507,000
1973	5,016,769	106,164,462	11,460,399*	78,516,219	68,160,683
1974	6,280,091	113,593,805	11,651,994	80,500,500	75,117,565**

*It should be noted that the gold reserve at $11,460,399,000 in 1973 reflects two 10% devaluations, placing it at $42.23 an ounce; at $35 an ounce, it would be only about $9 billion.

**1974 statistics from 61st *Annual Report* of Fed, 290–91.

assets and $5,930,977,000 in Reserve notes in print; in 1950, these totals had increased to $20.8 and $23.6 billion respectively; in 1960, to $26.5 and $28.5 billion; in 1965, to $39.1 and $37.4 billion; in 1970, to $57.7 and $50.5 billion; and in 1973, to $78.5 and $68.2 billion. We see, therefore, that the portfolio increased more rapidly than the note circulation, but that the growth of both has followed a definitely parallel pattern of expansion and inflation. In 1974, the totals were $80.5 and $75.1 billion.

HOW THE MEMBER BANKS OBTAIN RESERVES

While the Fed itself creates money by having it printed, its member banks* create checkbook money principally through their ownership of federal securities and Reserve notes. The method by which they obtain these is rather complicated, but the basis of it is their power to create credit out of nothing on their books.** They are thus able to obtain federal securities without cost, which they can then use as collateral, without even surrendering them, in order to get reserve notes from the nearest Federal Reserve branch bank.

In simplified form, and for the sake of clarity, let us assume that a member bank, such as the Chase Manhattan, desires $2 million in new currency; the following procedure will occur:

(1) Chase Manhattan enters on its books a credit of $2 million to the federal government;

(2) The Treasury Department delivers securities (bonds, notes, or bills) in that amount to the bank, which pays for them with a check created out of credit based on the new collateral.

(3) Using the new federal securities (or even commercial

---

*All national banks—4,659 on Dec. 31, 1973—must be members of the Federal Reserve System; 1076 state-chartered banks were also members at that time, making a total of 5,735 (*60th Annual Report*, 293).

** Patman stated: "On January 31, 1964, all commercial banks owned $62.7 billion in U.S. Government securities. The banks acquired these securities with bank-created money. In other words, the banks have used Federal Government power to create money without charge to lend $62.7 billion to the Government at interest." (*A Primer on Money*, 47.)

paper) as collateral, the bank then applies to the Federal Reserve agent, located in its district, for $2 million in new Federal Reserve notes, offering a short-term note—perhaps for fifteen days—in payment. The bank does not even need to surrender its federal securities.

(4) When the application of the member bank is approved, the Federal Reserve agent orders $2 million of new currency from the Bureau of Printing and Engraving and either delivers this to the member bank or retains all or a portion of it in its vaults as a reserve deposit.*

(5) The member bank then clears the obligation by writing a check made out to the Fed, using the new notes as reserve collateral.

In this transaction, the only cost is that of printing the notes (a fraction of a penny for each), which is fully paid by the Fed out of income received from the Treasury in interest on government securities, obtained by the Fed for nothing.

With this $2 million in new currency, the bank could advance (in 1973–1974) up to $20 million in new credits on real estate mortgages at an interest rate of perhaps 9 or 10%.

PROFITS FROM GOVERNMENT SECURITIES

TABLE FOUR indicates what a lucrative business commercial banking is and how holdings in government securities have contributed to the fantastic profits derived from this activity. No wonder, then, that banks can construct vast towers that pierce the very sky!

---

* As of Dec. 31, 1973, the Fed member banks had $26,759,986,000 on deposit as reserves in Fed branch banks, which enabled them to create checkbook deposits totaling $267,599,860,000. The purpose of maintaining this cash reserve in the Fed banks is to enable the commercial banks to draw down this amount should their loans be reduced or should there be a sudden necessity of meeting heavy cash withdrawals. The Fed has no difficulty supplying Federal Reserve notes, for it can order any amount of these it may wish from the Bureau of Printing and Engraving.

On the basis of reserves consisting of cash on deposit with the Fed and government securities kept in their own vaults, the member banks of the Fed were in a position where they could create credit in 1974 of nearly $1 trillion.

TABLE FOUR
PROFITS OF MEMBER BANKS
FROM GOVERNMENT SECURITIES [10]
(Dollar amounts in thousands)
(This indicates the banking profit made possible through government securities which banks obtain by bookkeeping entry, on which they collect interest, and on the basis of which they extend credit loans of six to ten times these reserves. The total profits thus obtained increased from just under $1 billion in 1920 to about $38 billion in 1972.)

ESTIMATED PROFITS

Year	Securities Held	Interest from Govt.	Rate	Interest on Credit Loans	Est. Rate
1920	$2,619,000	$91,665	4%	$900,000	6%
1930	4,125,000				
1935	12,268,000				
1940	15,823,000	632,900	3%	5,625,000	6%
1945	78,338,000	2,350,000	3%	23,500,000	5%
1950	52,365,000	1,570,900	3%	19,000,000	6%
1960	56,100,000	1,683,000	3%	20,000,000	6%
1972	61,700,000	4,320,000	7%	33,600,000	9%
1973	65,000,000	5,000,000	8%	39,800,000	10%

THE CREATION OF CREDIT MONEY

Section 19 of the Federal Reserve Act provides another means by which the Fed can control the economy—by creating inflation or deflation, through a lack, or by a superfluity, of credit. On June 21, 1917, reserve requirements were set at 13, 10, and 7, which enabled the commercial banks to advance credit equal to about ten times their reserves; and this helped finance WW I and contributed to the prosperity of the Twenties. Then, when the economy began to improve in 1936, the Fed increased the reserve requirements to 19, 15, and 10; and on May 1, 1937, to 26, 20, and 14;[11] in short, in order to prevent any return to better times, the Fed precisely doubled the reserve requirements, and thus forced the banks to call loans totalling billions of dollars and prevented them from making any new ones. When these ratios were reduced to 22.75, 17.5, and 12 on April 16, 1938, there was a noticeable improvement almost instantly in the economy.

When the reserve requirement is 16 or 17—as it continued to be for most banks between September 1, 1960, and November 9, 1972,[12]— the bankers could lend out six times as much as they had in reserve; and when this requirement was reduced to 10 in November, 1972, they could increase their loans by two-thirds.

This, of course, triggered an enormous inflation, which became fully effective in 1974. Since the banks were thus permitted to lend much more money, should it not have become more plentiful and therefore available at lower rates of interest? This would, indeed, have been the consequence had it not been for the enormous government deficits and general bursting inflation, which required twice as much money as was previously necessary for business and construction. An increase of 40% or even 50% in the money supply, therefore, fell short of meeting current needs; and for this reason the bankers were able to enrich themselves doubly or triply: first, by lending much more money; and, second, by extorting a far higher rate of interest on the total loaned. They have, therefore, been able to garner a harvest unparalleled in history. Where, for example, they were able to collect $1 billion by creating credit out of nothing in 1965, they were authorized to extort $3 billion by the same methods and from the same victims in 1974–75.

A book entitled *The Federal Reserve System,* published by the Board of Governors, explains how this fractional reserve system operates. When the reserve requirement is 20%, the bank can lend $500 for each $100 of currency or federal securities in its vaults or on deposit with the Fed; that is to say, it can create demand deposits of $500. A deposit of $10 billion in member banks will, therefore, create $40 billion of additional loan or investment money, and a total of $50 billion in demand deposits.[13] Whenever the Board determines that easier money or credit should prevail, it permits member banks to increase credit either by lowering reserve requirements or by permitting them to obtain more government securities, or both. When the reserve requirement is reduced to 10%, a deposit of $10 billion will create investment money totalling $100 billion; or, stated in more modest terms, $1,000 of cash or bonds will create credit money up to $10,000, which may be loaned at the highest rate of prevailing interest.

Let us suppose that a man is building a house worth $30,000. The bank takes a mortgage in return for a credit on its books of $20,000. Thereupon, the man uses the checkbook money thus created to pay his contractors and suppliers. With a reserve requirement of 10%, the bank needs only $2,000 on hand to obtain a first lien on property worth fifteen times as much; and it collects nearly $2,000 in annual interest on a loan created literally out of nothing.

The publication cited above explains also that when credit is restricted, "we see the powerful impact of reserve banking action, this time in the direction of contraction. A reduction of $5 billion in the reserves of member banks can bring about a liquidation of $20 billion in loans and investments and a reduction of $25 billion in demand deposits or money."[14] In other words, the banks must terminate loans during a period of contraction, and thus create a severe depression or even a destructive panic. This is what Congressman Charles Lindbergh meant when he said that panics are created scientifically under the Fed.

REQUIREMENTS DEALING WITH DEMAND AND TIME DEPOSITS

The *60th Annual Report* of the Fed—that for 1973—includes a section, pp. 288–89—called Member Bank Reserve Requirements, which pinpoints their history since 1917. These are of two kinds: (1) those governing the creation of credit, known as demand deposits or checkbook money, and (2) those governing loans based on time deposits. In 1917, the former were

13, 10, and 7; and, over the years, they have varied from a high of 26, 22, and 16—put into effect on September 24, 1949—and a low of 10, established on November 9, 1972, which created enormous inflation, followed by tight money and a depression, when the requirement was raised to 18 in April, 1974.

What we are dealing with here is the power of the Federal Reserve banks to create credit on their books on the basis of government bonds held in their vaults or of cash deposited by them with the Fed (the latter of which totalled $30,628,469,000 as of December 31, 1974). Such bonds and cash constitute the reserves on which loans may be made and which may range from less than five to more than ten times this base. If, therefore, a member bank has $2 million of government securities in its vault and $1 million of Federal Reserve notes on deposit with the Fed, it can lend up to $30 million on good security if the reserve requirement is 10; or it may lend up to $11,760,000 if it is 26. The cash kept by the Fed, and the federal securities held by the bank, are maintained as protection should a "run" develop, or should a shortage of currency arise.

The checkbook money created through loans against adequate pledges and based on cash or government securities are called Net Demand Deposits. However, just to the right of the section containing this information, we find another column under which requirements governing Time Deposits are listed; these, over the years, have ranged from 3 to 7 . This means that when a private depositor places money in the bank at interest, the bank may lend anywhere from 92.5 to 97% of this to clients. Such funds may not be used to create credit, and a portion of them must always be retained for emergency use. A similar restriction applies to all savings and loan associations and to credit unions.

Every member bank of the Fed, therefore, as well as commercial banks in general, make loans on two levels: (1) those based on time deposits, all of which may never be lent; and (2) those created out of credit based on Reserve notes, or government securities, which make possible loans ranging from less than four to a possible ten times of such reserves, depending on decisions promulgated by the Fed.

THE FED AT THE THROTTLE

Woodrow Wilson publicly deplored the fact that credit was in the hands of a few powerful men; and certain it is that, for better or for worse, the creation, extension, or contraction of credit is controlled by our Fed, a private institution, controlled by a few powerful men.

This power is to our nation and economy similar to that of the engineer who operates a great locomotive: he can open the throttle and the train gains speed; he can close it partially, and the train slows down; or he can shut it off entirely, and it stops. He can also open it wide going down the side of a mountain, and, as it careens around a curve, it may plunge over the precipice.

Our monetary system operates very much like this train and its engineer: by printing great quantities of Federal Reserve notes and reducing the reserve requirements, the Fed creates inflation; and when it attempts to curb investment by reducing them and increasing the rates of interest, it creates depression and more inflation at the same time.

By turning over our monetary system to private interests with ulterior motives for infinite profit, and permitting them to inflate our currency, control our rates of interest, determine permissible credit, and exact untold tribute from our people, we have embarked on a course which may well plunge our train of state into the abyss below the precipice.

THE DISTRIBUTION OF FEDERAL SECURITIES

TABLE FIVE (*see p. 76*) shows federal note ownership. As of mid-1973, when it totalled $469.2 billion, $291.1 billion, or 62.1%, was due to entities which had obtained the securities for nothing, or virtually so; state and local governments, $31.5 billion; commercial banks, $58.8 billion; the Fed, $75.2 billion; federal agencies, $125.4 billion, all contributed by citizens for specific purposes but appropriated and spent by the government for unauthorized activities or programs and replaced by IOUs.

TABLE FIVE
THE OWNERSHIP OF GOVERNMENT SECURITIES[15]
as of June 30, 1973
(In billions of dollars except percentages)

(Commercial banks obtain bonds from the government by bookkeeping entry and collect interest on them from the taxpayers; the securities owned by the Fed were purchased for the most part with newly printed Federal Reserve notes; those held by government agencies are IOUs given in return for trust funds collected from the people and intended for entirely different purposes, such as Social Security, highway construction, etc. Thus, $260.1 billion of the national debt as of June 30, 1973, could be expunged by a stroke of the pen and it would cost the taxpayers nothing. Bonds held by state and local governments and by "Other," which include government-sponsored agencies, could easily be liquidated in due course.

(In 1955, the OASI alone held $21,141 million; by June 30, 1973, this total had risen to $48,571 million, all appropriated by the government and used for other purposes.[16]

(We find, therefore, that $291.9 of the $469.2 billion, or 61.1%, could be expunged quickly and with little or no cost to the taxpayers.

(The money taken by the Treasury from the federal trust accounts for illegal purposes constitutes perhaps the greatest single theft in history. If this $125.4 billion were on deposit in private banks, it could be producing revenues of about $12 billion a year.

(This would leave $177.5 billion, which could be paid off in a few years through the savings in interest alone.)

TOTAL OUTSTANDING	$469.2	100%
Commercial banks	58.8	12.7
Federal Reserve banks	75.2	16.0
U.S. Government agencies	125.4	26.7
State and local governments	31.5	6.7
Sub-Total	291.1	62.1
PRIVATE NON-BANK INVESTORS		
Individuals	76.8	16.4
Insurance companies	6.3	1.3
Mutual savings banks	3.1	.7
Corporations	12.2	2.6
Other—including government-sponsored agencies	79.1	16.9
Sub-Total	177.5	37.9

According to the *Statistical Abstract,* published annually by the United States Department of Commerce, even a considerable portion of the $79.0 billion listed as "Other," is owned by government agencies. It appears, therefore, that at least two-thirds of the national debt could be expunged by a stroke of the pen without injustice to anyone and with little or no cost to the taxpayers.

It is obvious that the totals shown in TABLE FIVE will increase each year as long as present policies are continued. In fact, Congress has approved an incredible debt ceiling of $616 billion for the fiscal year beginning July 1, 1975, which demonstrates that politicians know of no cure for the disease that is eating away at our body politic other than more of the malady that is already threatening to destroy us. However, the proportion of this debt held by the Fed, its member banks, government agencies, by individuals, and others, remains substantially the same, and a similar solution for the problem created by this debt will be applicable at any time in the future.

WHO CONTROLS THE INDEPENDENT FED?

Although there has been some dispute as to the true ownership of the Fed, there is another and even more important question: who controls it—dictates policy—the private bankers, or the Congress of the United States?

On this point, there can be no valid difference of opinion, for the Fed is an absolutely independent, self-governing agency. The Congress can amend, alter, or repeal the Federal Reserve Act; but once it enacts a provision, it has no control whatever over its operation.

Some profess to believe that the Executive and Congress can exercise influence over the Fed because the Board of Governors is appointed by the President with the advice and consent of the Senate. Actually, public control or even influence in the Fed is a pure illusion. Six of the nine directors in each of the twelve branches are elected by the private member banks; and the majority of the Class C directors, appointed by the Board of Governors, have always, for the most part, been drawn from the banking community and therefore represent the same point of view. It is therefore certain that private bankers have total control over the Fed banks, which can dictate how much credit the member banks may extend.

The Federal Open Market Committee consists of nineteen members: the seven Governors and the executive officers (either the president or the vice-president) of each of the twelve branch banks. Of the latter, all have a voice in the deliberations of the FOMC, although only five of them may vote at any one time. However, since the chairman and several other Governors are always drawn from the financial community, it is obvious that this Committee also is controlled by private bankers.

And this brings us to the most crucial quesion of all, one which Wright Patman discusses at length in his *Federal Reserve System after Fifty Years* and his *Primer on Money,* both published in 1964. Since monetary policy is perhaps the most important constitutional function of the central government, and since the Fed is completely independent of Congress, it is, in effect, a fourth division of the federal establishment, and is in no way responsible either to the will of Congress or to the needs of the American people. Congress can pass laws affecting the general economy after long and arduous debate; but the Governors of the Fed can sit down in a brief session and nullify all of these entirely. For example, Patman notes[17] that he expected a definite upturn in the economy in 1936 when Congress gave the veterans several billions in cash; however, the Fed quickly cancelled the effects of this disbursement by increasing the reserve requirements for the extension of credit on August 16 of that year from 13, 10, and 7, to 19½, 15, and 10½, which forced the banks to call loans totalling billions of dollars.[18]

Thus, while Congress has no control over the Fed, this Agency can overrule Congress instantly in any economic action it may take. Our federal legislature has, therefore, not only farmed out to a privately controlled entity what is probably its most important constitutional function and power—it has even placed itself in subjection to the rule of this irresponsible agency. Finally, Fed officials, as such, are above the law; for they cannot be punished or even penalized for anything they may do in that capacity.*

We must, then, conclude that we are ruled primarily, not by our elected representatives, but by a consortium of international financiers who use their position to manipulate our currency for their own aggrandizement to a degree probably without parallel in the history of civilization.

Citations

1. Owen, *op. cit.* 100
2. 1956 *SA,* 430; *60th Annual Report* of Fed, 272
3. *Ib.* of 1971, 243; *ib.* 1972, 229; *ib.* 1973, 273
4. 1963 *SA,* 404; *60th Annual Report* of Fed, 272
5. 1973 *Annual Report* of Fed 273, 283
6. *Ib.* 282, 283
7. 1935 *SA,* 222; 1956 *ib.* 430; 1968 *ib.* 452; 1973 *ib.* 456; 1974 *ib.* 462
8. Index statistics from 1968 *SA,* 347; 1973 *ib.* 354; 1974 *ib.* 411
9. 1973 *Annual Report* of Fed 273, 282, 284–85; *Historical Statistics, op. cit.* 272, 273, 276; 1956 *SA* 382, 430; 1973 *ib.* 402, 444, 456
10. 1935 *SA,* 234; 1956 *ib.* 437; 1973 *ib.* 402
11. 1973 *Annual Report* of Fed, 288–89
12. *Ib.*
13. *The Federal Reserve System,* published by Fed, 63–78
14. *Ib.* 69
15. 1974 *SA,* 234
16. 1956 *ib.* 260; 1974 *ib.* 284
17. *The Federal Reserve System after Fifty Years,* 35
18. 1973 *Annual Report* of Fed, 288

* Wright Patman declared: "The heart of the matter is that the Federal Reserve's structural independence and insulation from the President and . . . Congress as well, mean that the . . . President cannot, as he is required to do under the Employment Act, submit a program that is likely to be effective . . . unless the Federal Reserve is willing to cooperate. There is no assurance that the required cooperation will be forthcoming . . . the President's program will not have even the proverbial 'ghost of a chance' if the Federal Reserve decides upon a perverse economic policy. Thus the President's program is really not a working program but a vision, the fulfillment of which depends on the policy of the independent Federal Reserve " (*The Federal Reserve System, op. cit.* 21).

CHAPTER V

The Federal Reserve In Action

THE UNHOLY TRINITY

We may regard 1913 as the Year of the Great Betrayal, because it brought about the establishment of an unholy trinity consisting of the Fed, the Sixteenth Amendment, and the foundation for the wars and debts which have tranformed the free American people into a nation of tax- and interest-paying slaves.

The Federal Reserve Act conferred upon a group of anonymous financiers the power to strangle our economy, exploit our citizens at will, and load our taxpayers with vast and perpetual debts. Through the ratification of the Sixteenth Amendment, the national government was empowered to extort from our producers the means of financing great and devastating wars, servicing an ever-growing and preposterous national debt, and filling the coffers of unknown bankers with tens of billions of American money.

THE GREAT APOSTLE OF PEACE AND WAR

Woodrow Wilson, that flaming crusader, that pious, passionate hypocrite with a flair for infinite deception, served his masters extremely well. After proclaiming his opposition to Wall Street so that he could force their legislation through the Congress, he turned his attention to the European War, which had begun in the Balkans in 1912 and had become a general holocaust in 1914. During his first term, he presented himself as the great apostle of peace and neutrality; and, running for re-election in 1916, he declared himself the spotless knight in shining armor who had preserved the American peace.

Scarcely had he taken his oath of office, however, when he became the fervent advocate of war. He dragged up the sinking of the *Lusitania,* which had occurred two years before (May 8, 1915), although Americans had been warned not to board her since she was loaded with contraband, and therefore legitimate prey for German submarines. The war would, he assured the deluded nation, put an end to all war; and, in addition, make the world forever safe for democracy!

He neglected to mention that American bankers had already absorbed French and English bonds totalling billions of dollars,* all of which might become worthless should Germany emerge victorious. The Fed even tried to cajole the American government into guaranteeing the payment of these securities.[1]

FINANCING THE WAR

The Fed supplied the machinery for financing** the conflict.[2] The reserve requirements of member banks were

---

* A single Anglo-French loan in 1916 totaled $750 million (Willis, *op. cit.* 1095). Lindbergh declared in *Your Country at War,* 134, that the war loans were the real cause of the war; that these totaled $3 billion before we entered it (*ib.* 129–30); and that the $6 billion of exports, for which we were never paid, caused domestic prices to rise by $17 billion (*ib.* 215).

** Milton Friedman and Anna Jacobson Schwarz state, *Monetary History of the United States,* Princeton University Press, 1963, 216: "The Federal Reserve became to all intents and purposes the bond-selling window of the Treasury, using its monetary powers almost exclusively to that end."

reduced on June 21, 1917, from 18, 13, and 10, to 13, 10, and 7,[*] which enabled them to extend billions of additional credits.[3] The first War Bond Act, passed on April 24, authorized the issuance of $7 billion at 3.5 per cent.[4] By discounting these bonds at member banks, the issue was soon oversubscribed.[5] On June 30, another was floated, which member banks purchased on the installment plan and gradually unloaded upon *their* customers.[6] As the war continued, short-term certificates were offered every two or three weeks to the banks,[7] which purchased them with down-payments of as little as 2%, and gradually resold them on credit to the clients and depositors.[8] Four issues of Liberty Bonds realized $16,937,491,850; the final Victory Bond drive netted additional subscriptions of $5,249,908,300.[9] The banks received generous commissions on bond sales totalling about $22 billion.

Without the Fed, the war could not possibly have been financed; nor could the debt have been serviced without the income tax. "The 12 Federal Reserve Banks," declares the *Encyclopaedia Britannica,* "were used as the central agencies in the 12 Federal Reserve Districts, and each of these banks formed Liberty Loan committees. To each district, a quota or proportional part of the whole issue was allotted, and the Treasury Department made use of every means of publicity."[10]

On August 11, 1919, the debt totalled $26,596,801,648, of which more than $10 billlion consisted of advances to foreign countries,[11] especially England and France, who, before long, began demanding the cancellation of the debt.[12] Private exporters and investors, however, were repaid in full with money advanced by the American taxpayers.

THE FED FINANCES INFLATION

Although the Fed had been established specifically for the purpose of preventing inflation and deflation, it did nothing to

---

[*]These requirements apply only to member banks of the Fed. Those in cities which have a branch bank of the Fed require the highest reserves; those in cities located in Fed districts, require the second highest; country banks have the lowest requirements.

discourage domestic speculation either during the war or the period immediately following; on the contrary, its member banks were the principal instrument of monetary expansion by making possible federal expenditures totalling almost $40 billion and by lending money at low interest rates for every kind of investment. The commodity price index rose from 102 in 1913, to 191 in 1918; to 202 in 1919, and to 226 in 1920.[13] Under the combined pressure of deficit spending and easy credit, wages, prices, and profits zoomed upward; some materials, such as steel and lumber, nearly tripled or even quadrupled in price.

During 1917–19, the member banks of the Fed found it more profitable to use discounted trade acceptances than government securities as collateral for reserve notes. In 1918, they held only $300,546,000 of the latter, but their discounted commercial paper, guaranteed by government obligations, totalled $1,400,371,000.[14] Through their instrumentality, the public debt rose from $1,225,146,000 in 1916 to almost $27 billion in 1919. Let us note that without the revenue from the income tax, which increased from $124,937,253 in 1916 to a combined total of $10,410,044,273 for the years 1918–20 inclusive,[15] the debt could not have been serviced.

In order to sell the Victory Bonds in 1919 at par and at a low rate of interest, the Fed could not then increase its rate of discount; large sums of money, available at low cost, therefore added more fuel to the raging fires of inflation.[16] Furthermore, as subscribers paid for their bonds at the banks, the latter "instead of paying off *their* loans at the reserve banks . . ." lent "the money in the stock market" for purposes of speculation. In fact, their borrowings actually increased, and the Fed did nothing to reduce them. The result was unprecedented inflation.[17] The wholesale price index rose from 98.9 in May, 1913, to 246.7 in May, 1920.[18] To make matters even worse, the government continued to guarantee huge additional loans to foreign countries, and great quantities of manufactured goods went abroad, for which no one, except the American taxpayers, ever paid a dime.[19]

In the fall of 1919, the stock market reached its highest peak; also in that period there were enormous increases in outstanding Federal Reserve notes,[20] and the cost-of-living index rose from 177.3 in June, 1919, to 216.5 in June, 1920.[21]

Since it seemed that this upward spiral might continue indefinitely, manufacturers continued to buy raw materials at high prices; when those at retail outran the ability of the public to pay, the warehouses rapidly filled with unsalable merchandise.[22]

THE FED CREATES ITS FIRST DEPRESSION

With the Victory Bonds safely tucked away in the hands of the public, there was no further need to hold down interest or discount rates; these were increased in November, 1919,[23] and reached 7% in the middle of 1920. There was at least one recorded instance in which a member bank of the Fed was required to pay 87.5% on "excess borrowings."[24] The larger banks began calling their loans in the stock market,[25] which crashed from a high of 138.12 in 1919 to a low of 66.24 in 1921.[26] The wholesale price index plummeted from 246.7 to 141.[27] The price of government bonds fell to 85[28] and even to 80, which reduced bank reserves drastically and thus forced them to call more of their loans. It was the first scientifically created panic in America, and thus fulfilled the prophecy of Lindbergh, Sr., written soon after the Federal Reserve Act was passed.

The magnitude of the boom-and-bust cycle was almost incomprehensible. Hundreds of thousands of farmers who had borrowed to pay for improvements lost everything.* Tens of thousands of businessmen and corporations, including the Ford Motor Company, which owed their suppliers for high-priced materials used to manufacture unsalable merchandise, either went bankrupt or survived as through fire.

As 1920 neared its close, the country was careening toward catastrophe. Not everyone, however, was a loser. The bankers had unloaded their now depreciated government securities. And when millions of debtors could not pay their notes or meet their other obligations, the bankers seized their assets and, in due

---

*Mullins, *The Federal Reserve Conspiracy*, 63, describes a secret meeting of the Fed Board held on May 18, 1920, where plans for the depression were completed.

course, repurchased the government bonds at heavy discounts, which they later resold at par when interest rates fell again in the Twenties.

THE COMPLEX EXPANSION OF THE TWENTIES

The period from 1922 to 1929 was probably unique in American history. Year after year, profits rose higher and activity in every economic field increased. Since most of the member banks of the Fed could lend ten times their reserves, credit expanded into a balloon; manufacturing plants, apartment buildings, shopping areas, and real estate developments were erected on every hand. Stocks, bought on small margins, made quick fortunes for lucky speculators while the market continued its ascent to dizzy heights.

But behind this glittering façade, built on overextended credit and speculative investment, yawned a fearful abyss; for, during each year following 1921, the productivity of industry rose rapidly; in 1923, 2,646,000 motor vehicles, produced by 241,256 workers, who received $406,730,000 in wages, had a wholesale value of $1,793,023,000; in 1929, 226,116 workers who received $366,379,000 produced 5,622,000 cars with a value of $3,675,646,000.[29] In 1923, the value added during manufacture was $1,015,655,000; in 1929, it was $1,321,282,000.[30] While the profits of the industry increased by $305,417,000, total wages actually declined by more than $40 million. The net profits increased from $35,751,000 to $410,000,000, or more than 1,000%. American manufacturing industry, therefore, with the inexorability of fate, was simply destroying its own domestic market.*

---

* It would be a mistake to consider the employers simply cruel and rapacious in their drive for doubled or tripled production at lower cost; what they did was their only means of survival. At least a thousand manufacturers of automobiles and parts went bankrupt in the fierce competition prevailing during this period. Since the industrial workers had no unions at that time, they had no protection or any means of enforcing a demand for a better share of the profits, which, if obtained, would have increased their buying power in the market place. Any employer who voluntarily raised the pay of his workers or reduced his production requirements was simply forced into bankruptcy.

Since these statistics are typical of the period, we need not wonder that the price of stocks rose from a low of 66.24 in 1921 to a high of 469.49 in 1929, and then fell to a low of 57.62 in 1932.[31]

Easy credit encouraged all and sundry to buy, expand, construct, invest. Take, for example, the manner in which houses, especially the popular three-unit structures, were sold in a typical city like Detroit: A builder would invest a total of about $12,000, get a first mortgage of $8,000, and then a second for $2,500, which required heavy monthly payments for fast write-offs. Such buildings brought $18,000 on contract with $2,000 down and monthly payments of about $175.00, in addition to taxes and insurance. The owner would occupy a six-room first floor flat, and rent two smaller apartments on the second floor, which would bring almost enough to meet all payments; the investor thought he had a home nearly free, in addition to amortizing his mortgage. The builder sold his paper at a discount of perhaps 50% and, when all was done, pocketed about $2,000 after paying sales commissions and other overhead.

Merchandisers developed an incredible system of installment selling until almost every family was making payments which consumed virtually every dollar of income in contractual obligations.

THE GREAT DEPRESSION

The cycle of inflation-deflation, with the consequent train of ruin and misery which occurred during the period 1918–21, was re-enacted on a far greater and more destructive scale between 1922 and 1941; and engineered by precisely the same forces and for the same purposes—namely, to denude our productive citizens of the wealth they had created by their toil, sweat, and tears.

A foretaste of what was to come occurred in July, 1929, when, after the contraction of credit had begun, Ford laid off some 50,000 men. In the fall, the Great Depression struck with the force of an avenging hurricane. Production and profits fell sharply. Installment payments could not be met. A huge inventory of repossessed merchandise, offered at less than bargain prices, soon drove new goods off the market. Factories reduced their hourly rates of pay and operated only one or two days a week, sometimes only two or three hours a day. Tenants could not pay their rents, and owners could not make payments on contracts or even their taxes. The price of the three-flat building dropped from $18,000, to $10,000 and then to $5,000 and soon became unsalable at any price. Men who had been millionaires in terms of contract paper, in which they had invested fortunes, lost everything. Then the holders of second mortgages were wiped out. Finally, the banks and the insurance companies foreclosed their first mortgages; and, since they could obtain virtually nothing for these properties, they could not pay their depositors. Thousands of banks were forced into bankruptcy. And where, exactly, was the "elastic" currency of the Fed?

Precisely what triggered the Great Depression has been the subject of much debate and it is undoubtedly true that several factors contributed. Analysis, however, indicates that the principal onus rests squarely on the Fed.* If the banks and their acceptance corporations had not encouraged the use of easy credit to finance installment buying, tens of millions would not shortly have faced bankruptcy. Had the banks made loans only to the purchasers of homes and apartments who obtained deeds instead of inflated contracts, the great bulk of real estate need not have been foreclosed.

The Fed banks could easily have prevented the speculative loans which led inevitably to the crash of the stock market in 1929, exactly as in 1921. Instead, especially between 1926 and 1929, they encouraged marginal buying with loans which rose from $3,111,000,000 in October, 1926, to a total of $8,549,000,000 in September, 1929, and thus drove the market to unheard-of

---

* Willis describes in an article published in the *North American Review*, May, 1929, how a group of bankers met in 1926 and planned the stock market speculation and boom, as well as the succeeding deflation, from both of which they reaped enormous profits.

levels. Those in the know began unloading in 1928, and especially in the early fall of 1929. On October 29, 1929, 16 million shares changed hands in a wild orgy of selling. By November, stockbroker loans were reduced to $4,071,000,000, and these continued to decline until December, 1932, when only $357,000,000 remained outstanding.[32] By January 1, 1930, values totalling $15 billion had been expunged; by 1932, losses reached $50 billion. The Dow Jones average fell from 366.29 to 93.63.[33] Bankruptcies and suicides were the order of the day.

Instead of performing the task for which it had ostensibly been established, the Fed put into operation what was known as the "Real Bills Doctrine," according to which funds were made available only to the extent required by current business activity.[34] As the Great Depression deepened and shock followed shock; and as the economy staggered from idleness into chaos, the Fed continued to make credit tighter until currency almost vanished from the American scene.[35] Total bank deposits fell from $935 billion in 1929 to $282 billion in 1933.[36]

In his *Memoirs*, Vol. III, *The Great Depression*, Herbert Hoover complains bitterly that the Democratic Congress elected in 1930 sabotaged every attempt to relieve the economic situation. He observed that the Fed proved a very weak reed on which to lean in time of trouble. Dominated by its banking ideology, it was primarily responsible for the tragic situation that continued year after year. Andrew W. Mellon, Pittsburgh financier, who was Secretary of the Treasury as well as Chairman of the Federal Reserve Board, was, according to Hoover, the leader of the "'leave-it-alone liquidationists' . . . who felt that the government . . . should let the slump liquidate itself. Mr. Mellon had only one formula: 'Liquidate labor, liquidate stocks, liquidate the farmers, liquidate real estate.' He insisted . . . that . . . a panic will purge the rottenness out of the system. High . . . living will come down. People will work harder, live a more moral life. Values will be adjusted, and enterprising people will pick up the wrecks from the less competent people."[37]

Inspired by Mellon's philosophy, the informed investors, who had sold while prices were high and had then precipitated the crash of the stock market, were the "enterprising people" who were to pick up the life's savings of the "less competent" at perhaps ten cents on the dollar, leaving the latter in penniless beggary which, it was hoped, would make them more moral; at all events, they would assuredly not be guilty of any high living, or, for that matter, of much hard work, simply because all kinds of industrial employment had virtually vanished from the land.

ECONOMIC DEVASTATION

Motor vehicle production fell to 1,431,000 units in 1932. In cities like Detroit, Penny Pantries were established where a meal could be obtained for ten or eleven cents. During the fifteen years following the stock crash of 1929, virtually no privately financed buildings (and very few of any kind) were constructed in the city; after eight years of constant and unparalleled expansion, economic death reigned supreme.

DR. HENRY PARKER WILLIS
REPUDIATES THE FED

It is worthy of note that some sixteen years after he prepared the text for the Federal Reserve Act, Dr. Willis was finally able to see what Lindbergh had understood so well from the beginning. In 1928 and 1929, he wrote articles in *The North American Review*[38] and in *The Journal of Commerce*,[39] of which he was the editor until 1931, condemning the operation, structure, and personnel of the Fed. He blamed it for the depression of 1920–21; he declared that the stock inflation following 1926 was the direct result of a bankers' conspiracy; and that the Fed had failed completely to accomplish any of the purposes or objectives attributed to it by its promoters and on the basis of which it had received support in 1913 from the business community and in Congress.* We wonder what Willis would

---

*Willis, who died in 1937, wrote in *The North American Review* of May, 1929: "Since the inauguration of the Federal Reserve Act, we have suffered one of the most serious financial depressions and revolutions ever known in our history, that of 1920–21. . . . One million farmers left their farms, due to difficulties with the

have written about the Fed had he published articles about it in 1933–34, after he had retired from the arena of public controversy.

Once again, the American people had been deceived, betrayed, and stripped of their hard-earned savings. The Great Depression left the great and silent majority almost totally dispossessed, not only of political influence, but of their property and means of livelihood as well.

THE UNITED STATES MONEY STOCK AND GOLD RESERVES

TABLE SIX gives statistics running from 1910 to the present showing the total money stock of the nation, the circulating currency, the gold reserves in the Treasury or the Fed, and the ratio of gold to the money stock and to the currency in circulation. Keep this information carefully in mind, because it is pertinent to other portions of this study, and should be consulted from time to time.

Citations

1. Willis, *op. cit.* 1095–1104
2. *Ib.* 1206,1298
3. *Ib.* 1196
4. *Ib.*
5. *Ib.* 1155
6. *Ib.* 1161
7. *Ib.* 1215, 1217
8. *Ib.* 1298–99, 1302
9. *Ib.* 1322
10. 14th Ed., Vol. 13, 1006
11. Willis, *op. cit.* 1320, 1398
12. *Ib.* 1411
13. *Historical Statistics, op. cit.* 231
14. 1925 SA 238

price of land and the odd status of credit. . . . We have suffered the most extensive era of bank failures ever known in this country. Forty-five hundred banks have closed their doors since the Federal Reserve began functioning."

TABLE SIX
UNITED STATES MONEY AND GOLD STOCK[40]
(In millions of dollars)

Note that between 1910 and 1929, the gold stock was generally equal to all other forms of currency combined—in other words, all of these could have been redeemed in gold. The ratio of gold to currency in circulation ranged from 50 to 60% during the period preceding 1920 and usually exceeded 90% during the Twenties. In 1930 and 1931, the ratio of gold to the money-stock—including all coined silver—was about 55%, and to the currency in actual circulation, more than 100%. Although this ratio declined in 1932 and 1933, it increased to 148.8% in 1934, and to 181.6% in 1935, and to 280.8% in 1940, when all Americans were still denied the right to own gold coin, although all the currency in circulation could have been redeemed three times over. Note that in 1934 and 1935, almost two-thirds and in 1940 almost three-fourths of the national money stock lay idle in the Treasury, withdrawn from circulation by the Federal Reserve System.

(Note how the total money stock increased by 1940 and especially after that date and following 1960; and how the ratio of gold declined to 51.6% in 1955; to 45.6% in 1960; to 27.7% in 1965; and to 13.3% in 1972.)

Year	Money Stock	Circu-lating Currency	Treasury Gold Stock	RATIO OF GOLD To Money Stock	To Circulat-ing Currency
1910	$3,467	$3,102	$1,636	47.2	52.8
1915	4,051	3,261	1,986	49.0	60.0
1920	8,159	5,467	2,866	35.1	52.4
1925	8,220	4,815	4,360	52.5	90.7
1929	8,539	4,746	4,324	50.7	91.1
1930	8,307	4,522	4,534	54.0	100.3
1931	9,080	4,821	4,956	54.6	102.9
1932	9,005	5,695	3,819	43.5	68.8
1933	10,210	5,806	4,323	42.3	74.5
1934	14,307	5,536	8,238	57.6	148.8
1935	15,113	5,567	10,126	67.5	181.6
1940	28,458	7,847	22,042	78.4	280.8
1945	28,009	26,746	20,083	71.7	75.1
1950	37,935	27,156	24,231	63.9	89.6
1955	42.045	30,229	21.678	51.6	71.8
1960	42,350	32,065	19,322	45.6	60.4
1965	50,239	39,726	13,934	27.7	35.1
1970	65,251	54,351	11,157	17.1	20.7
1971	68,929	58,393	10,184	14.8	18.5
1972	78,653	66,516	10,410	13.3	15.6
1973	85,888	72,497	11,567	13.4	15.9

15. *Historical Statistics, op. cit.* 304
16. Willis, *op. cit.* 1302
17. *Ib.* 1298–99
18. 1925 *SA* 311
19. Willis, *op. cit.* 1305
20. *Ib.* 1328
21. 1925 *SA* 322
22. Willis, *op. cit.* 1305
23. *Ib.* 1322
24. *Ib.* 1354
25. *Ib.* 1333
26. 1935 *SA* 285
27. 1925 *SA* 311
28. Lindbergh, *The Economic Pinch,* Omni 106
29. 1925 *SA* 770; 1935 *ib.* 353
30. 1925 *SA* 770; 1935 *ib.* 310, 738
31. 1935 *SA* 285
32. *Ib.* 284
33. *Ib.* 285
34. *The Federal Reserve Structure* 125 ff., a staff report by the House Banking and Currency Committee
35. Mullins, *op. cit.* 120
36. 1935 *SA* 264
37. *Memoirs,* Vol III 30, Macmillan, 1951, 1952
38. May, 1929
39. May 17, 1928
40. Statistics for 1910–35 from 1935 *SA* 222, 223; for 1940–55, from 1956 *ib.*430–31; for 1950–73, from 1974 *ib.* 462

CHAPTER VI

The Fed Under FDR

THE TRIBE OF POLITICIANS

Perhaps the art of politics should be defined as the Science of Deception as practiced by Nicolo Machiavelli and explained in *The Prince,* that handbook for wily tyrants. Certain it is that in America we have had no shortage of political skullduggery and betrayal. Is high office attainable only by proclaiming to a gullible public a set of principles which are the exact opposite of those the candidate intends to pursue? Or, are we to agree with the Italian cynic who said that "the way men live is so far removed from the way they ought to live that anyone who abandons what is, for what should be, simply pursues his own destruction rather than his preservation"?

It may well be that Richard Nixon was something less than an exemplary president; but a glance at his predecessors should be not only revealing but instructive. History demonstrates that Teddy Roosevelt was a complete fraud; that Wilson was a consummate hypocrite and betrayer; that Harding may have committed suicide because of Teapot Dome; that Truman obtained political office as the faithful servant of the Pendergast Gang; that Johnson may have been the biggest personal crook ever to occupy the White House, and that both he and Kennedy were elected by stolen votes.

FRANKLIN DELANO ROOSEVELT

Nevertheless, the policies and activities of these men, with the exception of Woodrow Wilson, were, compared to those of FDR, only slightly destructive in the general overview of American history. FDR stands alone and apart from all others; he was the supreme servant of the most evil and treasonous forces that operate on American soil—namely the international financiers, represented in classic American form by the Rockefeller interests, who work in close alliance with the Rothschilds and other European central banks.

Roosevelt's entry into the White House in 1933 heralded a complete revolution in American monetary policy and signalled the consummation of the work begun under Woodrow Wilson in 1913; thus, in 1934, the visions of Alexander Hamilton became realities and the American people were placed, at last, in total subjection to the world-wide monetary powers which have a stranglehold upon the governments of the western world. For 141 years, the dollar had usually been as good as the metal it represented; it guaranteed the integrity of contracts and produced a prosperous, solvent, and ever-expanding economy.

That this should continue, however, was contrary to the plans of those who placed FDR in his position of power. It is obvious that this financial oligarchy wanted all the gold for themselves and nothing but fiat currency for the people, thus made into pawns to be manipulated at will.

In his first campaign for the presidency, FDR promised to reduce taxes by 25%—and then he increased them by 3,000%; he said he would drive the moneychangers out of the temple—and then he *gave* the temple to them; he made solemn assurances that funds would be made available to business and to the people as needed*—and then, according to Percy L. Greaves, he reduced its supply from the $64 billion in 1928 to $30.8 billion in 1933–34.[1] Bank clearings dropped from a high of $695 billion in 1929 to $262 billion in 1934,[2] after which they rose only to $304 billion even in 1940.[3] He said he was raising the price of gold in order to increase domestic price levels, but since he banned it from domestic circulation, its price was irrelevant; he said he was spending federal money to prime the pump—to create prosperity—but the Fed made certain that there would be no return to it without a war;** he offered a managed currency which he said would guarantee a stable dollar for generations to come—but he created the basis for total monetary instability; he made it a crime for Americans to retain their own minted gold, and paid them only $20.67 an ounce for it—but he placed no restrictions on foreigners and paid *them* $35.00 for it; he posed as a great philanthropist and protector of the common people—but he loaded them with intolerable burdens of debts and taxes; he used the war emergency to establish price controls, ostensibly to equalize the war burdens—and by this means he destroyed millions of little people through rent control and other devices, while he made the financiers rich beyond the dreams of Croesus; he proclaimed that he hated war, loved peace, and would never send an American boy to fight on foreign soil—but he spent years conspiring to drag this nation into war; and when all else failed, he declared virtual war on the Japanese and so brought on the attack upon Pearl Harbor; he announced his Four Freedoms to the world—and then he confiscated the property of 130,000

*Wright Patman states that the money supply decreased by $8 billion—or one-third—between 1929 and 1933 and that 11,630 out of 26,401 banks went into bankruptcy during this period (*A Primer on Money*, 83).

** In 1933, the Federal Reserve Act was amended to give the Board of Governors discretionary power to adjust reserve requirements within wide limits. We note elsewhere also that when prosperity, in spite of FDR and the Fed, began returning in 1936 and 1937, the reserve requirements were doubled, which triggered a new and devastating depression. The forces then—as now—in full control of American life, had decreed that there must be no return of prosperity without war.

innocent American citizens of Japanese ancestry and sent them to concentration camps without charges, hearings, trials, or publicity;* he said he was opposed to Communism—and then he signed the Yalta Agreement, which enabled Stalin to survive, ceded a large portion of Germany to the Russians, and provided that some two million anticommunist refugees be forcefully returned to Stalin's power by the American army, there to be butchered or to die in the Gulag Archipelago. In his last appearance before the Congress, sick and emaciated, in a voice scarcely audible, he demanded that *the federal income tax be doubled,* and that a National Service Act be passed which would subject every American citizen virtually to military discipline and control.

These are only a few of the better-known stains which cast their dark shadows on the historical image of Franklin Delano Roosevelt. When, following his death, his casket was taken from Georgia to Hyde Park, it was never opened; and it was widely rumored that he had blown off his head with a shotgun and that his body had been cremated in Atlanta: a fitting end for a tyrant gone mad with egomania.

WHY, OH WHY?

That Roosevelt's overriding purpose was to plunge the nation into global war can scarcely be doubted; but then the question arises—why was he so desperately determined on a course which meant death to hundreds of thousands or even to millions, and frightful taxes for generations to hundreds of millions? Was he simply a human fiend?

Since we are living in an age in which it is impossible for anyone to reach the highest office in the United States without

---

*There were those who maintained (including Harry Elmer Barnes) that FDR was so determined to drag this nation into war that he had reconciled himself to permitting the Japanese to seize the whole western portion of the United States in order to accomplish his purpose; actually, there could have been little reason for interning all citizens of Japanese ancestry except a fear based upon such an expectation.

serving interests and powers that are inexpressibly evil, it is quite possible that he did merely what any other man in his position would have done. And his actions merely indicate that he was motivated by a burning desire for adulation and power; a determination to create a great central government with power to take from the people most of their production and to regiment their lives in perpetuity; and the unbending objective of amassing an enormous national debt in the form of interest-bearing bonds, which the financiers could then use in the creation of credit and the source of fantastic profits.

MONETARY POLICIES UNDER FDR

Destructive as were his other policies, the worst, we believe, were those that dealt such devastating blows to our monetary system. During his first week in office, he closed all the banks by executive order, which was not only unprecedented, but also without the slightest necessity. His purpose may have been to shock the nation into accepting laws which he quickly promulgated as executive orders or forced through a submissive Congress, which resulted in the economic destruction of millions of hard-working people, and the liquidation of labor, real estate, manufacture, agriculture, and home ownership (à la Mellon) on a scale previously unknown in American history.

On March 9, 1933, Congress approved the presidential proclamation of the 6th, which ordered all banks closed for four days "in order to prevent the export, hoarding, or earmarking of gold and silver coin or bullion or currency. . . ."

The fact is that those in the know had already removed more than $1 billion in gold from the banks; and now that the ordinary investors had learned that the dollar was to be devalued, it had become necessary to prevent them from imitating their betters who operated in the dizzy world of high finance.

By Executive Order dated March 10, the President empowered the Secretary of the Treasury to authorize the reopening of the banks, but only under special licenses, and prohibiting them from paying out any "gold coin, gold bullion, or

gold certificates, except in accordance with regulations prescribed . . . by the Secretary of the Treasury."

On April 5, the President, by still another executive order,
required every person or bank holding gold coin, bullion, or
certificates to surrender the same to the Federal Reserve banks in
return for Federal Reserve notes of the same face value, but
redeemable only in silver, and severe criminal punishments were
established for noncompliance.

On May 22, a rubber-stamp Congress enacted a law (48
Stat. 31) which declared all coins and currencies in circulation to
be legal tender, dollar for dollar, as if they were gold, and
empowered the President to reduce the gold content of the dollar
by not more than 50%, and authorized the Treasury to purchase
and mint certain quantities of silver.

On June 5, Congress declared by Joint Resolution (48 Stat.
112), that no one could legally demand payment in gold for any
obligation due him; and that all debts "shall be discharged upon
payment, dollar for dollar, in any coin or currency which at the
time of payment, is legal tender. . . ." It declared also (1) that
obligations which required payment in gold, or in currency
measured by gold, obstructed the constitutional power of
Congress to regulate the value of money; (2) that contracts
calling for payment in gold, or in currency measured by gold, be
henceforth prohibited; and (3) that gold coins, when below the
standard limit of tolerance provided by law, shall be legal tender
only at a valuation proportionate to their actual weight.

Congress thus contradicted itself by declaring on the one
hand that payment in gold could no longer be required or even
permitted; but, on the other, that the President had the power
and duty to reduce the gold content of the dollar, the value of
which must be determined by actual weight and fineness.

Then, on January 30, 1934, came the final crushing blow.
According to reliable testimony, the President never even read
the so-called Gold Reserve Act[4]—which carried no specific or
personal authorship—but signed it because it was prepared by
men in whom he had implicit confidence. This Act abolished
gold as domestic money; prohibited its coinage; provided that all

existing gold coin be converted into bullion; authorized the President to reduce the gold content of the dollar by not less than 40%; forbade the domestic exchange of other forms of currency among private individuals for gold coin or bullion, but permitted foreign governments and central banks to buy gold from, or sell it to, the United States Treasury at $35 an ounce. The Act provided also that the actual ownership of all gold be turned over to the Fed, which moved Congressman Louis T. McFadden* to declare on the floor of the House: "this bill . . . shall . . . give the Federal Reserve banks legal title to the gold, and the United States Treasury will be . . . nothing more than its physical custodian. . . . It is a fraudulent transfer."** Finally, the Gold Reserve Act authorized the Treasury to purchase or sell gold at home or abroad at any price deemed advantageous, notwithstanding any provision in the law relating to the maintenance of parity.

On the next day, January 31, 1934, the President proclaimed (48 Sta. 1730), that the dollar, fixed at 15 and $5/21$ grains of standard gold, would be the American unit of monetary value and that it would be the duty of the Secretary of the Treasury to maintain it at that level in perpetuity.

MONETARY SUBVERSION

Thus, in violation of ART. I, Sec. 10, Par. 1, of the Constitution, the integrity of every domestic contract entered into before the date of the Act was destroyed, since it became payable only in Federal Reserve notes redeemable in silver dollars, which then contained metal worth about thirty cents. It has been estimated that this debasement of the currency meant a loss to creditors of some $200 billion, taken without due process of law, in violation of the Fifth Amendment.

On February 18, 1935, the Supreme Court rendered three

---

* On two occasions assassins attempted to kill McFadden with gunfire; later he died, a few hours after attending a banquet, and there is little doubt that he was poisoned.
**From a speech delivered Jan. 30, 1934.

decisions (294 U.S. 240, 317, 330) upholding, by a vote of 5 to 4, the constitutionality of the June 5, 1934, Joint Resolution of Congress which authorized the devaluation of the dollar. The high court held that Congress had merely exercised its constitutional authority by regulating the value of coin, and that its decision was in accord with the Coinage Act of 1834 which reduced the content of the gold dollar from 27 to 25.8 grains of standard metal.

In this opinion, however, as Paul Bakewell points out in detail,[5] the Supreme Court was in error; for the Coinage Act of 1834 did not change the value of the dollar—Congress simply exercised its constitutional authority to regulate the exchange value of coins which did not serve as the basic unit. The Act had nothing to do with the value of the dollar, which was then a coin containing 371.25 grains of pure silver; it merely provided for the minting of a gold eagle of such value that it would be readily exchangeable for ten silver dollars.

POLITICAL CHICANERY ON A GRAND SCALE

The deceit and hypocrisy surrounding the passage of the Gold Reserve Act of 1934 are reflected in the declaration of the President describing its purposes. His objective, he stated, was to establish a sound currency "having a fairly constant standard of purchasing power." He proclaimed that the government had the inherent right to be "the owner of the base or reserve of precious metals" underlying the currency. He asked Congress on January 15, 1934, to deprive all American citizens of their monetary gold on the pretext that "the title to all the gold being in the government, the total stock will serve as a permanent and fixed metallic reserve."[6] In his Fireside Chat of October 22, 1933, he told the American people: "I repeat what I have said on many occasions that . . . it is the government's policy to restore the price level . . . and maintain a dollar which will not change its purchasing and debt-paying power during succeeding generations. . . . I am going to establish a government market for gold in the United States. . . . We are thus continuing toward a managed currency."[7]

The Preamble of the Act itself states that its purpose was "to protect the currency system . . . and to provide for the better use of the monetary gold stock of the United States. . . ."

The fact is that the Act abolished gold as a domestic currency; it made an outright gift (as McFadden declared)—and without so much as a receipt therefor—of the entire gold stock belonging to the United States government to the private bankers and financiers who operate the Federal Reserve System; it made the government into no more than the unpaid custodian of the gold owned by them, and it laid the foundations for the corrosive inflation that now threatens to destroy the entire economic fabric of the American nation.

A DUAL MONETARY SYSTEM ESTABLISHED

The Act of 1934 established a dual monetary system, based on the gold standard for foreigners, but consisting of fiat money for Americans, which meant that those who controlled the central banks of Europe could deal in any way they wished in gold with our Fed, while at home our own people would have to accept whatever these same international money-manipulators might dictate. Never, since the origin of civilization, has anything so absurd or outrageous been perpetrated upon a great nation; this provision in the law has enabled an interlocking fraternity of exploiters to rob the American taxpayers of hundreds of billions of dollars, and, as of 1975, there is no end in sight, unless Congress takes drastic and definitive action.

FURTHER SUBVERSION BY REGULATION

And there were other even more serious complications. While the Act itself authorized the Secretary of the Treasury to purchase gold at home or abroad at whatever price he deemed expedient, it also declared in Sect. 9 that he could sell it only to the extent necessary to maintain such currency at a parity with the gold dollar. This, of course, meant foreign redemption. In other words, the original Act placed no specific stricture upon the domestic production, ownership, or sale of any gold except coin—which no longer existed anyway. The moment Roosevelt took office, the public debt began rising sharply; during the Twenties, it had been reduced by nearly $10 billion; however, in the eleven subsequent years of peace between 1930 and 1941, it increased from $16,185,310,000 to $48,961,444,000—almost double the highest total of WW I. In 1936, the personal exemption was reduced to a point where very few could escape income taxation.

ANOTHER APOSTLE OF PEACE AND WAR

The period of the Thirties was one of prelude and conspiracy: while Roosevelt, like Wilson before him, was proclaiming his total commitment to peace and declaring that he would never send an American boy to fight on foreign soil, he was conspiring day and night to drag this nation into global war. Nor was this an easy accomplishment. When Charles Lindbergh, Jr., made speeches for the America First Committee, he drew immense and enthusiastic audiences, which moved the President to call him a "Copperhead." When Henry Ford offered to finance the Lone Eagle's campaign, it became necessary for the Man in the White House to deflect Mr. Ford from his purpose by an enormous bribe in the form of the $165 million Willow Run plant.[8] FDR conspired with Churchill in coded messages to bring America into the conflict; and when these were discovered by Tyler Kent,[9] a patriotic attaché in the office of Joseph Kennedy, our Ambassador to Great Britain and a known sympathizer with Germany, Roosevelt procured the silence of Kennedy by means which have never been fully revealed. Kent was left to rot in an English jail for the duration of the war.* Roosevelt finally ordered

* Interestingly enough, Mr. John Bryan Owen, grandson of William J. Bryan, became intrigued with the case of Tyler Kent, whereupon he was found dead in New York under peculiar circumstances, a reputed "suicide."

Cordell Hull to serve the Japanese with an ultimatum that was a virtual declaration of war,[10] and which resulted inevitably in the attack upon Pearl Harbor. With this consummation, FDR's fondest dreams were realized. Since the enemy code had been broken, it was well known in Washington where and when the attack would occur.*However, as the Japanese commander was ordered to return without action should the Americans be on alert, no warning was sent to Hawaii. Actually, the intelligence transmitted to them constituted aid to the enemy: it stated that there was danger of sabotage on the island, and therefore the American planes were drawn together as far as possible from the fence surrounding Hickam Air Field—which made them an easy target for the Japanese bombers.

THE WAR MUST GO ON!

The war could and should have ended in 1943: overtures for that purpose from high echelons in Germany reached the White House, but were ignored.[11] And when the German Air Force ran short of fuel, this was generously supplied from the great refinery belonging to the Standard Oil Company situated on the island of Aruba via Spanish tankers.**

It was of the utmost importance to the financiers that the war continue; otherwise, the debt would not rise high enough; nor would the American people be sufficiently enured to regimentation and confiscatory taxation.

*Cf. *The Final Secret of Pearl Harbor* by Admiral Robert Theobald; and various writings on the subject by Admiral Husband Kimmel, General Walter C. Short,and Harry Elmer Barnes, which lay bare in great detail the Roosevelt-Marshall conspiracy that plunged this nation into WW II.
**This writer was personally acquainted with a young man who enlisted in the U.S. Merchant Marine in 1942; who worked in the Caribbean area, and who saw many Spanish tankers leave Aruba—none of which were ever prevented by American submarines or other naval vessels from crossing the Atlantic in safety with their cargoes destined for Germany.

THE FED AND THE SUPERSTATE

In 1942, a "temporary" law was enacted to withhold income taxes and Social Security contributions from wages and salaries. Exemptions were reduced to $500; levies began at 20% and rose to 91%. In 1945, the federal government collected income taxes totalling $35,061,526,000; it had 3,526,000 civilian employees with a payroll of $8,019,000,000, and had increased the public debt to $258,682,197,000; Fed notes in circulation had risen to $24,649,132,000 and its assets to $5,062,808,000.

THE BANKERS MAKE A KILLING

The period immediately following the passage of the Gold Reserve Act were years of severe depression, when billions of currency were withdrawn from circulation. When the price of gold was increased from $20.67 to $35.00 an ounce, there was no increase in domestic prices—which FDR had proclaimed to be his objective—and, if anything, they continued to decline. The results of this devaluation are therefore most interesting and instructive to contemplate.

In 1930–31, the Treasury imported about $400 million more gold than it exported; but in 1932–33, the exports exceeded the imports by nearly $550 million. This trend, however, was sharply reversed in 1934, when exports fell to almost nothing ($52,759,000) and imports rose to $1,186,912,000,[12] and continued to increase thereafter until they reached $4,749,467,000 in 1940.[13] The Treasury continued to buy the yellow metal at $35.00 an ounce in considerable quantities until 1952–53. This was, indeed, a boon to the domestic mining industry, which increased its production from 2,412,000 ounces in 1925 to 3,075,000 in 1934,[14] and to 6,003,000 in 1940;[15] it received about $1 billion for the metal between 1934 and 1941. An infinitely greater bonanza, however, accrued to the international bankers and financiers who continued to obtain large quantities of gold from various sources at $20.67 or less an ounce, and to resell it in the United States at $35.00.

TABLE SEVEN

CURRENCY AND GOLD STOCK IN THE UNITED STATES[16]
(In thousands of dollars)

Year	Total Money Stock	Gold Coin & Bullion	% Gold	Circulating Fed Notes	Gold % Ratio	Gold Coinage
1910	$3,466,856	$1,636,043	47.19			$104,724
1915	4,050,783	1,985,539	49.02	$84,200		23,968
1920	8,158,496	2,865,482	35.12	3,064,700	98.6	16,990
1925	8,299,382	4,360,382	52.54	1,636,100	266.5	192,380
1930	8,306,564	4,534,866	54.59	1,402,100	323.9	2,440
1931	9,079,624	4,955,921	54.58	1,708,400	289.9	60,895
1932	9,004,505	3,918,596	43.52	2,780,200	140.7	66,665
1933	10,209,624	4,322,599	42.34	3,060,800	141.3	12,035
1934	14,306,814	8,237,967	57.58	3,068,400	268.3	
1935	15,113,035	10,126,000	67.51	3,492,854	290.2	
1940	28,009,400	22,042,000	78.58	5,481,778	402.2	
1950	52,440,353	24,230,720	46.22	23,602,680	102.7	

THE WORLD'S GOLD FLOWS INTO THE FED

TABLE SEVEN demonstrates that in 1925 the gold reserve was more than 52.5% of the total money stock, including the gold itself, and more than 100% of the remaining currency, more than enough to redeem all Federal Reserve notes; in 1931, the gold was sufficient to redeem all notes in circulation almost three times, and in 1940 more than four times over. We see, however, that between 1931 and 1932, in spite of substantial domestic production, the gold stock in the country declined by more than $1 billion, which means that the bankers and other depositors, expecting the metal to increase in price or the American monetary system to collapse, withdrew that amount from the banks or even the country, with the intention of reselling it later at a substantial profit.

What happened during the years 1934–1940 inclusive constitutes a profound lesson in international finance. Although American mines produced only about 3 million ounces of gold in 1934, the stock of this metal in the Treasury increased during that year by 111,867,000 ounces, on which the speculators made a net profit of more than $1.5 billion. In 1935, the profit was about $750 million, and during the five following years, when the gold reserve increased from $10,126,000,000 to $22,042,000,000, it exceeded $4 billion—a total of about $7 billion between January 31, 1934, and the outbreak of WW II. In 1940, the ratio of gold to the total money stock, including the gold itself, reached 78.58% and to all circulating currency no less than 370%; in spite of this, Americans were still denied the right to own gold coins, all of which had been melted into bars or ingots to be exported to foreign central banks, or simply stored in the United States at taxpayers' expense, and earmarked for foreign ownership.

Citations

1. *Understanding the Dollar Crises,* **235.** These totals include "checkbook" money.
2. 1935 *SA* 263
3. 1956 *SA* 429
4. Coogan, *op. cit.* 96
5. *13 Curious Errors about Money* 52–68
6. *Ib.* 20
7. Greaves, *op. cit.* 237–38
8. *The Wartime Journals of Charles A. Lindbergh* 487–92
9. *The Case of Tyler Kent,* by John Howland Snow
10. *Back Door to War,* by Charles Callan Tansill 63–52
11. *My Exploited Father-in-Law,* by Curtis B. Dall 146–59
12. 1935 *SA* 421
13. 1956 *SA* 749
14. 1935 *SA* 679
15. 1956 *SA* 748
16. 1935 *SA* 222–223; 1956 *ib.* 430–431

CHAPTER VII

The Fed and the American Dollar

THE MANIPULATION OF AMERICAN GOLD

Fantastic as were the profits of the international bankers through the sale of gold to our Federal Reserve between 1933 and 1941, this was only prelude to what has taken place since. To believe all this purely accidental places a heavy burden upon credulity; and we can only conclude that what has occurred has been the result of astute and far-seeing conspiracy.

Following the passage of the Gold Reserve Act of 1934, our government continued to sell gold to licensed industrial users in the United States at $35 an ounce and to buy it at the same price from foreigners and from domestic mines. In these transactions, the international financiers were simply trading American gold back and forth among themselves at enormous profit. As prices rose after 1954, and inflation became more and more severe, the flow of gold was reversed, and its ratio to our money supply became less and less.

TABLE EIGHT
MONETARY STATISTICS: 1950-1973[1]
(In millions of dollars)

Year	Money Stock*	Circulating Reserve Notes	Gold Stocks**	RATIO OF GOLD To Money Stock	To F.R. Notes Circulating
1950	$37,935	$23,880	$24,231	63.9	101.4
1955	42,045	26,793	21,678	51.6	80.9
1960	42,350	28,995	19,322	45.6	66.6
1965	50,239	37,416	13,934	27.7	37.2
1970	65,251	50,507	11,157	17.1	22.1
1971	68,929	54,599	10,184	14.8	18.6
1972	78,653	62,563	10,410	13.3	16.6
1973	85,888	68,238	11,567	13.5	16.9
1974	93,766	75,116	11,652	11.1	15.5***

*Money stock includes all kinds of currency—coin, Greenbacks, National Bank Notes, Federal Reserve Notes.
**For 1972, its value is computed at $38.50 an ounce; for 1973, at $42.23. If it were still valued at $35.00, the ratio of gold to the money stock would be only 10.8% in 1973.
***Statistics for 1974 from 61st *Annual Report* of Fed, 290–91. Total for Money Stock estimated.

THE WEAKENING DOLLAR

We note from TABLE EIGHT that in 1950 the gold reserve totalled 63.9% of the money stock, and 101% of the Federal Reserve notes in circulation. Why, then, could not the Treasury have redeemed all such notes in specie? Obviously, it could easily have done so at that time, and this would have prevented the ensuing inflation by placing the domestic dollar on the same footing as on foreign soil.

However, even though the currency could still have been sound as late as 1960, the omens of deterioration were even then becoming evident; for in that year the money stock was almost $15 billion greater than in 1950; and the gold stock had declined from $24,231 to $19,322 million and its ratio from 63.9 to

45.6%. In 1972, the gold reserve had fallen to 13.3% of the money stock and to 16.6% of the Federal Reserve notes in circulation.

THE DEATH OF AN INDUSTRY

While the Gold Reserve Act of 1934 permitted the operators of mines to sell their silver and gold where they pleased, this freedom was abrogated by the Secretary of the Treasury by regulation after the price of the metal rose above parity. Whereas neither the Constitution nor the Act itself gives this official the power to determine the price of commodity gold, he did so by decrees issued in 1954, which provided that gold could be mined only by those holding licenses to do so and that it could be sold only to those authorized by the government to handle or process it. The regulations provided also that Treasury mints would purchase all gold offered them at $35 an ounce, and sell it to anyone licensed to buy it at virtually the same price. Competition and freedom were thus destroyed.

As inflation following 1954 increased the cost of production, all gold—and then silver—mining ceased in the United States; tens of thousands of people were thrown out of work; untold millions invested in these industries were left to deteriorate; the nation was deprived of metal worth countless billions; and, in time, the dollar fell to 35 cents or less at home, and gold payments abroad had finally to be terminated, suddenly and peremptorily.

We believe that at least $100 billion dollars of recoverable gold—even at $35 an ounce—lies underground in the United States, and that enough of this could be extracted within a few years to serve as a 50% or even a 100% reserve for all the currency necessary for our monetary operations.

After his mining enterprise was bankrupted as a result of these Treasury regulations, one miner sued the federal government, claiming that by issuing a patent it had guaranteed him the right to operate on an economic basis. He maintained that a patent so issued cannot be divested or altered by subsequent Congressional or executive act; that he had a right to operate at a profit; that such right is inherent in the Constitution, since it protects the right to property as one inalienable in a citizen's relation to a physical thing, with the right to possess, use, and dispose of the same; when the government, by its act, deprives an owner of such rights, the act amounts to a taking without compensation or due process, even though the government does not actually seize the property; that the deprivation of the owner constitutes the "taking"; that the right to dispose of property and to determine the price at which it shall be sold is an essential attribute thereof, protected by the Constitution; and that it cannot be clothed with such public interest as to require that the price of its product must be fixed by regulation.

In his defense, the litigant cited many Supreme Court decisions.

Nevertheless, on September 15, 1959, the Circuit Court of Appeals for the Ninth District upheld the Regulations which determine the price of gold, who may produce it, and to whom it may be sold. The Court justified its position by declaring that even though the Gold Reserve Act does not specifically authorize price control of gold, nevertheless the Regulations by which the Secretary of the Treasury sets the price, are within the delegation of authority contained in the statute.[2]

THE INTERRELATIONSHIP OF SILVER AND GOLD

TABLE NINE shows that in 1920, when the population of our country was only 105 million, it produced nearly 5 million ounces of gold; and in 1940, more than 6 million; but in 1971, with a population exceeding 200 million, this production had dropped to less than one quarter of what it was before WW II.

Although the Treasury minted no gold coins and Americans were prohibited from possessing them after January 30, 1934, the Treasury was authorized to purchase and mint considerable quantities of silver. Since the price of this metal was very low at the time, the seigniorage was substantial.

TABLE NINE
PRODUCTION AND VALUE OF GOLD AND SILVER IN THE
U.S.[3]
(Domestic gold mines virtually ceased operation about 1955-56; thereafter, very little gold was extracted in the territories of the United States, except as a by-product of other metallurgical operations, such as in copper, zinc, lead and iron.
(Note how the price of silver has fluctuated from $1.323 an ounce in 1840 to 35.1 cents in 1940 and to dizzy heights in recent years; and note how its ratio of value to gold varied from 15.62 in 1840 to 33.33 in 1900 and to 99.76 in 1940. Note also that gold production, which averaged about 4.5 million ounces annually before WW I, increased to more than 6 million in 1940, and then fell almost to one-sixth of this amount in 1973. Note also how the production of silver increased from 30.7 million ounces in 1954 to 45 million in 1970, after which it fell slightly because of the drop in price. However, it will certainly increase dramatically in 1975-76.)

Year	Silver Price	Gold Ratio to Silver	ANNUAL UNITED STATES PRODUCTION IN OUNCES		Total World Gold Production
			Gold	Silver	
1840	$1.323	15.62			
1890	1.046	19.75	1,589,000	54,516,000	
1900	.620	33.33	3,830,000	57,647,000	
1910	.541	38.22	4,657,000	57,138,000	
1920	1.019	20.28	2,476,000	55,362,000	
1930	.385	53.74	2,286,000	50,748,000	
1940	.351	99.76	6,003,000	69,586,000	
1950	.742	47.14	2,104,959	42,309,000	32,700,000
1960	.905		1,666,722	30,766,000	38,000,000
1961	.924		1,548,270	32,166,000	
1962	1.080		1,542,511	36,798,000	46,200,000
1964	1.293		1,456,308	36,334,000	46,300,000
1970	1.771		1,743,322	45,006,000	47,500,000
1971	1.542		1,495,108	41,561,000	4,500,000
1972	1.665		1,450,000	37,000,000	44,700,000
1973	2.535		1,166,000	37,000,000	43,500,000
1974	5.580 —Oct. 9 Jan. futures				

Silver is quite different from gold in various respects. Gold, for the most part, is either hoarded or used for purposes which, in due course, cause it to return to coinage or bullion; it is estimated that 60% of all the gold extracted from the earth in 7,000 years is presently stored in the vaults of central banks. Its rate of production, furthermore, has varied so little over the millenniums that its value has changed only slightly. Silver, on the other hand, presents a very different image: in the first place, its price fluctuates far more rapidly and widely and its industrial consumption is very heavy; furthermore, once used—again unlike gold—almost all of it disappears forever. Consequently, there must be a large and constant production of new silver to meet the needs of industry. In 1972, for example, while the United States produced 37 million and imported 65 million ounces of silver, it consumed 147 million; and since it exported about 28 million,[4] it was necessary to draw upon existing stocks for about 60 million ounces.

TABLE NINE demonstrates why a bimetallic monetary standard is impractical or even impossible over any extended period of time. Although the ratio of gold to silver remained quite stable between 1790 and 1870, thereafter as one metal or the other became either more scarce or plentiful, the ratio varied excessively. Between 1840 and 1870, the metal in a silver dollar remained stable at about $1.025. In 1880, however, it fell to $.886. During the depression years, processors of used metals paid as little as 15 cents an ounce for silver, and in 1930 the value of the metal in a minted dollar fell to 29.8 cents and in 1940 to 27.1 cents; at the same time, the commercial value-ratio of gold to silver zoomed to 99.76.[5]

Then, however, with the increasing industrial consumption and the declining domestic production of silver, its price rose from 35 to 74 cents between 1940 and 1950; in 1954, it went to 90 cents, where it remained for a few years. In 1961, it reached .924 cents and in 1962, $1.08. When it rose to $1.293 in 1964, the economic facts of life made the cessation of silver coinage in the United States mandatory. The system of managed currency had simply brought on its own destruction.

In 1970, the price of silver soared to $1.771 an ounce; but

this was only a premonition of what was to come. During the two years following 1971, wild speculation in the metal sent it to dizzy heights; it has been reported that certain multi-millionaires are buying such quantities of it so as virtually to corner the market. On April 4, 1974, the average price hovered somewhere over $5.00 an ounce; and futures were selling at from $508 to $572 per hundred ounces.

THE DRAMATIC STORY OF OUR GOLD AND MONEY STOCK

The history of gold since 1934 is even more dramatic and instructive and demonstrates what happens when a managed currency replaces one redeemable in specie. During the early Sixties, as we have seen, the ratio of gold in the Fed to its money supply continued to decline, and by 1967–68 reached a condition of crisis.

TABLE TEN reflects the tragic situation into which monetary mismanagement has plunged the United States. In 1920, the money stock totalled $8,158,490,000, the gold reserve $2,639,000,000, and the portion earmarked for foreign ownership only $13 million, which was only one-fiftieth of one percent. In 1955, the money stock was about $42 billion, and the gold reserve still exceeded 50%; but the foreign liabilities had risen to almost $12 billion, and the gold earmarked to foreigners had increased to nearly $7 billion, more than 30% of our total (*see p. 114*).

Even this, however, was only the beginning. By 1965, the money supply had been inflated to more than $50 billion, the gold reserve had fallen to $14,715 million, and foreign obligations had risen to $25,561 million. In 1973, the Reserve notes alone totalled well over $68 billion; the devalued gold stock had fallen to $11.4 billion; foreign liabilities exceeded $65 billion; and gold earmarked to foreign ownership had risen to about $18 billion.

EXCURSUS ON THE DOLLAR

Since the Constitution declares that Congress shall have the power to coin money and regulate the value thereof; and then

TABLE TEN[6]
RESERVE NOTES, GOLD STOCK, FOREIGN LIABILITIES,
AND GOLD UNDER EARMARK
(In thousands of dollars)

(Note that in 1925, the Federal Reserve notes in circulation totalled only $1,636 million, while the gold in the Treasury totalled $4,112 million, and that only $13 million was under earmark, and this fell to $8.8 million in 1930. In 1940, the Federal Reserve notes still totalled only $5.5 billion, while the gold reserve was four times as great. In the meantime, however, gold earmarked to foreign ownership had increased to $1.8 billion. Between 1940 and 1945, Federal Reserve notes increased to $23.6 billion and earmarked gold to $4,293 million. Note what happened between 1955 and 1973-74: Federal Reserve notes increased from $26.6 to $68.1 billion, foreign liabilities from $11.9 to $72.9 billion, and earmarked gold from $6.9 to $18 billion, while our own gold reserves declined from $21.7 to $10.4 billion. In 1973, therefore, obligations to foreigners were almost seven times greater than our gold reserves and exceeded all Federal Reserve notes in existence.)

Year	Reserve Notes	Gold Stocks	Foreign Liabilities	Gold Under Earmark
1920	$3,064,700	$2,639,000		$22,000
1923	2,234,700	3,784,652		
1925	1,636,100	4,112,000		13,000
1930	1,746,501	4,306,000		8,800
1935	3,492,854	10,126,000		137,000
1940	5,481,778	22,042,000		1,807,700
1945	23,650,975	20,083,000		4,293,800
1950	23,602,680	22,820,000		5,625,700
1955	26,629,030	21,753,000	$11,895,000	6,941,000
1960	28,449,000	17,954,000	18,701,000	
1965	37,074,000	13,799,000	25,561,000	
1970	50,323,000	11,105,000	41,761,000	
1972	58,757,000	10,410,000	60,722,000	
1973	68,160,783	11,460,399	69,218,000	
1974	75,117,563	11,651,994	72,936,000	18,000,000 (Est.)

adds that no state shall make anything but gold and silver legal tender for the payment of debts, constitutionalists declare, as we shall see, that it means at least this: first, that Congress alone may, and is required to, establish a coin either of silver or of gold of a certain fineness and weight to serve as our unit of value; and, second, that it must require that notes circulating as currency be redeemable in specie.*

Jefferson and Jackson were bitter opponents respectively of the First and the Second United States Bank because these institutions were organized for private profit at public expense and were endowed with powers which Congress alone can exercise and may, therefore, not delegate to any other authority. In his Second Inaugural Address, Jackson stated his opposition to state-chartered banks of issue; and Jefferson declared over and over that the federal government alone should have power to coin money or issue circulating currency of any kind.

Since it seems to have been the position of the Founding Fathers that the Treasury should emit no currency except coin, and since they assuredly envisioned the existence of paper money, it may be that they intended the latter to be issued by state-chartered institutions; and they probably intended that all such notes be guaranteed by metallic reserves of 100%, for there is nothing to indicate that those who framed the Constitution would have tolerated what is known as fractional reserve banking.

It is certain that no fully constitutional paper currency has ever been issued in America except the Lincoln greenbacks, and even these qualified as such only after 1879 when they became fully redeemable in gold on demand. Between 1791 and 1811, and again between 1816 and 1836, the principal form of circulating

---

*Inflation does not mean that values or real prices have increased—only that money has been cheapened. For example, in 1940, a loaf of bread cost 10 cents—ten loaves for a dollar. In 1974, the same loaf cost 50 cents—two for a dollar. However, in 1940, a silver dollar exchanged for a $1 Fed note; in 1974, five such notes were necessary to obtain the equivalent of one silver dollar, which means that an ounce of silver bought the same amount of bread in 1974 that it did in 1940.

notes consisted of issues from the two United States banks; and from 1811 to 1816 and from 1836 to 1863, the only notes circulating as currency—all theoretically redeemable in silver or gold—were those emitted by state-chartered institutions.

Between 1863 and 1909, most of the notes circulating as money, in addition to the greenbacks, were issued by the federally chartered associations of banks authorized by the National Banking Act of 1863, which issued currency based on federal bonds.

When the Aldrich-Vreeland Act was passed in 1908, Congress created the precursor of the Federal Reserve System, which confers upon a consortium of private banks monopoly power for the issuance of currency notes, for the control of credit, and the determination of rates of interest. In 1934, this power was enormously enhanced by giving these banks the ownership of the government gold stock and the complete control over American international monetary operations.

Since January 31, 1934, there has been no such thing in the United States as a lawful domestic dollar. Although Congress at that time gave the Treasury the power to purchase silver and mint silver dollars of the kind authorized in 1791, it did not make these the unit of value; on the contrary, it declared specifically that the dollar would consist thereafter of a coin containing 15 and 5/21 grains of standard gold, but at the same time forbade all gold coinage and made it a crime for any American citizen to retain possession of his own coin or bullion.*

It is therefore obvious that the only constitutional dollar ever circulated in the United States was the coin containing 371.25 grains of pure silver which was the official unit of value from 1791 to 1873; and the coin of 25.8 grains of standard gold, which replaced it between 1873 and 1933.

---

*It is indeed interesting to note that in 1929 the Communist government of Russia made it a crime for any Russian to retain gold in any form. Solzhenitsyn related (cf. *Gulag Archipelago*, 52–54) how literally thousands—even tens of thousands—were tortured, sent to Siberia, or shot, who were found in possession of gold, or who were merely suspected of hiding it. Tyrants know the value of gold.

THE PROGRESSIVE DEGENERATION OF OUR CURRENCY

Between 1914 and 1934, every Federal Reserve note promised to pay the bearer on demand at the United States Treasury or at any Reserve Bank the full value of the document in gold or silver. Between 1934 and 1963, the note promised to pay the bearer "in lawful money"—which meant that it was redeemable in silver. Beginning with the latter date, the currency states only that "This Note is Legal Tender for All Debts, Public and Private." In other words, it can be exchangd for nothing except other similar pieces of paper, or for goods and services that other persons are willing to surrender in return. And since a "note" by definition is "a written or printed paper acknowledging a debt, and promising payment" with something of value on demand or at the expiration of a certain period of time, Federal Reserve issues are not only unconstitutional as money—they are a total fraud; they have no stability or assurance of future value; they can be printed like newspapers and could become as worthless as the assignats of the French Revolution.

Under the Gold Reserve Act of 1934, the Fed was required to maintain a reserve of 40% in gold certificates against its circulating currency notes; on June 24, 1945, however, this was reduced to 25%; and on March 3, 1965, all such requirements were abolished entirely. In 1965 also, the Treasury began issuing the debased sandwich dimes and quarters and the silver content of dollars and half dollars was reduced by 40%. On June 24, 1968, silver certificates were, by presidential proclamation, declared irredeemable. On December 31, 1970, the Secretary of the Treasury authorized the issuance of dollars and half dollars of the same composition as dimes and quarters. On March 17, 1969, a 2-tier gold system was established, under which only central banks could obtain American gold at $35 an ounce—while the dollar and the metal were set free to float for others. In August, 1971, the American gold window was slammed shut for all purposes except to clear balances of international trade. On May 8, 1972, the gold dollar was officially devalued by 10%—from

$35.00 to $38.50; and on February 1, 1973, by another 10%, to $42.23 an ounce.

However, even at that level, the Federal Reserve notes were still enormously overpriced; and, when, on March 16, 1973, Congress approved the executive order of February 22 setting the dollar completely afloat, gold had already established its true value in the open market. Since then, it has been selling at prices ranging from about $150 to $200 an ounce. The gold stock held by the Fed in 1973 is valued at $11,460,399,000, but is actually worth, in terms of Fed notes, approximately $45 billion; and the gold stores in the vaults of the New York branch of the Fed is now, at $200 an ounce, worth about $100 billion.

When the dollar was set afloat officially, the pent-up inflationary forces of the preceding fifteen years were released to wreak their destruction upon all the monetary systems of the world's important free nations; this was inevitable, since we live now in an integrated global economy.

UNILATERAL REPUDIATION

Thus the American government, which had repudiated its obligations to its own citizens in 1934, finally perpetrated the same offense against its foreign creditors. It was, however, an act of absolute necessity: for had this not been done, the Fed would shortly have been without so much as an ounce of the precious metal—a catastrophe simply incomprehensible in scope.

However, the fierce, deep bitterness felt by many left holding our depreciated notes can easily be understood; for many of them had exchanged the equivalent of an ounce of gold for $35.00, and were now to discover that this currency had been debased somewhere between 300 and 400%.

DEVASTATION AT HOME

Before the American dollar was repudiated in Europe, we had creeping inflation at home—steady and inexorable; but with this renunciation, it became a galloping disease in 1975. The consequent losses and suffering of Americans have been fearful indeed; and the end is not in sight. Yet there is one group of powerful men who have amassed profits that stagger the imagination: they are the same financiers who brought the Fed into being and who control the Banque de France, the Reichsbank, the Bank of England, and the Bank of Italy. As inflation intensified between 1960 and 1973, as more and more billions of United States currency were exported, and as the obligations of the Fed grew into astronomical proportions, the operators of those banks exchanged their United States currencies for gold in ever-increasing quantities. In the vaults of the New York branch of the Fed—stored there presumably at the expense of American taxpayers—lie approximately 18,000 tons of ingots,[7] worth about $18 billion at $35 an ounce, and about $22 billion at $42.23.* None of this belongs to the American people or its government; it does not even belong to the Fed; it is the property of the foreign investors who purchased it at $35 an ounce even after its true value was well above $125. At $200, it will bring more than $100 billion, a windfall of about $85 billion, which, under Section 895 of our Internal Revenue Code, is not only tax-free, but also exempt from disclosure. So, when this gold is resold in America, not even the IRS will be able to discover who made these fantastic profits.

In 1950, when the gold reserves totalled $25,505,000,000 and comprised 63.9% of the total money stock, including circulating coin and Reserve notes, a sound currency could certainly have been maintained. By 1970, however, when most of the gold was owned by European banks, it had fallen to $10,459,000,000 and the ratio to 15.5%. During this period, the reserve notes in circulation rose from $27,156,000,000 to $57,093,000,000—an increase of 129%. We find, meanwhile, that fiat money proved a great boon to American bankers; for their cash dividends, which were only a small portion of their total profits, increased from $346,000,000 to $1,754,000,000.[8]

---

*Cf. *The Politics of Money*, by Brian Johnson, McGraw-Hill, 1970, 114–15. See TABLE ELEVEN (p. 121) for statistics concerning the profits which have been made by the gold manipulators at the expense of the American taxpayers.

THE FLIGHT OF CURRENCY AND CREDITS

According to the *Wall Street Journal* of May 25, 1972, the dollar holdings of all foreigners totalled $57.67 billion at that time, of which $53 billion was held by central banks; and our total foreign liabilities had reached the astronomical total of $65,680 million.[9] Since our own reserves declined by $15 billion in twenty years, all of the gold now remaining with the Fed would fall short by almost $55 billion of being sufficient to redeem, at $35 an ounce, all the currency and credit now held by foreign central banks.

This ominous situation has developed in large part because of the enormous flight of industrial capital to foreign countries, where it has taken refuge because of cheaper labor and materials; or it consists of deposits in American banks sent abroad by them in order to enjoy the higher rates of interest there available. However, several billion dollars are said to have taken wing through unknown channels to unknown destinations.

It is certainly true that capital has fled because of high domestic production costs. Plants built with American money in Japan, Germany, Italy, England, Spain, etc., disgorge their niagaras of goods which are sold, not only in the international market, but are also shipped back to the United States. It should be obvious that, unless this flow of capital and goods is reversed, our economic future is dim indeed. We have few exports except raw materials and subsidized agricultural products. Is it not ironic that the most highly industrialized nation in the world has come to so desperate a pass?

When American industry again competes successfully in foreign markets, gold will once more flow from abroad back into the United States Treasury; only then will we again have a stable dollar; only then can the perils of financial collapse be avoided.

WHAT IS A DOLLAR IN 1975–76?

Interestingly enough, although Americans have not been permitted to own a lawful dollar since 1934, this has always been

TABLE ELEVEN
PROFITS FROM GOLD MANIPULATION
(During 1932, bankers withdrew more than $1 billion in gold from American banks and then returned it to the Fed after Jan. 31, 1934, at a profit of 66%. Between 1934 and 1940, foreigners sold so much overpriced gold to the Fed that its stock increased from about 200 to 630 million ounces, with an approximate profit of $20 to the sellers per ounce, or $8 billion.

(After 1952, a reverse movement set in: inflation reduced the buying power of the dollar so that gold became more and more underpriced. However, foreigners—particularly central banks—were still permitted to cash in their U.S. currency at the Fed at $35 an ounce for gold; and, as a result, between 1953 and 1972, the gold stock fell from 700 to 270 million ounces; and, since foreigners held U.S. currency or credit equal to 6 and a half times our entire gold stock, the American government was finally forced to set the dollar afloat by repudiation and bring on the inflation that has since resulted throughout the world.

(When the foreign bankers who own about 18,000 tons of gold stored in the vaults of the New York branch of the Fed decide to sell at perhaps $200 an ounce, they will make a clean profit of about $80 billion, which they can use to buy American industries. Under section 895 of Internal Revenue Code, this profit will not only be completely exempt from taxation, but from disclosure also.)

Year	GOLD STOCK	ESTIMATED PROFIT
1932	$3,819,000,000	
1940	22,042,000,000	$8,000,000,000 (1934-40)
1950	24,231,000,000	
1971	10,184,000,000	Estimated Potential
1972 (at $35.00)	9,350,000,000	Profit by Selling Gold
1972 (at $38.50)	10,410,000,000	at $200 an Ounce
1973 (at $42.23)	11,460,393,000	$80,000,000,000 (1954-73)
1973 (at $35.00)	9,168,000,000	

defined. It consisted of 15.238 grains of standard gold until May 7, 1972, when it was reduced to 13.712 grains; on February 1, 1973, it was further reduced to 12.342 grains—which is its official content in 1975.

And this poses an extremely intriguing and interesting question: since the federal government imposes percentage taxes upon "dollar incomes," are not all American citizens justified in reporting these in terms of standard metal? With gold at $200 an ounce, a taxable income of $20,000 translates into one of about $4,000. Why, then, should not the taxpayer subtract all the exemptions and allowances in terms of Federal Reserve notes to which he is entitled from his Gross Income, report the remainder as Adjusted Gross, compute the value of this in terms of official gold dollars, subtract his exemptions from this amount, and pay a tax on the remainder, which would be his Taxable Income?

The computation in TABLE TWELVE would therefore indicate the kind of report the taxpayer might file with the Internal Revenue Service.

BONDS VS. CIRCULATING NOTES

It is, of course, more inflationary for the government to issue large amounts of noninterest-bearing notes than to emit interest-bearing certificates in the same amount; and when the

---

TABLE TWELVE
INCOME TAX DUE UNDER AN OFFICIAL DOLLAR

GROSS INCOME	$25,000.00
Deductions for taxes, interest, charitable contributions, etc.	5,000.00
RESERVE NOTE ADJUSTED GROSS INCOME	20,000.00
TRUE INCOME, IN TERMS OF GOLD DOLLARS	4,000.00
Deductions for 5 exemptions, at $750.00	3,750.00
TAXABLE INCOME	250.00
Tax in terms of Gold Dollars	35.00
Tax in terms of Reserve note dollars	185.00
TAX IN RESERVE NOTE DOLLARS UNDER IRS COMPUTATIONS	3,330.00

Fed,through the FOMC, purchases great amounts of federal securities in the open market, as it does constantly with newly printed Federal Reserve notes, it is, in reality, liquidating a portion of the national debt by placing excess currency into circulation and thereby creating runaway inflation. However, there is no economic reason why all privately held bonds, etc.—which now constitute only a fraction of the national debt—could not be replaced gradually over a period of time with United States currency: we emphasize *gradually* because a huge and sudden conversion would be disastrously inflationary, while a gradual liquidation would not, since the same currency would be used repeatedly to make the additional purchases. And note that we say *no economic reason:* for the obstruction would be political, namely, the stranglehold which the financiers have on the American government, and their determination to continue the government debt to be utilized by them for banking profit.

The liquidation of the national debt is now a realizable objective; for the assets of the Fed could be assumed by the nation without cost, except to purchase at par the stock owned by the member banks. The Fed could then be replaced by, or transformed into, a publicly-owned institution of issue performing for the people as a whole the functions that it now performs in the interest and for the profit of its private owners. The present Reserve notes could easily be replaced by true United States currency; and it is at least possible that redeemability could be restored, as mandated in the Constitution. Almost two-thirds of the federal obligations, which constitute the public debt, are held by government agencies, by the Fed, or by private institutions which obtained them without cost. Since this is true, this portion of the burden could be expunged virtually for nothing; and it is still not too late to avert total disaster. The debt could thus have been reduced to about $160 billion, as of 1973, or to comparable amounts in later years, and this too could be liquidated progressively by the issuance of noninterest-bearing notes. And we see, finally, that if there is any silver lining in the inflation that has overtaken us, it consists of the fact that the national debt can now be repaid in depreciated

Fed notes, which in itself would be a colossal form of repudiation.

CONGRESSMAN RARICK'S BILL

On January 22, 1971, Congressman John R. Rarick introduced H.R. 351: "To vest in the Government of the United States the full, absolute, complete, and unconditional ownership of the twelve Federal Reserve Banks." The bill states that "the Secretary of the Treasury of the United States is hereby authorized and directed herewith to purchase the capital stock of the twelve Federal Reserve Banks and branches and to pay the owners thereof the par value of such stock at the date of purchase."

It should be pointed out, however, that unless the Federal Reserve Act is repealed and another monetary system established to replace it, a mere change of stock ownership would have little substantive effect on its operation. The preparation and enactment of a law which will transfer the control of our currency and credit into the hands of a federal agency, such as is envisioned in the Constitution, looms, therefore, as one of the most important and difficult objectives facing constitutionalists at this juncture of American and world history.

CONGRESSMAN PATMAN'S BILL

On the very same day in 1971, Congressman Patman introduced H.R. 11, which would effect far-reaching changes in the Federal Reserve Act, but would not repeal it or transfer ownership of the system to the government. This would be done by

(1) Retiring Federal Reserve bank stock and giving member banks certificates of membership in return;
(2) Abolishing the Federal Open Market Committee;
(3) Coordinating Federal monetary with other economic policy;

(4) Establishing financial accountability via audits;
(5) Requiring congressional checks, through normal appropriations procedures;
(6) Reappraising the tight-money policies and the high interest rates established by the Fed; and
(7) Reducing private banking influence in the System.

It is interesting and informative to contemplate the fate of the men who oppose the policies of those who control and manipulate American monetary policy through the Fed. Enormous sums of money, poured into John Rarick's congressional district in Louisiana, brought defeat at the polls to this stalwart and outspoken patriot. When the same tactic failed to accomplish the same result in regard to Wright Patman in Texas, he was summarily removed from his position as Chairman of the House Banking and Currency Committee (a post he had occupied for decades) and replaced by another man, known to be friendly to the banking interests and the men who operate the Federal Reserve System.

THE UNCONSTITUTIONALITY OF THE FED

A central bank of issue controlled and operated by the federal government would, of course, be necessary in our complex economy if the functions of the present Fed were to be replaced by a practical and constitutional agency. As the present operation of the Fed is efficient and successful, its physical plant could be utilized by a United States Monetary Authority operated in the interests of the public, instead of those serving international private bankers. The situation which existed after the Second United States Bank was abolished or even while the National Banking Act of 1863 was in operation, would be intolerable. The fatal flaw in the Fed consists in the fact that it operates as an independent agency for the benefit of the private financiers who own the member banks and are thus able to control credit, interest rates, and our entire economy. As various statesmen have pointed out, Congress alone is given the authority in the Constitution to coin or issue money and regulate the value thereof; the Federal Reserve Act is therefore unconstitutional on its face; and our Reserve notes do not qualify as true legal tender, no matter what words are printed upon them, and no matter what laws are passed by Congress.

This does not mean, however, that the federal government should in any way go into the banking business; this ought to remain a private operation. The government is to coin money, and determine the value thereof by weight and fineness; it may also issue regulations setting forth the conditions under which banks may lend money and extend credit.

OUR ULTIMATE OBJECTIVE

The purpose of this study is to make some contribution to the establishment of a monetary system which will restore constitutional money; to promote prosperity; guarantee stable prices; protect the people who have invested in bonds, bank accounts, insurance policies, annuities, etc.; create a favorable balance of international trade; increase the export of American manufactures in the world market in return for raw materials; liquidate the national debt; and remove the danger of inflation, deflation, depression, and panics.

THE FEDERAL RESERVE SYSTEM

We believe that the Federal Reserve Act should be replaced by a constitutional monetary system, not only because it is in violation of our basic law but also because it gives a cabal of private, international bankers the means of issuing our currency, controlling our credit, determining rates of interest, and thus enslaving our people. They have used their power to drag us into one war after another; to load us with confiscatory taxation and astronomical debt; to construct a monstrous federal bureaucracy; to create inflation, followed by frightful depressions, in which tens of millions lost their possessions; and to concentrate the wealth of this nation in the hands of an all-powerful oligarchy of irresponsible and parasitical exploiters.

A CONSTITUTIONAL MONETARY SYSTEM

Since constitutionalists agree that the Federal Reserve Act should be repealed, our problem centers around three questions: (1) what kind of monetary system should replace it? (2) should the dollar represent or consist of a definite standard of intrinsic value, such as gold, and be redeemable in specie? and (3) what should be the relationship between the United States Treasury and the private banks?

When ten individuals meet who agree that the Fed should be abolished and who have studied the monetary problem carefully, it is quite possible that no two of them will agree on the legislation that should be enacted to replace the Fed, especially in respect to the monetary question and redeemability. However, after extensive study and many conferences, we can offer the following as a general consensus: Congress, we believe, should

(1) Repeal the Federal Reserve Act;
(2) Purchase from the member banks at par value their stock in the Fed;
(3) Replace the Fed with a publicly owned facility which would
  (a) Repossess without further compensation all the assets of the Fed, including all its gold certificates, government securities, cash, buildings, personal property, and any other tangible or intangible property it may possess;
  (b) Repossess in the same manner all securities now owned by the member banks of the Fed and obtained by them through the creation of credit on their books;
  (c) Replace such securities with government certificates of deposit to whatever extent necessary in order to enable the banks to continue in business; and require them to pay interest on such certificates to the United States Treasury exactly as they now do on time deposits placed in their care by private individuals;
  (d) Replace all present Federal Reserve notes with government issue;

(e) Gradually reduce the total of government securities in private hands by redeeming and replacing them with noninterest-bearing government notes;

(f) Establish reserve requirements for all commercial banks;

(g) Issue rules and regulations governing lending and the control and creation of credit by private banks;

(h) Re-establish a lawful currency based on a stable dollar;

(i) Be subject to independent audit and be financed by regular government appropriations.

An Act replacing the Fed would, of course, have to be an elaborate piece of legislation, roughly comparable to the original Federal Reserve Act itself. However, a reconstruction of the national monetary system along the lines indicated above would transform it substantially into what Charles A. Lindbergh, Sr., and Ollie M. James wanted in 1913, and what the deluded William J. Bryan and Robert L. Owen said the Federal Reserve Act was designed to accomplish.

HOW THE FEDERAL RESERVE CREATES INFLATION

During the Sixties and Seventies the role of the Fed, as always, continues to be destructive of the general welfare. By maintaining exorbitant interest rates, it has created a continuing depression; but, at the same time, by financing the huge deficits of the federal government and emitting a flood of fiat currency, it has created and continues to create irrepressible pressures for inflation, which, unless curbed and terminated, will bring this nation to economic ruin.

At least indirectly, the Fed is also responsible for the enormous federal bureaucracy that is now strangling the American people, for without this agency, it would be impossible to finance it. And we should understand that the bureaucracy itself contributes enormously to our progressive inflation. It may be said that its cost merely transfers buying power from one class of individuals to another, and therefore does not inject additional purchasing power into the market; but this argument ignores completely one decisive fact: for when an auto worker, for example, receives his pay, he has produced a thing of physical value which represents the money he has received and balances it in the market place. But since three million federal bureaucrats produce nothing, the $65 billion necessary to maintain them, their overhead, and their retirement program, competes with the money received by productive workers in the market place, the federal money is almost as inflationary as if it had just emerged from the printing presses and were being added to the total money stock of the country. If one million bureaucrats were transferred from parasitical to productive employment, more goods and services would be available in response to the same buying power, and this would reduce inflation drastically.

PERSONAL MEMORIES FROM ANOTHER GENERATION

In 1923, this writer, a newly spawned Ph. D., took a job at what is now Eastern Michigan University at a salary of $2,500. Extension courses on Saturdays and work as a summer salesman increased the annual income by $1,800. My wife earned $1,500 as a teacher.

Total income was therefore $5,800. There were no sales taxes, no income taxes, no social security taxes, or other deductions.

Early in 1924, we purchased a fine lot for $1,200 on which we built a house, 26' × 40', with two stories, a full basement, central heat, four bedrooms, a bath, a powder room, a commodious dining room, a good kitchen, a library, and a living room 15' × 26', adorned with a large brick fireplace and lighted with four double windows.

The total cost, including the lot and garage, was $5,440.

Expenditures for food, clothing, property tax and incidentals were about $1,000, which meant that we drew about $700 from previous savings to pay for the new home, *in toto*, out of current earnings in a single year. We sold it a year later for $12,000 cash, and built another similar home, using only the profits (untaxed) on the sale of the first to pay for it entirely.

Had we come to Michigan in 1974 and built the same house in that year, we could have expected the following: my salary might have been about $11,000 and my wife's about $8,000; but from these sums, at least $5,000 would have been taken for state and federal income taxes, for sales taxes, and for Social Security contributions, leaving us about $12,500. Since our living expenses would have been about $8,000, we would not have had more than $4,500 or so for capital expenditures or savings.

The lot we purchased in 1924 for $1,200 would have cost at least $10,000; the house and garage at least $35,000. Since we would not have had very much money, we would need a mortgage of more than $35,000, which, with interest at 10% for twenty-five years, would have involved annual payments of about $5,000.

Is this progress? The young couple who could pay completely for a good house in 1923–24 from the income of a single year, would, fifty years later, not only have to settle for a much less desirable residence, but, even so, would become the slaves of the bankers and the tax collectors for most of their productive lives.

Citations

1. 1974 *SA* 462
2. Bakewell, *op. cit.* 111–117
3. 1935 *SA* 695; 1956 *ib.* 431, 748; 1963 *ib.* 713; 1966 *ib.* 703; 1973 *ib.* 649, 666; 1974 *ib.* 678
4. 1973 *SA* 666
5. 1956 *SA* 431
6. 1935 *SA* 222, 223; 1956 *ib.* 430, 431; 1973 *ib.* 444, 456, 768; 1974 *ib.* 780
7. Brian Johnson, *The Politics of Money* 114–15
8. 1972 *SA* 433
9. 1973 *SA* 768

PART TWO

THE DEBATE OVER THE CURRENCY

THE FRENCH ASSIGNATS

The following by Andrew Dickson White, published in
The Freeman in 1945, describes the French experience with fiat
money between 1791 and 1796:

From the early reluctant and careful issues of paper we saw,
as an immediate result, improvement and activity in business.
Then arose the clamor for more paper money. At first, new issues
were made with great difficulty; but, the dyke once broken, the
current of irredeemable currency poured through; and the breach
thus enlarging, this currency was soon swollen beyond
control. . . .

The government . . . continued by spasms to grind out
still more paper; commerce was first stimulated by the difference in
exchange; but this cause soon ceased to operate, and commerce,
having been stimulated unhealthily, wasted away. . . .

New isues of paper were then clamored for as more drams
are demanded by a drunkard. New issues only increased the evil;
capitalists were all the more reluctant to embark their money on
such a sea of doubt. Workmen of all sorts were more and more
thrown out of employment. Issue after issue of currency came; but
no relief resulted save a momentary stimulus, which aggravated
the disease. The most ingenious evasions of natural laws in finance
which the most subtle theorists could contrive were tried—all in
vain. . . . All thoughtful men lost confidence. All men were
waiting; stagnation became worse and worse. At last came the
collapse and then a return, by a fearful shock, to a state of things
which presented something like certainty of remuneration to
capital and labor. Then, and not till then, came the beginning of a
new era of prosperity.

As soon as Napoleon came to power, he re-established a
solid specie currency; he paid all his bills in cash; nevertheless it
took the French nation nearly 40 years to recover from the
desolation caused by the 7-year experiment with the irredeemable
currency known as Assignats.

CHAPTER VIII

The Case for a Managed, Fiat Currency

A. INTRODUCTORY

WHAT FDR PROCLAIMED

When Roosevelt announced that he was moving the country toward a managed currency, with a dollar that would remain stable for generations to come, he formulated the hopes and visions of those who believe that redeemability is entirely unnecessary to prevent monetary erosion.

DEFINITION OF FIAT MONEY

According to Webster's *New Collegiate Dictionary*, fiat money is "paper currency of government issue which is made legal tender by fiat or law, does not represent, or is not based upon, specie, and contains no provision of redemption." Since all who propose that the government issue notes based upon its credit and power of taxation alone, advocate precisely such currency, we must recognize them as proponents of fiat money.

THE SCHOOL OF FIAT CURRENCY

In the field of monetary reform, there is an important and very influential school consisting of proponents with widely varying theories, but who agree in believing that a stable fiat currency can be established, provided only that it is handled honestly and intelligently, is issued by a sovereign government, and is based on the national credit and power of taxation. Its advocates proclaim themselves strict adherents of the Constitution and declare that the power to coin money and regulate the value thereof, conferred therein upon Congress in ART. I, Sec. 8, Par. 5, is the same as issuing legal tender notes not redeemable in specie. Such theorizers, however, rarely make any reference to ART. I, Sec. 10, Par. 1, which declares that no state shall "make any Thing but gold and silver coin a Tender in Payment of debts. . . ."

It is interesting to note that the French Assignats were proposed by able financiers; issued by the national treasury;1 guaranteed by the full credit of the nation; bottomed on the unlimited power to tax; and made redeemable in recently confiscated properties worth many times their face value. Finally, the most solemn promises were made by the government that no excessive emissions would ever take place.

In the present chapter, we present the views of those who advocate a fiat currency; in the next, we reproduce the arguments of those who are convinced that only a specie currency is constitutional and that no stable monetary system is possible without redeemability. In the final chapter of PART TWO we summarize the pros and cons of the two sides.

B. PROFESSOR IRVING FISHER

THE GREAT REVERSAL

Irving Fisher, for many years professor of economics at Yale University, who was loaded with so many degrees, titles, and honors that they fill almost an entire printed page, must be ranked as one of America's most celebrated monetary theorists. Interestingly enough, he advocated one definite theory or concept until the advent of FDR; but shortly thereafter, we find him reversing himself almost completely. During most of his life he was an advocate of what we may call the Variable Gold Standard; but since, in the end, he advocated what is in effect a commodity dollar based on price indexes and a system of 100% reserves for bank loans based upon the monetization of all bank resources, we must classify him among the principal protagonists of a managed currency.

THE VARIABLE GOLD STANDARD

In his pre-New Deal writings, Fisher offers a monetary system based on a definite gold dollar, but one that does not determine the prices of other commodities: on the contrary, *their* prices would determine the quantity of gold in the dollar, which will continuously vary in weight to conform with the cost of goods in the market place. Just how *their* prices are to be determined, however, remains obscure, if, indeed, they are to be controlled at all.

THE FLUCTUATING VALUE OF GOLD

Contemplating the general decline in the price level between 1880 and 1900, and its subsequent increase during the following twelve years, Professor Fisher declares that "no other units of measure are so unstable as units of money. . . ." While the weight of the dollar remains fixed, he observes, its purchasing power varies from year to year.[1]

Although other factors may be involved, Professor Fisher declares that gold becomes cheaper and all other commodities increase in price when large deposits are discovered, or more efficient methods of extraction are developed. "Whenever there have been rapid outpourings from mines," he explains, "following discoveries of the precious metals used for money, prices have risen with corresponding rapidity. This was observed in the sixteenth century, after great quantities of the precious metals had been brought to Europe from the New World; and again in the nineteenth century, after the California and Australian gold mining of the fifties . . .; and still again . . . after the South African, Alaskan, and Cripple Creek mining of the nineties."[2]

His plan, declares Fisher, "would not destroy the gold standard, but merely stabilize it. Gold bullion would still be the ultimate concrete basis of every dollar; but instead of being fixed by weight, and varying in purchasing power, it would be fixed in purchasing power and varying in weight."[3]

In *Stabilizing the Dollar,* published in 1920, Professor Fisher states that the recent war had caused the greatest upheaval in prices that the world had ever seen;[4] and he declares that a gold dollar varying in weight but constant in purchasing power could be established through the use of index numbers,[5] which "can control the price level. The more gold in the dollar, the greater its buying power and the lower the price level. . . ."[6] The process by which this will be accomplished, he maintains, "is as simple as clock-shifting for daylight saving. . . ."[7]

Under this plan, gold coin would be abolished; gold certificates would be redeemed in bars of bullion; the dollar's weight would be adjusted according to its index value; a brassage fee would be imposed; and the gold clause in all contracts would be abrogated.[8]

In order to establish a gold dollar of constant purchasing

power, it should represent a composite corresponding in value to an imaginary goods-dollar consisting of about thirty products in constant use.[9]

"By all means," he declares, "let us keep the metal gold for the good attributes it has—portability, durability, divisibility, salability," but let it vary in weight to conform with the goods-dollar.[10]

He then offers his tentative draft of an Act to Stabilize the Dollar,[11] with seventeen sections setting forth his monetary theories. All gold would be melted into bars of not less than 5 ounces and convertible on demand in return for circulating currency; the existing gold certificates would be replaced with gold-bullion dollar certificates, certifying their redeemability according to the varying price of gold. Gold would no longer be legal tender, but all debts would be payable in currency based on the Variable Gold Standard; there would also be a 100% gold reserve against all circulating certificates.

In *The Money Illusion* published in 1928,[12] Professor Fisher reiterates that since gold fluctuates in value more than commodities in general, the gold standard is to blame for sharp losses or gains to lenders and borrowers alike.[13] "As things are now," he concludes, "every contract in a gold-standard country is a gamble in the future value of the dollar . . .[14] every contract is necessarily a lottery. . . ."[15]

THE CREATION OF 100% RESERVES

When we turn from his earlier works to the *100% Money* of 1935,[16] we find that Professor Fisher has become a crusader against fractional reserve banking, has invented an entirely new monetary system, and proposes a novel method by which banks may be supplied with 100% reserves for all their loans. "Under our present system," he declares, "the banks create and destroy checkbook money by granting, or calling, loans. . . . Thus our national circulating medium is now at the mercy of loan transactions of banks; and our thousands of checking banks are, in effect, so many irresponsible mints,"[17] which lend, not money, but promises to supply money they do not possess. On meager cash reserves, banks create investment pyramids; and can therefore inflate or deflate the volume of currency at will.[18]

A CONGRESSIONAL CURRENCY COMMISSION

Fisher therefore proposes that a Currency Commission be created by Congress with authority to convert into cash "enough of the assets of every commercial bank to increase its cash reserves up to 100% of its checking deposits" by the issuance of United States Currency Notes. "In other words, let the government, through the Currency Commission, buy some bonds, notes, or other assets of the bank or lend it to the banks on their assets as security. Then all checkbook money would have actual money—pocketbook money—behind it."[19]

THE MONETARY SOLUTION

If this were done, declares Fisher, there would be no more runs on banks; no more bank failures; the government debt would be reduced or liquidated; we would have a simplified monetary system; inflation and deflation would be reduced; and there would be no more cycles of boom and bust. Gold would then be used only for the settlement of international balances;[20] Congress would no longer be farming out to private banks its prerogative—conferred upon it in ARTICLE I, Section 8, of the Constitution—of coining or creating money, and regulating the value thereof, which the Professor regards as identical functions.

To recapitulate: under Professor Fisher's plan, the Currency Commission would issue new currency to purchase from its member banks and from the Federal Reserve System itself enough United States bonds, or assets in the form of mortgages, commercial acceptances, etc., to provide each of them with 100% reserves in the form of circulating currency against all their demand liabilities; purchase from all other banks carrying checking accounts sufficient United States bonds or other assets to provide each of them also with a similar 100%

reserve; and purchase from the general public government bonds in an amount such that the Commission could, with these as reserves, issue $30 billion of fiat money, which would, thereafter, be maintained rigidly at that level, unless the Commission determined that the needs of business required additional currency. Under this system of managed currency, the Professor believed that there could be no danger of inflation.

THE RETURN TO THE GOLD STANDARD

Professor Fisher declares that a return to the gold standard would have to provide a 100% reserve, not only for all currency, but also for all loans; and this might actually be accomplished, he concludes, but only by reducing the gold content of the dollar sufficiently so that the gold hoard could be minted into $30 billion dollars.[21] How such miniscule dollars could constitute a barrier to inflation remains entirely obscure.

POPULAR FALLACIES[22]

There are, states Professor Fisher, many false ideas abroad, among which he enumerates the following:

(1) That the value of the dollar never changes;

(2) That the price of any commodity is determined solely by supply and demand;

(3) That the government should leave the expansion and the contraction of the currency and of credit to the banks;

(4) That gold is the best standard of value; and

(5) That gold is inherently stable and that fiat currency is inherently unstable.

Citations

1. Irving Fisher, *The Instability of Gold,* 5
2. Fisher, *Stabilizing the Dollar,* 29
3. *The Instability, op. cit.* 14
4. *Stabilizing, op. cit.* vii
5. *Ib.* xxvi-xxvii

6. *Ib.* xxvii
7. *Ib.* xxviii
8. *Ib.* xl, xliv
9. *Ib.* 85-86
10. *Ib.* 88
11. *Ib.* 205-13
12. The Adelphi Co., New York
13. Fisher, *The Money Illusion,* 17
14. *Ib.* 85
15. *Ib.* 86
16. The Adelphi Co.
17. Fisher, *100% Money,* 7
18. *Ib.* 7-8
19. *Ib.* 9
20. *Ib.* 11
21. *Ib.* 19
22. *Ib.* 199

C. JOHN MAYNARD KEYNES

KEYNES VS. KEYNES

The principal writings of Lord Keynes, after he became a proponent of fiat currency and government economic control, are *A Treatise on Money*, 1930, and *The General Theory of Employment, Interest, and Money*, 1936. Gone is the realist of 1920 who spoke in forthright terms in *The Economic Consequences of the Peace:* instead, we find now a theoretician who had repudiated his own earlier convictions,[1] whose ideas are clothed in abstruse formulas, and who admits that he cannot attain his objective without "a highly abstract argument . . ."[2] His general philosophy entails staggering consequences; and since it has been accepted, in varying degrees, by most nations in the western world, we are justified in placing at his door whatever of good or evil has emerged from the establishment of a managed currency.

THE SOCIALIST

If anyone doubts that fiat theories are likely to be socialistic, or that Keynes was at least a Fabian after 1929, he need only read the last chapter of *The General Theory*, where he declares that the basic faults of existing society consist in its failure to provide full employment and to equalize wealth among its different classes.[3] He states that the "controls necessary to insure full employment will, of course, involve a large extension of the traditional functions of government."[4] This, he believes, can be attained by means of "comprehensive socialization," which can be introduced so gradually that there will be no break in the general traditions of society.[5]

Again and again Keynes declares that the investments of the rich make little or no contribution toward full employment;[6] and, this being true, he proposes the termination, by a process of economic euthanasia,[7] of all income now derived from rents, interest, or dividends—a completely Marxian proposal. Vast social changes, he notes, will result from the disappearance of returns "on accumulated wealth."[8] However, even though nonrisk investments would no longer offer any return, there would still be the possibility of savings from skill and enterprise.[9]

MONETARY GOLD BANISHED

Keynes has neither need nor use for gold as a means of exchange in his socialist society. Writing in 1929,* he declares that the metal is so scarce that the total dug up in 7,000 years could be carried in the hold of a single transatlantic liner.[10] Thus the long age of commodity money, he concludes, has now been replaced by representative money; gold, withdrawn from circulation, is now stored, as it should be, in the vaults of the great central banks.[11] It is an illusion to suppose that gold can furnish a stable standard of value, any more than could any other commodity of which the world's annual increment is slight.[12] It is a mistake to permit private ownership of gold or to allow it to circulate as money (as it was still doing at that time in the United States); all countries must agree to prohibit the use of gold or gold certificates as a means of private exchange; central banks must convert to some substitute for gold as a reserve for money; and they must be able to create their own currencies irrespective of the gold in their possession.[13]

Whereas gold has been considered traditionally as a stabilizer of prices because of its inelasticity, this very quality has proved to be at the bottom of the current monetary troubles in England and America.[14] Agreeing with Fisher, prices, says Keynes, should be determined by index numbers or the tabular standard, based on sixty representative commodities.[15]

*A Treatise on Money, consisting of Vol. V and VI, of Keynes Collected Writings, in 8 volumes, Macmillan, Great Britain, 1971.

RAISING PRICES BY GOVERNMENT INTERVENTION

One of Keynes' most frequently repeated theories is that government should intervene in the economy to raise prices during a recession because workers and unions will resist bitterly any attempt to reduce money wages even in the midst of falling prices; but they will not refuse employment at existing pay levels when prices rise.[16] Since the monetary authority, once freed from the shackles of the gold standard, can issue fiat currency at will, it has the power to increase prices to any desirable point by expanding the money supply; and this is the remedy which Keynes proposes. Even in 1929, he declared that prices should be raised so that it would be easier for debtors to discharge their obligations.[17]

THE GENERAL THEORY

Keynes' basic thesis, as stated in *The General Theory*, is as follows: "There will be an inducement to push the rate of new investment to the point which forces the supply-price of each type of capital-asset to a figure which, taken in conjunction with its prospective yield, brings the marginal efficiency of capital in general to approximate equality with the rate of interest. That is to say, the physical conditions of supply in the capital-goods industries, the state of confidence concerning the prospective yield, the psychological attitude to liquidity and the quantity of money (preferably calculated in terms of wage-units) determines, between them, the rate of new investment."[18]

Reduced to less abstract language, this means that in order to create full employment, we must have a rate of interest which will encourage capital investment to the point where the declining rate of return—called marginal efficiency*—will equal

---

*This theory of the declining rate of capitalist profit is virtually identical to the Marxian dogma concerning the falling rate of capitalist profit or return, which was expected to bring about the automatic destruction of the system.

this rate of interest. At this point, a proper ratio of production will go into consumption and investment respectively, with a resulting condition of equilibrium that will create full employment. But since private lenders always demand too high a return for the use of their money, government must step in and supply it for capital expansion and replacement, or for public works, so that the economy will operate at full or near capacity. The private investor, no longer necessary, will be relegated to the dust bins of history. In short, public capital, created by fiat, will replace all private investment.

From this premise, two corollaries follow: there must be a great central bank with power to issue inconvertible currency and to determine credit and rates of interest—which is precisely what the American Fed does.

Keynes elaborates the theory: with the increase in employment, aggregate real income also increases, but not as rapidly or as much; it would, therefore, be an error should employers limit production to meeting the demands for immediate consumption. There must be a sufficient amount of new investment to absorb the excess of total output over what the community chooses to consume, otherwise full employment cannot continue. Employment, interest, and money are inextricably intertwined, for unless investment continues, there will be no outlet for employer income above the sales for consumption. It therefore follows that the equilibrium level of employment will depend on current investment, which, in turn, will depend on the inducement to invest which in its turn will depend on the relation between the schedules of marginal efficiency of capital and the rate of interest on various kinds of loans.[19]

In this system, there will be no difficulty in supplying industry with all the capital it needs at low interest to finance expansion, which will result in full employment. "A change in the quantity of money is already within the power of most governments by open market policy, or analogous measures," declares Keynes; and "It can only be a foolish person who would prefer a flexible wage-policy to a flexible money-policy . . . a method . . . comparatively easy to apply. . . ."[20]

Monetary stability will be achieved by controlling the quantity of currency to be allocated to expansion or public works so that the rate of interest and the marginal efficiency of capital will always be in equilibrium.[21]

In order to bring about recovery from a depression, it will be necessary to reduce the rate of interest;[22] by so doing, a condition of quasi-boom can continue indefinitely.[23]

However, since "the rate of interest is not self-adjusting to a level best suited to social advantage," a wise government will control it by statute;[24] assuming that steps can be taken to ensure a rate of interest consistent with a rate of investment that will create full employment, the beneficent state will provide the balancing factor for the proper growth of capital so that this, approaching saturation, will guarantee full employment.[25]

The Keynesian system obviously envisions total control of the money, the economy, and the people by an all-powerful state.

HOW TO AVOID INFLATION

Inflation, of course, should be avoided, which Keynes says would result only if lending for further industrial expansion or expenditures for public works were to continue after full employment is attained.[26]

HOW TO ACHIEVE FULL EMPLOYMENT

Keynes explains that in a country where 5 million are working and consuming the entire production, there will be no investment; but if an additional 100,000 were given work, only 99% of their production would be consumed; and if 9 million were employed, investment would rise to 9%.

However, should investment then fall by two-thirds,

employment would decline to 6,900,000.[27] Keynes does not explain how he arrived at these computations.

WEALTH FROM UNECONOMIC PROJECTS

Keynes explains the enormous utility of employment on nonproductive public works, even when they are ill-conceived and totally useless. Since these produce nothing for resale in the market place, an addition of 100,000 workers in such endeavors will increase employment from 5,000,000 to 6,400,000.[28] It is therefore extremely profitable for a nation to engage hundreds of thousands, or even millions of persons in such pursuits as raking leaves or leaning on shovels.

Keynes' economic theories are, to say the least, distinctive; for, according to him, the key to wealth production would consist in an enormous government bureaucracy. When men dig holes to extract useless gold, he declares, the nation becomes rich: Egypt, for example, was "doubly fortunate," because she not only built pyramids, but was also constantly searching for and extracting precious metals from the earth. During the Middle Ages, Europe became wealthy by building cathedrals and singing dirges.[29]

Building a house, however, or a second railroad between York and London has an opposite effect on the economy; for these reduce the value and the income derived from all existing facilities and investments.[30] It would seem, therefore, that if people would simply spend their entire lives and energy in building pyramids, carving tombstones, and constructing highways in trackless jungles, they would all become infinitely wealthy.

THE CAUSE OF THE AMERICAN DEPRESSION

Keynes has a novel way to explain the American depression of 1930–32: for five years prior to 1929, he says, industry had expanded so rapidly and had set up such large depreciation schedules and sinking funds that further investment was virtually impossible.[31] However, it was not overinvestment, he declares elsewhere, in a strict sense; for the boom could have continued, perhaps indefinitely, had proper foresight been exercised, and had low interest financing been available from a central bank with power to create fiat money.[32]

FIAT VS. COMMODITY MONEY

Keynes' entire economic system rests on the premise that commodity money may and should be replaced by fiat currency which will be managed by the State in order to create full employment. Redeemable or convertible money cannot be produced without labor or be turned on at will by the entrepreneurs; however, when we have an inconvertible currency controlled by the State, there is no problem at all.[33] If money could be produced like a motor car or a crop of corn, we could easily prevent depressions simply by diverting more labor into its production.[34] As it is, however, there "is no remedy" for unemployment "but to persuade the public that green cheese is practically the same thing" as redeemable money "and to have a green-cheese factory (i.e., a central bank) under public control" to produce such fiat currency.[35]

THE ALL-POWERFUL BANK AND STATE

The central bank, says Keynes, will be the instrument for controlling interest rates and, in general, the terms upon which money is to be lent.[36] When the State has complete control over both wages and currency, it can by decree adjust the supply of money so that a desirable rate of earnings and investment will result; and it can do whatever it may desire to stabilize the purchasing power of money without danger of social disruption. However, it must also have power to control wages, investments, and money; otherwise, it cannot ensure the equilibrium which will result in stability and full employment.[37]

Banks must not be permitted to create inflationary credit, i.e., loans resulting in capital expansion beyond the needs of full employment; nor must they be permitted to curtail credit to a degree which will cause deflationary pressures.[38]

One of the most important functions of the central government bank will be to buy and sell gilt-edged bonds of all maturities at stated prices in order to stabilize interest rates.[39] Thus, corresponding to the quantity of money created by the central bank, we would have predetermined rates of interest for various categories of debt.[40] And, insofar as the people and the economy are concerned, the controlled fiat money issued by the central bank will serve precisely the same function as do gold coins; the new money printed by the government "wherewith to meet its current expenditures" always "accrues as someone's income,"[41] and is, therefore, as good as gold.

THE KEYNESIAN NEW DEAL

Even a cursory examination of the preceding demonstrates that these Keynesian proposals appeared again and again during the Roosevelt administration and, in fact, to a considerable degree, formed the basis of New Deal Economic Policy and constituted the instruments by which it consolidated its control over our economy and the regimentation of our people.

It is also obvious that the practical implementation of the Keynesian theories is in complete accord with the 5th Secton of the *Communist Manifesto*, which calls for the "Centralization of credit in the hands of the state, by means of a national bank with State capital and an exclusive monopoly."

We note furthermore that various monetary theorists—some of them with a conservative label, as we shall see in the following pages—lean heavily in the direction of Keynesianism. Such individuals are perhaps well meaning, but, if so, involved in basic confusion, for they do not understand or distinguish between two all-important functions: (1) the issuance of currency and the regulation of its value—a power conferred upon Congress by our Constitution; and (2) the business of handling checking accounts, lending money to private individuals, or supplying funds for capital expansion, which, under the American system of free enterprise, must remain a private function to be performed by private banks.

Citations

1. John Maynard Keynes, *The General Theory* v, vi, 175, 351
2. *Ib.* v
3. *Ib.* 372
4. *Ib.* 379
5. *Ib.* 378
6. *Ib.* 373
7. *Ib.* 376
8. *Ib.* 221
9. *Ib.*
10. John Maynard Keynes, *A Treatise on Money* Vol. VI 259
11. *Ib.* 260, 262
12. *Ib.* 261
13. *Ib.* 355
14. *General Theory, op. cit.* 235-36
15. *A Treatise, op. cit.* 351-2
16. *General Theory, op. cit.* 9, 15, 253
17. *A Treatise, op. cit.* 353
18. *General Theory, op. cit.* 248
19. *Ib.* 27-28
20. *Ib.* 267-68
21. *Ib.* 270
22. *Ib.* 306
23. *Ib.* 322
24. *Ib.* 351
25. *Ib.* 220
26. *Ib.* 118-19
28. *Ib.* 127
29. *Ib.* 130-31
30. *Ib.*
31. *Ib.* 100
32. *Ib.* 323
33. *Ib.* 230
34. *Ib.* 230-31
35. *Ib.* 235
36. *A Treatise, op. cit.* V 147
37. *Ib.* 151-52
38. *Ib.* VI 197
39. *General Theory, op. cit.* 206
40. *Ib.* 205
41. *Ib.* 200

D. THE HONORABLE JERRY VOORHIS

VOORHIS, AUTHOR AND DEFEATED CONGRESSMAN

Mr. Jerry Voorhis of Claremont, California, is a man of deep personal integrity who, in 1946, after a bitter campaign, lost the seat he had occupied in Congress for ten years to Richard M. Nixon. Mr. Voorhis has written a number of books, including *Confessions of a Congressman,* 1947, and *The Strange Case of Richard Milhous Nixon,* 1973. Here, however, we are primarily interested in his *Out of Debt, Out of Danger,* written in 1943, which contains perhaps the best-reasoned and most forthright plea for a managed, fiat currency that we have seen.

THE THEORY OF MONEY

Mr. Voorhis declares repeatedly that neither gold nor silver is in the least necessary for a stable currency, nor need the government maintain any metallic reserve in order to prevent either inflation or deflation. "Gold," we read, "may someday be useful once again in the settlement of international balances, but it is fervently to be hoped that no great nation will ever again tie its currency to gold and thus make it possible for international financial interests to make a most profitable business for themselves by artificially shipping gold back and forth between the nations and thus forcing the value of the currencies up and down."[1]

Anyone who believes that government should not or cannot constitutionally create and issue money is, says Mr. Voorhis, "afflicted with the great deception"; and, he adds, "such a person is laboring under a great delusion when he says: 'All this is very well, but you are proposing that the government create money. And if it does so, that will be inflation.' And so for his benefit there is one thing we must make clear. . . . Any nation can safely credit itself with new money income and pay it out into active circulation up to a certainly easily determined total amount. That is the number of dollars that can be put into circulation without increasing prices."[2]

Mr. Voorhis was certain in 1943 that a great collapse, depression, and deflation would follow the Second World War[3] because the bankers would make certain that money would not become cheap.[4] Nowhere do we find any suspicion that FDR was the servant of the financial interests or that the Gold Reserve Act of 1934 was for their benefit; on the contrary, the author declares that both WWI and WWII were the instruments used (and presumably the only ones that could be) to end depressions.[5] In 1943, Mr. Voorhis evidently held FDR in the highest esteem; and he supported his theory concerning fiat money by explaining how Hitler was able to put Germany back to work and create great prosperity without the use of either gold or silver* in, or as a reserve for, its currency.[6]

Again and again, in spite of the dictionary, Mr. Voorhis says that the coining of money and the issuance of fiat currency constitute basically identical operations; and that when the Constitution declares that Congress shall have power "to coin money and regulate the value thereof," this means simply that it shall have the power to issue whatever quantity of irredeemable currency it may desire, and to regulate its buying power by limiting the money supply to current needs, based upon the national production.

"Money," writes Mr. Voorhis, "is anything which people generally use to . . . pay debts or buy goods. . . .

" 'To coin money' means, therefore, if it means anything,

---

*We should note, however, that German government spending resulted in a 1,000% inflation and the redemption in 1948 of all circulating marks at a ratio of 10 to 1.

not only the minting of metal coins, but the issuing of bank notes, and the creation of checkbook money or any other substitute which performs the function of money."[7]

Making no differentiation between money in general and currency in particular, Mr. Voorhis continues: "The credit of the United States Government is the credit of the American people as a whole. It rests squarely upon two things: (1) the ability of the American people to produce and (2) the power of the government to tax. The sovereign right of the nation to coin or issue money is an unlimited right, but prudence and sound judgment and a concern for the future will always dictate that the right be not exercised beyond the amount of credit which the nation possesses. . . ."[8]

A SPECIFIC MONETARY PROPOSAL

Since our government, according to Mr. Voorhis, has the power under the Constitution to create and issue fiat money without limit, and since specie is unnecessary in order to maintain a sound and stable currency, he offers the following proposal: "Now, the perfect money system for this or any other nation contains two parts: (1) By order of the nation's Congress—and it alone—enough new money should be created from time to time to keep the volume of the people's total buying power increasing just as fast as their production of goods and services increases. And (2) by action of the same Congress taxation should be used to take out of circulation any amount of money necessary to keep the supply of money from getting ahead of the supply of goods produced for sale."[9]

Nowhere does Mr. Voorhis mention the constitutional provision that no state shall make anything but gold and silver legal tender for the payment of debts; nor is there any attempt to define the dollar in specific terms or to guarantee that a monetary authority with unrestricted control over the currency will not inflate it. He declares that the prevention of inflation as well as repudiation "will only be possible if control over the creation and destruction of money in America is in the hands of a responsible governmental agency operating under a direct mandate from Congress and according to statutory rules and procedures calculated to give America a dollar of sustained and stable buying power from one generation to the next. Even in the midst of war, these things can be achieved."[10]

Mr. Voorhis explains that "men of reasonable judgment and decent interest in the public welfare could write a law creating, as a public body, a monetary agency of the Congress and giving it exclusive power to create money or any substitute for money in the United States. Such a law would also have to contain explicit instructions to the agency to issue money or set up national credit on the books of the Treasury at such times and in such amounts as to provide the same percentage increase in money volume as the increase that was taking place in the national capacity to produce goods for sale. And . . . if this were done, there is no reason in the wide world why either inflation or deflation should ever visit America again.

"Sound money is money which bears a constant relationship to, and value in terms of, actual goods and services. That is all there is to it. It makes no difference what the money is made of. . . . Sound money is money that does the job money is supposed to do. And that job is to enable the business of the nation . . . to be carried on in an orderly and effective way."[11]

THE CREATION OF CREDIT MONEY

When bankers lend checkbook credit through fractional reserve banking, this is like the creation of money by forgery;[12] but when governments do so, they are merely exercising their sovereign authority to coin and issue money. In order to establish a sound and constitutional currency, then, under the plan proposed by Mr. Voorhis, "It becomes necessary that legislation be passed setting up, as a direct agent of the Congress, a nonpolitical public body of outstanding citizens whose sole duty it shall be to 'coin money and regulate the value thereof.' Such an agent might be called a Monetary Authority. It might be a transformed Federal Reserve Board, if the central banks were made the property of the people. Such a monetary agent of Congress must be given the sole and exclusive right to create the money of the American people and it must be given a privileged position with regard to making recommendations to Congress as to taxes.

"For without these powers it could not discharge its primary duty which is to provide the people of the United States with a dollar 'whose purchasing and debt-paying power will not change from one generation to another,' as President Franklin D. Roosevelt once proposed.

"The Monetary Authority would from time to time create new money in the form of credits on its books to the account of the United States Treasury. The Federal Reserve Board does that very thing right now every time it buys bonds from the Treasury.* The only difference here between our scientific system and the present one would be that the people would need to incur no interest-bearing debt to their own monetary agent when the money their industry and productiveness had earned was placed to their credit.

"But the Monetary Agent of the Congress and the people would not create money at will. Neither would it create it simply to pay the bills of the government. It would create it in accordance with the provisions of the law. And those provisions would require that as much new money be created as was necessary to prevent a fall in average commodity prices, and to secure continued full employment and full production—and no more."[13]

PROPOSED LEGISLATION

On January 3, 1945, Mr. Voorhis introduced H.R. 153 into the House of Representatives "A BILL, To restore to Congress

---

*It seems to us that there is here some confusion between checkbook credit money created by the banks through fractional reserve banking, and the United States notes that would be issued by the Monetary Authority and which would go into immediate circulation. Does Mr. Voorhis distinguish properly between bank credit and currency notes?

the sole power to issue money and to regulate its value, as provided in ARTICLE I, section 8, of the Constitution of the United States; to improve the banking system; to aid in maintaining or restoring full employment and production; to reduce the public debt; and to provide a stable currency."

This Bill, which has thirteen sections and many subsections, calls for the repeal of the Federal Reserve Act and the creation of a Monetary Commission with power to control credit and issue the national currency. We believe that because of this proposal, powerful financial interests rallied behind Mr. Nixon to defeat Mr. Voorhis in 1946, and so eliminated from the halls of Congress the most articulate voice calling for drastic reform in our monetary system.

On September 18, 1971, Mr. Wright Patman entered into the *Congressional Record* a statement by Mr. Voorhis which repeats in some detail the proposals set forth in *Out of Debt, Out of Danger,* and the Voorhis Bill of 1945.

Citations

1. Jerry Voorhis, *Out of Debt, Out of Danger,* 170
2. *Ib.* 211
3. *Ib.* 129, etc.
4. *Ib.* 68
5. *Ib.* 63
6. *Ib.* 75, 83
7. *Ib.* 97
8. *Ib.* 151
9. *Ib.* 134-35
10. *Ib.* 197-98
11. *Ib.* 126
12. *Ib.* 203
13. *Ib.* 204-206

E.   GERTRUDE COOGAN

A STAUNCH ADVOCATE OF FIAT MONEY

Another proponent of fiat currency is Gertrude Coogan, whose book, *Money Creators,* first published in 1935, has gone through a number of printings and is now distributed by Omni Publications.

It may be that her opinions have altered over the years; in her book, however, where she refers repeatedly and contemptuously to those who advocate redeemability as "the gold crowd,"[1] she is an uncompromising advocate of fiat, managed currency. (Interestingly enough, she declares "that all money is fiat money," since *"fiat* is a Latin word meaning 'so be it'.")[2] She declares that "In reality, convertibility into gold is a myth and a fetish," for the reason that there existed in 1929 $53 billion bank deposits, in addition to $5 billion in currency and $225 billion in bonds; and since obviously the gold stock was insufficient for the conversion of nearly $300 billions of obligations into gold, the statement of the banks that we then had sound money was an obvious fraud.[3]

CONCERNING CONVERTIBILITY

Miss Coogan propounds that gold is the weapon of the internationalist bankers, and that convertibility, which exists only for their aggrandizement, is used by them whenever they desire to collapse the money structure of a nation,[4] as they did in the United States following 1930, when they shipped such large quantities of the metal abroad[5] that the "Gold Standard completely evaporated. . . ."[6] Elsewhere she states that a return to the gold standard would be "a direct step backward into the clutches of the financial bankers of bolshevism [who] are at the center of the abuses of the money creation powers, as attested by amazing archives of the United States government."[7]

ATTITUDE TOWARD FDR

Miss Coogan seems to be in basic agreement with most of Roosevelt's policies, especially when he raised the price of gold and then embarked upon a domestic experiment in managed currency.[8] She says that since increasing the price of gold in 1934 from $20.67 to $35 an ounce did not cause an increase in retail prices, it could not have reduced the value of savings accounts or insurance policies. That it constituted a 41% capital levy was, she states, "a malicious lie foisted upon the American public by the international bankers and the *parrot section* of the *press. . . .*"[9] It was, she further states, mandatory that the price of gold be increased in order to facilitate foreign trade.[10]

Furthermore, there is no implication in Miss Coogan's book that FDR was a servant of the financiers; on the contrary, we are told that he was opposed to them: "despite the lies shouted ever since by the money powers and their unwitting parrots," the President "caused raw material prices to rise and come into equitable relation with the price of finished goods"—a highly desirable result.[11]

INTERPRETING THE CONSTITUTION

Miss Coogan declares that the Constitution never intended convertibility into gold, and that the United States government has no right to make any contract binding either on the government or any private individual to repay dollars convertible into this metal. "Whatever is legal tender at the time of payment," she writes, "is all that could humanly or legally be used by *the debtor.*"[12] She goes on to say that the power to create money is conferred upon Congress by the Constitution[13] and that the power to coin money is identical to the power of creating it,[14] or of issuing it in any form, which, when created by

Congress, must be entirely divorced from metals,[15] since gold and silver should be used only for the settlement of international trade balances.[16] Neither is necessary as a base for domestic currency.[17] In time, there will be no monetary use for it at all, even for international purposes; for when we learn how to use clearing-house certificates as between nations, gold will be used only to fill teeth.[18]

ON BIMETALLISM

Miss Coogan states that we had a bimetallic currency before 1873;[19] that a silver currency would be highly desirable because that metal exists in our country in great abundance,[20] and that the demonetization of silver in 1873 was the result of a conspiracy concocted by international bankers.[21]

GOVERNMENT MUST NOT LEND MONEY

In one respect, Miss Coogan differs drastically from most proponents of fiat currency; for, although she insists that our legal tender currency shall be issued by the government, she is equally adamant in opposing the lending of money as a national function, for this, she holds, would be the final step in turning America over to the Socialists.[22] Although she believes that no private bank should have the power to create money,[23] she does not seem to make it quite clear whether she means by this the creation of credit through a fractional system of lending money. However, the national government should only create the currency—not lend it—for "to place the merchandising of money in the hands of the national government . . . would give the internationalists their final weapon to destroy property and the personal rights of loyal Americans."[24]

THE STABLE COMMODITY DOLLAR

Essentially, what Miss Coogan advocates is what may be called a "commodity dollar . . . which will, over succeeding generations, purchase about the same average amount of food, clothing, houses, automobiles, etc. The supreme importance of the commodity dollar is shown by the determined resistance of the money creators to all efforts of those who are seeking to force Congress to resume the money creation powers so that stable general price levels can be maintained."[25]

A stable currency, we read, can be established and maintained without redeemability so long as the supply of it bears a scientific relation to the volume of goods purchased and available for distribution in the nation.[26] The only way to regulate the value of money is to regulate its quantity, a duty mandated to Congress in the Constitution.[27]

THE FEAR OF UNCONTROLLED INFLATION

Miss Coogan feared even in 1934–35 that the money creators would, when the time was ripe, "start their privately controlled printing presses and turn out private money by the bale, as was done in Germany in the early 1920s." Far better, she declares, would it be if the government were to pay off its entire debt in new currency, "which common sense tells us is exactly as good as the bonds it would replace."[28] (We wonder what she would say in regard to this in 1975, when the same debt is rising toward $616 billion.)

MISS COOGAN'S PRACTICAL PROPOSALS

Miss Coogan proposes the following steps:

(1) Congress should appoint a group of individuals to be known as Monetary Trustees who would be guided by the mandates of Congress in establishing a constitutional monetary system.

(2) Each Trustee should be at least thirty-five years of age, appointed for life, receive ample compensation, and be of unquestionable honesty and integrity.

(3) These Trustees would maintain scientific records of prices as general averages and supply whatever amount of money

may be required to maintain a desirable price level so that business activity will absorb the unemployed but will not cause inflation.

(4) With the increase in national production, the Trustees would control prices by releasing only proportionate amounts of money into circulation.

(5) Currency increases would be made to meet government expenses. Excess funds would be recaptured through taxation.

(6) Banks would be privately owned and would lend money, but have no power to manufacture or cancel it by expanding or contracting credit. The nation would create its own currency, the value of which would be determined by its acceptability.

(7) Gold and silver should be used only to settle international balances; the domestic money supply should be completely independent.

(8) The National Monetary Trustees would publish monthly reports showing the currency outstanding, when and to whom issued.[29]

THE ULTIMATE UTOPIA

Miss Coogan assures us that although the power to lend money by the national government would lead inevitably to Socialism or Communism, we could place implicit confidence in Monetary Trustees put in power by statesmen who represent the people; and that "If the power to create money were honestly managed by Monetary Trustees" so appointed, "civilization could then actually strive for its Divinely ordained objectives—universal peace and brotherhood under the Golden Rule. . . ."[30]

Citations

1. Coogan, *op. cit.* 187, 284, 295
2. *Ib.* 283
3. *Ib.* 120-1, 296

4. *Ib.* 165
5. *Ib.* 152-3
6. *Ib.* 157
7. *Ib.* 289
8. *Ib.* 127
9. *Ib.* 153
10. *Ib.* 127
11. *Ib.* 268
12. *Ib.* 234
13. *Ib.* 271
14. *Ib.* 201
15. *Ib.* 288
16. *Ib.* 240-41, 253
17. *Ib.* 240-41
18. *Ib.* 167
19. *Ib.* 219
20. *Ib.* 220 ff.
21. *Ib.* 219 ff.
22. *Ib.* 253
23. *Ib.* 334
24. *Ib.*
25. *Ib.* 284
26. *Ib.* 247
27. *Ib.* 188
28. *Ib.* 309
29. *Ib.* 250-55
30. *Ib.* 265

F.   SILAS WALTER ADAMS

WRITER AND PUBLISHER

Another articulate advocate of Treasury fiat currency was Silas W. Adams, born in 1879, who for thirty years edited his own weeklies in Texas, called himself a Money Analyst, and published a variety of tracts, flyers, and booklets, attacking the existing monetary system; among these, his *Legalized Crime of Banking,* 1958, was perhaps the best known. In the same year, he republished the 1939 issue of *The Federal Reserve System, Its Purposes and Functions,* together with his comments on fractional credit-creation and the general practices of the commercial financial institutions.

EXTRAORDINARY COMPUTATIONS

Some of Mr. Adams' computations are truly dazzling. He explains how the Rockefeller billions are created by parlaying a $500 million deposit into a profit of $6,250,000,000 in a single year. In his 16-page, closely printed brochure, *The United States Treasury System,* dated February 12, 1959, which contains his definitive position, he states that the Reserve banks have, over a forty-year period, received bonds totalling $288 billion from the United States government in return for bookkeeping entries; that they have thus obtained free bank credit totalling $2.88 trillion, plus $3,019,600,000,000 in interest, all for nothing, thus making a profit of nearly $6 trillion,[1] every penny extorted from the American people. However, since the total wealth of the United States in 1959 was only $1,682 billion,[2] these computations seem somewhat surprising.

GOLD UNNECESSARY FOR CONSTITUTIONAL MONEY

Mr. Adams declares that "The bankers are trying to make you believe that gold gives the dollar value. How could gold," he asks derisively, "buried in Kentucky, impart value to cash or deposits?"[3] "We must dissociate gold, silver, and other metals," he continues, "from our money. The present system of personal bank clearing has proven that gold and silver have no place in our monetary system."[4]

WHO CAUSED THE PRICE OF GOLD TO RISE?

Under the monetary system advocated by Mr. Adams, we would have token coins of differing sizes, the penny being the smallest, and one about the size of a quarter being the largest. Gold, silver, and nickel would be returned to industry where it belongs, since "we have learned that bullion, or cash as 'security and guarantee of deposits' is the rarest bunk, peddled by gold miners," who took advantage of the 1930 depression by persuading Congress to increase the price of the metal from $20.67 to $35.00 an ounce. The result was that it became so plentiful that tractors were plated with it.[5]

ALL MONEY FIAT MONEY

Mr. Adams agrees with Miss Coogan that "to coin is to issue" money, for "The terms are synonymous!"[6] There is no difference between coining money and printing notes. "Both are the creation of money by fiat of the government."[7] Further: "If our nation can issue a dollar bond, it can issue a dollar bill,"[8] the one being as good as the other.

THE TREASURY AS NATIONAL BANKER

Mr. Adams declares that Congress through the Treasury should "take over the issuing of ALL OUR MONEY into circulation, take over the keeping of the people's deposits, cashing and clearing of checks."[9] Congress should issue all money into circulation, which "would save the people the interest costs, plus the principal of the loan."[10] Instead of the debt dollars which now circulate and constitute our entire money supply, we would have a currency given to the people without either debt or interest.

Under Mr. Adams' plan, Congress would "take over the coining and printing of our cash, creating deposits, cashing and clearing all checks; in other words, take over the functions of banking, except the lending of money. . . ." We could then "have immediately *a debtless nation and a debtless economy,* and the bank-made boom and bust would disappear."[11]

REGULATING THE VALUE OF THE DOLLAR

Mr. Adams believes that it would be a simple matter for Congress to establish and maintain a stable currency for it "can easily regulate the value of the dollar, its purchasing power, simply by keeping the volume of money equal to the volume of business money must do."[12] Since it costs no more for the Treasury to place its fiat on a note for $1 million than it does to do the same for one of $1, there need never be any shortage of money.

THE EXPANDED TREASURY FUNCTIONS

Under Mr. Adams' system, the Treasury would, therefore, assume all the functions now exercised by the Federal Reserve System and most of those performed by commercial banks. The Treasury would issue checks,[13] similar to traveler's or bank cashier's checks, which "will be transferrable from buyer to seller" and "will be the best money man has yet invented." Such currency, paid into circulation, would be "enough to provide the buyers with adequate funds to buy their necessities and luxuries."[14]

HOW MONEY WOULD BE PAID INTO CIRCULATION

We learn, however, that this "does not mean that Congress may or shall *give* the people the money. It shall require every person, every firm, corporation, or association to surrender goods and services for every dollar received. Then, in as much as goods or services were surrendered for the money, it ceases to belong to the government, but belongs to the people and no man can demand that they give it up; therefore, the people keep it and it continues to circulate perpetually. Of course, the government can take it as taxes, but then it returns right back to the people for their goods and services as costs of Government,* and it continues to circulate from buyers to sellers, doing the labor money is designed to perform."[15]

HOW THE NEW TREASURY SYSTEM WOULD OPERATE

In order to perform its vastly expanded role, the Treasury would establish offices in all portions of the country. "Under the United States Treasury System," we are told, "the individual Depository would function exactly as post offices function. A one-story building would meet the demands of the people. All they would need would be deposit windows where they could go and deposit their cash . . . or cash their checks. . . .[16] Bank robberies would disappear," for "few would dare to rob the United States Depositories."[17]

Mr. Adams envisions a rapid transformation of our

---

*However, if the people must surrender their property and their services to the government in return for circulating medium, would they not then become the servants of an all-powerful state and would not the government become the owner of all the property so obtained? And when this money is retaken by the government via taxation, would not the producers be forced to surrender their labor and possessions in perpetuity in order to obtain the means of buying and selling?

monetary system from the deceitful extortionist scheme based on debt-financing, now operated by private banks, into a beneficent institution under the aegis of the United States Treasury. The transfer would occur in a series of steps called "Days" under orders from Congress.

FIRST DAY. All private banking institutions carrying deposits of the people would be required to transfer these to the nearest Treasury Depository. All cash not immediately delivered would become worthless. (The same provisions would apply to other securities or evidences of assets held by the banks, which would also be deposited with the Treasury under pain of confiscation.)

SECOND DAY. All individuals and other institutions would be required to deliver all cash in their possession, and receive therefor either deposit credits or new Treasury cash, dollar for dollar.

THIRD DAY. All owners of United States securities would be required to deliver them to the nearest Depository, where they would receive deposit credit for them at par, plus accrued interest, after which the securities would be burned. However, banks and other financial institutions which paid for them with credit created by the bonds themselves, would receive nothing. Thus, the debt of $288 billion—as of 1958—would be expunged entirely, and the $10 billion of annual interest on it would no longer be charged to the American people.

FOURTH DAY. All holders of corporation stock, all forms of industrial indebtedness, would be required to bring their shares, debentures, etc., to the Depositories, where deposit credit would be entered for the owners on Treasury deposit books; all such evidences of indebtedness would then be burned.

FIFTH DAY. All holders of city, district, county, and state securities would be required to deliver the same to the Depositories; if they had been purchased with current money, they would receive deposit credit for the full market value of the bonds, plus accrued interest; but financial institutions which obtained them by creating deposit credit, would receive nothing. All such public securities would then also be burned.[18]

Any securities not promptly delivered would be declared worthless.

Only personal debts, contracted between individuals, would be permitted to remain; but even these would be placed under the most careful scrutiny.[19]

All public and most private debt would therefore be wiped out at a single stroke; and all stock market operations would cease. There would be no unemployed, because the Treasury would supply business with all the money necessary for full employment in industry and elsewhere—somewhat à la Keynes.

Thus, the United States Treasury System would be established. "When the Treasury submitted to Congress both the volume of deposits plus money out of Depositories and the volume of business of the nation, if the Congress found that there were too many deposits, say $20 billion too much, it would pass an act instructing the Treasury to take deposit credit for a billion dollars of the total income each year for twenty years."[20]

If the deposits were less than required by the volume of business, a reverse action would be taken. "That would eliminate all public and industry debt.* Only a personal borrower to meet his personal necessities would remain in debt."[21]

The disposition of mortgages held by private institutions or individuals against real estate seems to remain obscure.

*This transfer of money and other obligations would necessarily entail the disbursement of hundreds of billions or even trillions of dollars in cash, and concentrate nearly all the assets of the nation on the books of deposit issued by the Treasury. Since such deposits would carry no interest, we would necessarily find perhaps $2 trillion dollars of spendable currency in the hands of individuals and private nonbanking corporations, who would certainly seek to place it in circulation as quickly as possible, since otherwise it would lie useless and unfruitful. If federal expenditures of perhaps $250 billion above revenues and the purchase of $50 billion of government bonds by the Fed between 1962 and 1974 caused our currency to inflate more than 50%, what would $2 trillion of new fiat money suddenly injected into the monetary stream of the nation do to the purchasing power of the dollar?

It would seem that the net result of Mr. Adams' ambitious scheme, when fully implemented, would simply be that the government would come into possession of virtually all the property in the United States through the disbursement of printing press money which cost nothing in the first place and which would quickly fall in purchasing power to that of the Continentals in 1787 or of Confederate money in 1866, or of the French assignats in 1796.

Citations

1. *The United States Treasury System,* 2
2. 1963 *SA* 346
3. *A Debtless Nation*
4. *The United States Treasury, op. cit.* 6
5. *Ib.* 11
6. *Ib.* 10
7. *Ib.* 3
8. *Ib.* 9
9. *Ib.* 5
10. *Ib.*
11. *A Debtless Nation*
12. *The United States Treasury, op. cit.* 10
13. *Ib.* 7
14. *Ib.* 14
15. *A Debtless Nation*
16. *The United States Treasury, op. cit.* 11
17. *Ib.* 12
18. *Ib.*
19. *Ib.*
20. *Ib.* 13
21. *Ib.*

G. PETER COOK

THE CREATION OF UNITED STATES FIAT CURRENCY

Mr. Peter Cook, who operates the Monetary Science Institute in Wickliffe, Ohio, is a prolific correspondent who has written a number of publications, of which *The Magic of Reserve Banking* is the most elaborate, and in which he mentions Silas Walter Adams as a source of inspiration.[1] It is, however, in a brochure entitled *Constitutional Money* that Mr. Cook sets forth his own theories concerning a monetary system which will require no specie. Congress, he declares, has "the power to coin and create Money."[2] Now, then, he asks, "What does [or will] Congress do with the money it is empowered to create? . . . exactly what the banks have been doing for centuries. Congress is to pay all its expenditures and obligations with the money it is empowered to coin or create." Congress being so endowed, "we could run rings around the Communists with our National Defense posture . . . without incurring a debt to anyone."[3]

Congress, then, "by asserting its sovereign prerogative to create its own money" can, "simply by using its own ballpoint pen . . . designate to the Treasury the maximum amount of funds to be disbursed with Treasury checks."[4]

The Fed and the fractional system of credit-lending now practiced by private banks will be abolished and monopolized by the federal government.

THE DISBURSEMENT OF CONSTITUTIONAL MONEY

Mr. Cook explains that in "a privately monopolized money and banking system . . . in order to obtain money or funds from the bankers . . . real wealth or property must always be pledged or mortgaged." However, under a constitutional monetary system, Congress would be "much like a father interested in his own family." It would not be "interested in [seizing] the public's wealth and property"; and "When there arises a national or popular need . . . the public then simply petitions Congress for the required funds . . . which Congress then creates . . . to finance the required or desired programs or projects—without incurring a debt or issuing any bonds or mortgaging anybody's property."[5]

Anyone needing money, therefore, will merely ask Congress for it, which, like a loving and generous father, will provide the same without being so harsh as to require any security for repayment.

Since the national debt would be expunged by the issuance of fiat currency, the interest on this, which has always been "the greatest single escalating factor" in creating the obligation, will no longer be due; and this will automatically so reduce expenditures that great savings will follow even if much of the money advanced upon request is recaptured by taxation.[6]

THE BLESSINGS OF FREE MONEY

The power of Congress to create and disburse currency, declares Mr. Cook, will be a universal blessing. "Take for example the city of Cleveland, Ohio . . . where the municipal transit system" is bankrupt because it "operates to the tune played by the banker creditors. Under the Constitutional money system, the people of the city . . . would simply petition" their "Congressman to arrange for an interest-free long-term loan from the United States Treasury to refinance the transit system. And when that interest-free loan was due . . . if the Cleveland transit system was still in trouble . . . the Congressman . . . would have authority to renew the loan as often as necessary."[7]

In short, every municipality and other level of local

government could have all the interest-free loans they might need, which would never have to be repaid.*

"Under the Constitutional monetary System; the state and local governments . . . when they were in need of funds . . . could simply go and petition their Congressman —either for interest-free loans or direct grants of funds to meet their needs or emergencies. And Congress . . . would have the power and authority to grant the state and local government's petitions and requests."[8]

Mr. Cook notes that hospitals and medical costs have skyrocketed "because of the compounded interest charges."[9] Under a Constitutional monetary system, however, funds would be supplied without interest** and thus cut the cost of medical care by 50 to 70%.[10]

THE WELFARE STATE SUPREME

We would thus be able to establish adequate programs for every kind of social welfare without cost to the people.[11] Since local capital expenditures would be met in this manner, "the real estate taxes on homes and small farms could be cut at least 50%.[12] Because the schools, which are the greatest portion of local real estate taxes, would also be financed with Congress-created funds; and, if necessary, even with grants of free Congress-created money."[13]

---

*Actually, this is the very method used by the federal government to finance to a large degree the Salt River Project of Arizona, the Tennessee Valley Authority, and other similar installations; these have contributed heavily to the creation of the national debt and to the current inflation.

**We should note that since 1947, under the Hill-Burton Act, about $6 billion has been given as outright grants to hospitals; and that during the same period their fees have increased approximately 1,000%. These hospitals pay no taxes of any kind, nor are they required to make any financial reports to the IRS or anyone else.

LOW INTEREST RATES FOR EVERYONE

"The interest rates on Congress-created funds issued through the United States Treasury, can range anywhere from no interest to a moderate interest, as it may be required, to regulate and maintain an orderly and stable currency.

"For example: The private home ownership and family farm development must always be a prime priority. And for all such dwelling homes and family farm loans of the Constitutional money, the interest rates shall never exceed 1%.

"For all local family operated food, clothing, and services establishments and the like, the interest rates on the Constitutional money shall not exceed 2%."[14]

HOW BANKS WILL OPERATE

However, Mr. Cook assures us that the banks will not suffer, because they will still be "free to do exactly what they always claim they are doing, and that is: to compete for the public savings, and invest them for a profit. . . ."[15]

The banks will obtain funds from two sources: the people's savings, as just indicated, and the United States Treasury, from which they will be permitted to borrow "on the same terms as any other industry,"[16] which, we presume, will not exceed 2 or 3%. Since fractional reserve banking would be outlawed, they would always have 100% reserves against their loans, such funds to be obtained either from the government or private long-term deposits. However, since the banks might be unable to lend as much money as business would require, "the public can go to the United States Treasury and there borrow newly issued funds . . . at about 2% higher interest than would be charged for similar general purpose retail financing."[17] The Treasury, therefore, would not, Mr. Cook assures us, be in competition with private banks.[18]

THE TREASURY AS THE GREAT MONEY LENDER

Why the Treasury would charge 2% higher interest than the banks when it has already loaned unlimited amounts of money at 1 or 2%, or entirely without interest, remains obscure. At any rate, under Mr. Cook's system, the Treasury would certainly become the principal money lender, if, indeed, it did not achieve complete monopoly in this field; for, with such competition, it is difficult to see how any private banking could survive at all. How could banks, borrowing their 100% reserves from the government at 2 or 3%, compete with the federal government, which would be lending money without interest or security, or at rates not exceeding 1 or 2%?*

FINANCING THE FEDERAL BUDGET

Above and beyond all this, however, we have the federal government itself for which "there is usually a certain fixed annual operating budget" which will be met by levying "duties, imposts, excises, and the like . . . on the total population, to remove out of circulation the excess funds that have accomplished their purpose; because, a new round of funds is continually being spent into circulation, to replace the withdrawn and extinguished funds."[19]

We note, therefore, that the federal income tax would be abolished and that taxation would be limited to the forms specifically enumerated in the original Constitution.

Citations

1. Peter Cook, *The Magic of Reserve Banking* 39
2. *Ib. Constitutional Money* 3

*Once the Treasury has paid off the entire national debt with fiat currency and injected perhaps another two or three trillion dollars of immediately spendable money into the financial arteries of the nation, precisely what would happen to the purchasing power of the dollar?

3. *Ib.*
4. *Ib.*
5. *Ib.*
6. *Ib.* 4
7. *Ib.*
8. *Ib.*
9. *Ib.*
10. *Ib.*
11. *Ib.*
12. *Ib.* 5
13. *Ib.* 6
14. *Ib.* 5
15. *Ib.*
16. *Ib.*
17. *Ib.*
18. *Ib.*
19. *Ib.*

H. CHARLES S. AND RUSSEL L. NORBURN

BASIC PROPOSALS

The Norburn brothers, authors of *Mankind's Greatest Step,* published in 1971, declare that gold is a monetary fetish which should be discarded in word as it has been in fact;[1] that a United States Treasury Bank should issue its own fiat currency in any amounts deemed desirable;[2] that this institution should lend money to all other levels of government; that it should provide commercial banks with loans sufficient to create reserves of 100% for them;[3] that all such loans should require the payment of interest, and that commercial banks should be prohibited from creating credit on the basis of marginal reserves.[4]

THE FIRST TRUE MONEY

The Norburns describe the manner in which the Massachusetts colony established its own mint in 1652; but, since the coins produced there were seized by agents of the English crown and exported to England, the Colony began issuing its own paper notes in 1690 and then made them full legal tender in 1692. "This," declare the Norburns, "was the first true money the world had ever known—it has been the last."[5]

A LEGISLATIVE PROPOSAL

The book contains considerable discussion dealing with monetary history; but its most significant portion is found in Chapter 5, where we find a rough draft of proposed legislation which we summarize as follows:

(a) The Federal Reserve Act is repealed.

(b) All its property is surrendered to the Secretary of the Treasury.

(c) The Secretary is directed to take charge of the Federal Reserve surplus and pay its member banks for their stock.

(d) All government bonds retrieved from the Fed are to be burned.

(e) The name of the System is changed to "The United States Treasury Department of Money."

(f) The System is to be remodeled by the Secretary under the direction of Congress and the House Banking and Currency Committee. The only currency to be issued thereafter will be the "United States Note." The headquarters of the new System shall be located in the nation's capital and shall have a governing body consisting of a board of three governors (to be appointed by the President with the advice and consent of the lower house of Congress), who, together with the Secretary of the Treasury, shall operate the System.

(g) The System shall be operated so as to show a large profit from interest on funds loaned to banks, etc.

(h) The United States Treasury Bank, replacing the twelve Fed banks, shall issue all the money and credit the nation requires.

(i) The System, with its Central Office located in Washington, D.C., will operate essentially as the Fed now does—only the beneficiaries thereof will be changed. [However, the Fed does not lend money.]

(j) The Secretary shall prepare a list of United States Monetary requirements pursuant to Congressional appropriations and shall transmit such list to the Central Office of the System, which will supply money as needed in the form of cash, checks, or vouchers to all departments of the government.

(k) This Central Control Office shall make interest-bearing loans as necessary to State, County, and Municipal governments, such loans to be guaranteed by local taxation.

(l) The true ownership of all privately owned financial institutions shall be recorded in the office of the United States Treasury.

(m) All commercial banks shall become national banks, and their only source of lendable funds shall be the United States Treasury Banks. No private bank shall be permitted to relend any customer's money.

(n) Every commercial bank shall have a Loan Department, the sole function of which shall be to borrow from the United States Treasury Bank and then lend the same money, dollar for dollar, to its customers. [Why could not the Treasury make the loans directly in the first place?]

(o) The money thus loaned to private banks and then reloaned to their customers is the Credit of the Nation—the labor of all its people, which makes pieces of paper the representatives of actual wealth.

(p) When the note from the United States Treasury Bank falls due, the commercial bank must pay, whether or not its customers have met their obligations.

(q) Uniform interest rates for different types of loans shall be established for the whole country by Congress.

(r) The United States Banks shall supply currency and coin to all commercial banks.

(s) As soon as this legislation is enacted, all commercial banks shall furnish the United States Treasury Banks with full details concerning outstanding loans, which shall then be refinanced with dollar-for-dollar interest-bearing loans from the United States Treasury Bank. The interest differential shall be sufficient to enable the commercial banks to operate at a profit.

(t) Neither the United States government nor any of its agencies, or any other level of government, shall make loans to private individuals or to any corporation except a commercial bank.

(u)   (v) The United States Treasury Banks shall act as a clearing house for checks and shall perform this service at a charge to its customers sufficient to cover the cost thereof.

(w) Severe penalties shall be provided against any person or institution which fails to comply with the provisions of this Act.

(x) The Board of Governors shall determine how much

money is to be placed in circulation, what the rate of interest shall be, and how much shall be withdrawn as federal taxes in order to maintain a stable dollar.

(y) This Act shall never be repealed; any effort to do so or to weaken its provisions shall be considered *prima-facie* evidence of bribery and punishable as such.[6]

SUMMARY

The Norburns are certain that once our government is freed from its present shackles, it can create happiness and prosperity by lending fiat money to liquidate the national debt, clear away every kind of pollution, construct a pipeline to bring water from the Northwest to the arid Southwest, rebuild our cities, care for the old and infirm, and perform a myriad of other welfare services that would bring security and happiness to our people.[7]

Citations

1. Norburn, Charles S. and Russel L., *Mankind's Greatest Step* 126
2. *Ib.* 102
3. *Ib.* 106, 108, 110
4. *Ib.* 114
5. *Ib.* 12
6. *Ib.* 98–118
7. *Ib.* 120–123

I. THE GUERNSEY EXPERIMENT
WITH FIAT MONEY

Guernsey, one of the Channel Islands under British sovereignty and located near the coast of France, contains less than 25 square miles. It had been the resort of smugglers, bootleggers, and privateers until the War of 1812–14 between England and France, when its income was derived from military occupation. With this withdrawn, however, virtually all sources of income were terminated, and the population of some 6,000 or 7,000 were faced with a crisis of devastating poverty. (The population doubled by 1821 and stood at 38,283 a century later.)

According to a pamphlet by Olive and Jan Grubiak written about 1944, and reprinted by Omni Publications, the States of Guernsey solved their problem by printing fiat currency; and the authors suggest that other communities—for example their city of Glasgow—should issue vouchers, similar to the scrip used by various American cities in 1932–33 to pay their school teachers and other public employees.

The Grubiaks grow quite lyrical in their praise of a debt-free, fiat currency issued by the government. "Debt, private and public," they declare, "is the cancer that preys on the vitals of our civilization, not only in Britain, but throughout the civilized world. Must we wait till our own great civilization follows its predecessors into limbo, or can we learn the lesson in time to prevent disaster?. . . .

"The flaw is in [private debt-based] money-creation. Guernsey creates its own money as a Credit; the so-called nationalized Bank of England creates our money as a Debt. Guernsey lit the torch of freedom from debt one hundred-thirty years ago, and it is reaping the benefits in present prosperity. Guernsey leads the world in common-sense finance—shall we follow, or shall we continue to flounder ever deeper into the quagmire of debt, taxation, and final extinction? *The decision is yours."*

The first note issue was for £4,000 in 1816, all to be redeemed in less than two years. In 1819, there was another issue, of 4,500, redeemable in ten years. Other issues followed, and in 1821, 10,000 were in circulation; in 1826, 20,000; in 1829, 48,000; and in 1837, 55,000. By 1918, the total had risen to £142,000 and in 1937 to £175,000.

The only important historical document reprinted in the pamphlet is the 1829 "Reply of the States of Guernsey to the Privy Council Justifying the Guernsey Experiment." From this and other information, we can make the following reconstruction of what happened.

Faced with literal starvation, the inhabitants of Guernsey voted in 1815 in favor of issuing fiat money on the condition that it be redeemed in less that two years, and that it be invested in roads, schools, markets, rentable buildings, and port facilities. Actually, they had little choice, for the alternative was starvation or abandoning their homes forever.

For example, the only passage across the island was a rutted road barely seven feet wide, and scarcely passable by ox cart. The harbor had fallen into decay and nearly all buildings had deteriorated to the point of uselessness. The debt was so great that the interest on it almost equalled the public income; and increased taxation was simply impossible. There seems to have been no agriculture or production of any kind; and the famous Guernsey cattle and dairy industry was not yet developed.

The note issues were actually very similar to the emergency wartime noninterest-bearing bills or notes advocated by Jefferson which, however, were to be solidly bottomed on taxes and redeemable in a short time.

We need not be surprised that the results on Guernsey were beneficial. None of the money, so far as we can tell, was spent for government overhead or administration. A law was passed in 1814 placing a duty of one shilling on every gallon of spiritous liquor produced and sold for a period of five years. In

1819, this was extended for ten years and in 1929 for another fifteen. The income from this tax was sufficient to guarantee the integrity of the notes.

During the period 1815–30, roads and schools were built, public markets were constructed, business facilities leased, and port facilities which, in turn, served as the basis for considerable construction in the private sector. Meanwhile, revenues from the liquor tax, rentals from markets and other buildings, and increased maritime trade was sufficient to redeem the notes and support the government.

However, as we learn from the 1829 document, by no means all of this expansion was financed by the issuance of fiat money. Large loans at 3% interest, obtained from individuals and savings banks, were used to build the markets and finance most of the other expenditures. Liquor taxes and business revenues sufficed to finance the government and redeem its obligations.

Actually, the Guernsey project was an experiment in public ownership and operation of commercial investments rather than in the use of fiat money, which served primarily to initiate all that activity and expansion. However, it certainly demonstrated that under certain conditions people will, at least for a time, accept noninterest-bearing government paper similar to small bonds and use it as legal tender until the economy improves.

Whether such a solution could be applied succesfully on a permanent basis in a large, industrialized nation is a question which as yet remains unanswered.

J. AN ARGUMENT FROM RHODESIA

The following article appeared in the May, 1974, issue of
Rhodesia and World Report, in answer to a letter which
advocated a return to the gold standard in that country.

To insist on a currency convertible to gold is to demand a
gold currency standard. We must therefore ask ourselves whether
(a) a gold standard would get rid of inflation and ensure us a stable,
honest monetary system; and (b) whether it is possible for
Rhodesia to adopt a gold standard on her own. We shall now deal
with these queries.
Gold Check on Inflation
    Firstly, a thorough-going gold standard would keep
inflation on a tight rein, but could never get rid of it. We all know
that gold cannot be multiplied ad lib—as paper money and bank
credit can—to cause inflation; but nevertheless, the gold standard
has an inherent weakness which will always render it unable to
ensure monetary stability. This weakness consists in the fact that
the gold standard entails two different values for gold, viz. a
commodity value and a *monetary* value. Inevitably, the
commodity value would be governed by one set of factors and the
monetary value by another. This conflict could never be resolved
for it has always been, and still is, beyond the wit of man to tie the
two permanently together. The discovery of new gold deposits, the
rate of gold abstraction, the cost of mining and such-like factors,
which govern the amount of gold produced, are not naturally
linked with the factors which govern the volume of money
required by the development of trade and industry. Thus the
increments of the new gold and new money tend to drift apart.
    Money, as we all know, is the catalyst of expansion and
must precede expansion. Thus, where money is tied to gold, the
supply of monetary gold and the value of money in use must
always be the same—to ensure monetary stability. Unfortunately,

this does not happen in real life, for money tends to increase in volume faster than new gold is mined. Thus a continuing problem is posed, viz., whether to limit the volume of money by increasing the 'fixed' price of gold, thus making full economic expansion possible, but introducing instability to the system of money.

Gold Standard Obsolete

This problem underlines the great anachronism of the gold standard and demonstrates that it is merely an expedient, not a scientific instrument. The gold standard survived for many years of borrowed time simply because the world's economies were sluggish and the amplitude of its own eccentricities was so small as not to call for its sudden and total removal. But it has been removed nevertheless, bit by bit, and no better standard found. Modern economic expansion has put too great a strain on the inherent weakness of having two separate values. Gold has not been allowed to dictate the rate of the world's economic expansion and never will be; nor will any other commodity for the same reason. The vaunted gold standard is at last the mere shell of an extinct creature mourned by some, but never to be revived except with dishonest intent. We must look to another standard to ensure monetary stability.

The Ratio Standard

What we must have is a scientific standard and one is, in fact, readily available. It is the ratio of commodities available to money available for buying them. The value of this ratio should be 1.

Money is the means by which production is distributed and the producers rewarded. It may be likened to food without which we cannot be healthy; too little debilitates and could kill, too much hurts in as many ways. A scientific food standard demands the equating of food value to food needs. So with money. Too little depresses the body economic; too much generates inflation, which is monetary obesity. A scientific standard equates an economy's supply of money with its need of money. . . . Mr. Richard C. Haw . . . puts it like this: '. . . the purchasing power [must] be in balance with the wealth-on-sale.' He goes on to say, 'Inflation and deflation would be impossible so long as this balance between money and goods were maintained.' Let us repeat: The scientific monetary standard is a RATIO, viz., Commodities to Money, or C/M, which must be maintained at a value of 1. It is to this mathematical ratio standard, *not to gold,* that we must look for monetary stability in the future.

And now we deal with the second question, viz., is it feasible to adopt a gold standard on our own?

In view of what we have just learned, a gold standard UDI would seem to be pointless. However, some of our readers may feel that an imperfect gold standard is preferable to our existing paper-drunk system. We need not list the technical difficulties of adopting a gold standard unilaterally. These, in to-day's context, although not beyond our ability, are really beside the point. What we must consider is the certain and venomous opposition which would come from the Banking Establishment, which in this day holds the world to ransom. Let us take a lesson from what this financial coterie did to the Thirteen Colonies of America. (Here follows a citation from the Norburn book, discussing the manner in which the English government seized and exported the coins minted in Massachusetts and thus controlled its economy.)

Any Rhodesian gold standard rebellion would invoke the opposition of this same ruthless coterie. Can anyone doubt that our own coins would in their turn be collected by agents 'almost as fast as they were minted,' and melted down? Our chances of winning through would be slight indeed.

Such might not be the case, however, for the ratio standard which subsists in reality, for even the Establishment itself is desperately struggling to save its own run-away monetary machine. It may yet be compelled to adopt a ratio standard in the effort to save itself. Yet nothing will save it, and the Establishment itself is doomed, for both are inherently self-destructive. There are already signs that the world's trade unions, so long and barbarously exploited by this moneyed junta for its own ends at a great cost of human misery, may soon turn and rend their masters. It should comfort us to reflect that the noblest achievements of the great unions lie ahead, not behind. If they can succeed in wresting economic freedom for the great masses of the world's people from the most ruthless and cunning oppressors in all history, it will go a long way towards atoning for their past irresponsible conduct.

As for little, but significant, Rhodesia, let us bring pressure on our government to adopt the ratio monetary standard and thus point the way to monetary stability for all the world to see.

We note, then, that the author's objections to the gold standard are (1) that the price of the metal fluctuates; (2) that there is not enough of it to supply monetary needs; (3) that it is manipulated by vicious financiers; (4) that its return would be opposed by these same enemies of the people with such force and virulence that it could not be accomplished; and (5) that it could not be re-established successfully in a small country like Rhodesia on a unilateral basis.

CHAPTER IX

The Case for the Gold Standard

A. INTRODUCTORY

Some of the proponents of the gold standard differ significantly from each other in regard to marginal reserve banking, how commercial institutions should be supplied with reserves, who should control the national credit, how the banks should be chartered, and what should be done with the national debt; nevertheless, most of them are in basic agreement concerning the techniques of restoration and various other fundamentals, to wit: (1) that neither bankers nor politicians, or, indeed, anyone appointed by the government, can be trusted with discretionary power in the issuance of currency; (2) that the value of money, by its very nature, can be established only by economic law—namely, the cost of reproducing whatever is to serve as the official medium of exchange; (3) that only by anchoring the dollar in a base of intrinsic value, can its integrity be insured; and (4) that every form of fiat money serves always and even primarily as a means of manipulating the economy and making the people the pawns of politicians and financiers.

Those who advocate a return to the gold standard declare also that there is no issue before the American people at this time more important, more crucial, than the monetary problem; and that unless we find a firm and permanent solution for this in the foreseeable future, our nation may be plunged into chaos with the possibility of violence and ultimate revolution—perhaps involving the total destruction of all the liberties and blessings our Founding Fathers conferred upon us.

They maintain, finally, that a return to the gold standard is not only entirely feasible and practical, but mandatory if our nation is to avoid the fearful catastrophes which have overtaken so many others in the course of history because of the same problems that now are eating the vitals of American life like a spreading cancer.

Those who believe in the gold standard declare that although the metal has fluctuated somewhat in "value," such variations have been minimal or localized; that nothing else can compare with gold as a monetary reserve or yardstick; and that there is no other means of insuring society equally against inflation and panics. They remind us of what happened after Solon "lifted the burdens"; how Roman civilization was destroyed when its currency was utterly debased; how the theories and experiments of John Law plunged France into chaos in 1717–19; and how the French financiers—reputedly the most astute and knowledgeable in Europe—carried their nation into economic ruin in a few years when they attempted to guarantee the value of the assignats by anchoring them in the lands confiscated by the government during the Revolution, but succeeded only in raising prices by several thousand per cent and causing almost universal starvation.

B. THOMAS JEFFERSON

THE IMPORTANCE OF THIS FOUNDING FATHER

Since Jefferson was the most important of our Founding Fathers; since he, in a real sense, created the philosophical basis on which this nation was established; and since, finally, he spelled out his convictions concerning banking, monetary problems, and the issuance of currency in many passages, we feel that we should reproduce his ideas rather fully, which are scattered throughout his works, but expressed in concentrated form in three lengthy letters composed in 1813 and addressed to his son-in-law, John W. Eppes, then Secretary of the Treasury under James Madison.

OPPOSITION TO PRIVATE BANKS OF ISSUE

We should note first that Jefferson above all was adamantly opposed to the emission of paper currency by any private entity, whether chartered by state or national authority. In a letter to Albert Gallatin of October 16, 1815, we read: "We are undone, my dear Sir, if this banking mania [in favor of the Second United States Bank] be not suppressed. . . . Put down the [private] banks, and if the country could not be carried through the longest war . . . without ever knowing the want of a dollar and without loading the public with an indefinite burden of debt, I know nothing of my countrymen. . . ." And, he continued: "If the Treasury had ventured its credit in bills of circulating size, as of five or ten dollars, they would have been greedily received by our people in preference to bank paper. But unhappily . . . the country [has] delivered itself bound hand and foot to the bold and bankrupt adventurers" who pretend "to be money-lenders, whom it could have crushed at any moment."[1]

On January 1 of the same year, Jefferson wrote James Monroe: "The dominion which the banking institutions have obtained over the minds of our citizens . . . must be broken, or it will break us."[2]

In another letter, dated March 6, 1813, addressed to Eppes, he wrote: "After the solemn decisions of Congress against the renewal of the charter of the United States Bank," in 1811 because of lack of constitutional authority, "I had imagined that question at rest, and that no more applications would be made to them [the members of Congress] for the incorporation of banks. . . ."[3]

At times, Jefferson waxed satirical: "Here," he wrote Eppes on November 6, 1813, "we have a set of people . . . who have bestowed on us the great blessing of running in our debt about 200 millions of dollars, without our knowing who they are or what they are. . . . And to fill up the measure of blessings, instead of paying, they receive an interest on what they owe. . . . And they are so ready still to deal out their liberalities to us that they are willing to let themselves run in our debt ninety millions more, on our paying them the same premium of six or eight percent interest. . . ."[4]

After the First United States Bank was abolished in 1811, there were only state-chartered banks of issue. In a letter to John Taylor, dated May 28, 1816, Jefferson wrote: "The system of banks which we have both equally and ever reprobated, I contemplate as a blot in all our [state] constitutions, which, if not corrected, will end in their destruction." This system, he continued, is operated "by the gamblers in corruption, and it is sweeping away in its progress the fortunes and morals of our citizens" as well as our Republican form of government itself.[5] And he observed in a letter to Eppes "that the toleration of banks of paper discount, costs the United States one-half of their war taxes;* or, in other words, doubles the expenses of every war."[6]

---

*The reason for this was that these private banks loaned the government their fiat currency, but required that the obligations be repaid in specie, which was worth twice as much, in addition to the heavy interest exacted.

THE ISSUANCE OF CURRENCY AS A FEDERAL MONOPOLY

Convinced that the emission of currency should be a monopoly of the General Government, Jefferson condemned the issuance of currency by the private banks chartered by the states; and again and again he urged them to relinquish their authority to authorize them. "If Treasury bills," he wrote further to Eppes, "are emitted on a tax appropriated for their redemption in fifteen years and . . . bearing interest of six percent, there is no one who would not take them in preference to the bank paper now afloat. . . .* Their credit once established, others might be emitted bottomed also on a tax, but not bearing interest; and if ever their credit faltered . . . these bills alone should be received as specie." And finally: "The States should . . . transfer the right of issuing circulating currency paper to Congress exclusively, in perpetuum. . . ."[7]

THE PERILS OF INFLATION

Jefferson described to his son-in-law what had happened in France under the Duke of Orleans in 1717;[8] again and again, he emphasized the dangers of fiat currency. In a letter to Monroe, dated January 15, 1815, he wrote: "Although all the nations of Europe have tried and trodden every path of force and folly in a fruitless quest of the same object, yet WE still expect to find in juggling tricks and banking dreams, that money can be made out of nothing, and in sufficient quantity to meet the expenses of a heavy war. . . ."[9]

In 1813, the national debt had risen sharply because of the war with England; and because depreciation had reduced the purchasing power of American currency by half, inflation had become a serious problem.[10] "In this state of things," wrote Jefferson, "we are called upon to add ninety millions more to the

---

*These bills would be a kind of combination bond and circulating currency, issued in small denominations and bearing interest at the rate of 6 percent.

circulation. Proceeding in this career, it is infallible that we must end where the revolutionary war ended. . . ."[11] Let us suppose that the panic will arrive when three hundred millions of paper currency is in circulation. No one dreams that the private banks possess "three hundred millions of specie to satisfy the holders of notes. . . ." When these are repudiated, desolation and universal bankruptcy will follow.[12]

OPPOSITION TO FRACTIONAL RESERVE BANKING

Jefferson was among the first who condemned fractional reserve banking: "No one," he emphasized, "has a natural right to the trade of money-lender, but he who has money to lend. . . . The unlimited emission of bank paper has banished all her [Great Britain's] specie, and is now, by depreciation . . . carrying her rapidly to bankruptcy as it did France, and as it did us, and . . . every country permitting paper to be circulated, other than that held by public authority, rigorously limited to the just measure for circulation. Private fortunes, in the present state of our circulation, are at the mercy of these self-created money-lenders, and are frustrated by the flood of nominal money with which their avarice deluges us. . . ."[13]

OPPOSITION TO HEAVY NATIONAL DEBT

Jefferson had an almost preternatural horror of a large national debt. "It is a wise rule," he wrote to Eppes on June 24, 1813, "never to borrow a dollar without laying a tax at the same instant for paying the interest annually and the principal within a given term. . . .[14] The earth belongs to the living, not the dead. . . . We may consider each generation as a distinct nation, with a right to . . . bind themselves, but not the succeeding generation, any more than the inhabitants of another country. . . .[15] The modern theory of the perpetuation of debt has drenched the earth with blood, and crushed its inhabitants under burdens ever accumulating."[16]

Jefferson continued: "We shall consider ourselves unauthorized to saddle posterity with our debts, and morally bound to pay them ourselves. . . . We must ourselves raise the money for this war, either by taxes within the year, or by loans; and if by loans, we must repay them ourselves. . . ."[17] And creditors must be repaid in full, for our debts are "our risk, not theirs. . . ."[18]

Jefferson once wrote to John Taylor: "I wish it were possible to [amend our] constitution with . . . an additional article taking from the federal government the power of borrowing."[19]

On October 11, 1809, he wrote Albert Gallatin: "I consider the fortunes of our republic depending in an eminent degree, on the extinguishment of the public debt . . . ; because, that done, we shall have revenue enough to improve our country in peace, and defend it in war, without incurring either new taxes or loans. But if the debt should once more be swelled to a formidable size, its entire discharge will be despaired of, and we shall be committed to the English career of debt, corruption, and rottenness, closing with revolution. The discharge of the debt, therefore, is vital to the destinies of our government. . . ."[20]

THE QUESTION OF FIAT CURRENCY

Since Jefferson sometimes advocated the emission of paper currency during a war emergency by the General Government without specific reference to specie, some have mistakenly concluded that he was advocating fiat money.* He

*A syndicated article written by Jeffrey St. John and published by the Copley News Service (April 15, 1974) states: "Jefferson strove to solve his own problems and those of the young republic . . . by enunciating a plan based on the gold standard." Leslie Snyder wrote in a book published in 1973: "gold and silver was as important to the Founding Fathers as were their other rights. Gold and silver money was incorporated into the body of the Constitution before the Bill of Rights was written." (Exposition Press, *Why Gold?*) In his monumental biography of Jefferson, Merrill D. Peterson notes that "Monetary expansionists, from the Greenbackers to the free silverites," have repeatedly quoted from the Eppes letters in support of their position; however, "Jefferson's letters, whatever their

wrote Eppes, for example, that "A nation . . . making purchases and payments with bills fitted for circulation thrusts an equal sum of coin out of circulation. . . . And so a nation may continue to issue its bills as far as its wants require, and the limits of circulation will admit. . . . But this, the only resource which the government could command with certainty, the States have unfortunately fooled away, nay corruptly alienated to swindlers and shavers, under the cover of private banks."[21]

In another letter to his son-in-law, Jefferson wrote again in a vein which has been interpreted as advocacy of federal fiat currency: "Bank paper must be suppressed, and the circulating medium must be restored to the nation to whom it belongs. It is the only fund on which they can rely for loans; it is the only resource which can never fail them, and it is an abundant one for every necessary purpose. Treasury bills, bottomed on taxes . . . thrown into circulation, will take the place of so much gold and silver. . . ."[22] However, as Merrill Peterson points out, such Treasury bills would be only an emergency emission, and would quickly be honored with full redemption.

HOW MUCH SPECIE IS NECESSARY?

Jefferson estimated that only one-thirtieth of all exchanges were accomplished by means of currency;[23] and he found in this fact a powerful argument in favor of specie—gold or silver. Some argue, he noted, that we should not use coin because of its intrinsic or capital value; but, since only $15 million of such metal, or the one hundred and thirty-third part of $2 billion, would be required, it is ridiculous to hold, because of this petty

---

purport as to banks, were a powerful indictment of paper money, which he seemed willing to risk in a wartime emergency, provided specie payment was speedily restored. Of the three financial proposals of the Bryan Democracy of 1896—suppression of private bank issues in favor of government control of the circulating medium, regular government issue of paper money as legal tender, and free coinage of silver at the legally fixed ratio of 16 to 1—only the first had clear warrant in the Eppes letters. . . ." (*The Jefferson Image and the American Mind*, Oxford University Press, New York, 262-3.)

sum, that we should "give up our gold and silver medium, its intrinsic validity, its universal value, and its saving powers in time of war, and to substitute for it paper, with all its term of evils, moral, political, and physical; which I will not pretend to enumerate."[24]

"There is, indeed, a convenience in paper," he continues, such as "its easy transmission from one place to another. But this may be mainly supplied by bills of exchange [certificates redeemable in specie on demand], so as to prevent any great displacement of actual coin."[25] Thus we see that the acute and capacious mind of Jefferson encompassed every important subject under the sun.

THE DESIRABILITY AND NECESSITY OF SPECIE

Over and over, Jefferson declared that the redeemability of the currency on demand in specie was not only desirable, but mandatory in order to prevent inflation. "It is a litigated question," he stated in one of the Eppes letters, "whether the circulation of paper, rather than of specie, is a good or an evil. . . ." However, "excepting England and her copyist, the United States, there is not a nation existing, I believe, which tolerates a paper circulation."[26] And he continued: "one of the great advantages of specie as a medium is, that being of universal value, it will keep itself at a general level. . . . This is agreed to by Smith, the principal advocate for a paper circulation; but . . . on the sole condition that it be strictly regulated. He admits, nevertheless, that the commerce and industry of a country cannot be so secure when suspended on the Daedalian wings of paper money, as on the solid ground of gold and silver; and that in time of war, the insecurity is greatly increased. . . ."[27]

Jefferson reasoned that, should the States concede to Congress their power to charter banks, then shortly "the medium of gold and silver will be universally restored," which "is what ought to be done." Otherwise, "merchants, speculators, and prospectors, will drive us before them . . . until . . . our citizens will be overtaken by the crush of this bankers' fabric, without other satisfaction than that of execrations on the heads of those functionaries who, from ignorance, pusillanimity, or corruption, have betrayed the fruits of their industry into the hands of prospectors and swindlers."[28]

Again and again, Jefferson excoriated the private banks of issue because they inflated the currency by banishing specie: "If the debt which the banking companies owe be a blessing . . . it is to themselves alone, who are realizing a solid interest of eight to ten per cent on it. As to the public, these companies have banished all our gold and silver medium, which . . . before we had without interest, which never could have perished in our hands, and would have been our salvation now in the hour of war; instead of which they have given us two hundred millions of froth and bubble, on which we are to pay them heavy interest. . . ."[29]

THE GOLD AND SILVER STANDARD

Jefferson declared that "specie is the most perfect medium, because it will preserve its own level; because, having intrinsic and universal value, it can never die in our hands, and is the surest resource of reliance in time of war; that the trifling economy of paper . . . weighs nothing in opposition to the advantages of the precious metals; that [paper currency] has been, is, and forever will be abused, in every country in which it is permitted; that it is already at a term of abuse in these States, which has never been reached in any nation, France excepted, whose dreadful catastrophe [under John Law] should be a warning against the instrument which produced it; that we are already at ten or twenty times the due quantity of [necessary] medium; insomuch that no man knows what his property is worth. . . . Instead, then, of yielding to the cries of scarcity of medium . . . no endeavors should be spared to begin the work of reducing it by such gradual means as may give time to private fortunes to preserve their poise, and settle down with the subsiding medium; and that, for this purpose, the States should be urged to concede to the General Government . . . the exclusive power of establishing banks" with power to issue currency.[30]

SUMMARY

We find, then, that Jefferson wished to abolish all private banks of issue—state or national; that he advocated a solid currency to be emitted exclusively by the federal government; that, in time of war, this authority might issue circulating currency bottomed solidly on taxes, which might or might not bear interest; that any cost incurred in time of war should be met by current taxation or by short-term loans; that creditors must be paid in solid currency; and that all money issued by the federal government must be in the form of gold or silver or in paper currency redeemable in specie on demand.

Citations

1. Jefferson, Library Edition, *op. cit.* Vol. XIV 356–57
2. *Ib.* 227
3. *Ib.* Vol. XIII 409–410
4. *Ib.* 420–21
5. *The Writings of Thomas Jefferson,* H.W. Derby, Vol. VI 605–6
6. Jefferson, Library Edition, *op. cit.* Vol. XIII 364
7. *Ib.* 275–75
8. *Ib.* 419
9. *Ib.* Vol. XIV 227
10. *Ib.* Vol. XIII 427
11. *Ib.* 426
12. *Ib.* 427
13. *Ib* 277–78
14. *Ib.* 269
15. *Ib.* 270
16. *Ib.* 272
17. *Ib.* 358
18. *Ib.* 366
19. *The Writings of Thomas Jefferson,* Grey and Bowen, Vol. III 404
20. *Ib.* Vol. IV 136

21. Jefferson, Library Edition, *op. cit.* Vol. XIII 274
22. *Ib.* 361
23. *Ib.* 414–15
24. *Ib.* 416
25. *Ib.*
26. *Ib.* 409
27. *Ib.* 412
28. *Ib.* 429
29. *Ib.* 423
30. *Ib.* 430–31

C.   LUDWIG VON MISES

AN EMINENT ECONOMIST

Ludwig von Mises' principal work, *Theorie des Geldes (The Theory of Money),* was first published in Austria in 1912, translated into English in 1934, and produced in an updated edition in 1953 by the Yale University Press, which also published his monumental *Human Action* in 1963. Von Mises declares that the basic purpose of economics must be to re-establish the gold standard and explode the fallacies that have confused a multitude of authors from John Law to Lord Keynes.[1] "The gold standard," he declares, "made the marvellous evolution of modern capitalism possible. It led to the establishment of the modern methods of banking. But the businessmen who had developed them lacked the intellectual power to resist successfully the attacks upon the operation of the monetary and banking principles, the strict observance of which is absolutely necessary to make the system work and to prevent its catastrophic breakdown. If the determination of the quantity of money—the generally employed medium of exchange transactions—were subject to actions on the part of any individuals or groups of individuals whose material interests would be affected by changes in the purchasing power of the monetary unit, the system would not have been able to avoid a complete collapse. Neither inflation nor deflation is a policy that can last.

"The eminence of the gold standard consists in the fact that geological conditions strictly limit the amount of gold available. This has up to now made the operation of the gold currency possible."[2]

THE ORIGIN OF THE GOLD STANDARD

Gold, says von Mises, achieved historic monetary pre-dominance by automatic development. It was never the intention of governments to establish the single, but rather a bimetallic, standard, which was intended to maintain a rigid exchange ratio between gold and silver; all such attempts, however, failed completely;[3] and, as a result, the gold standard emerged from empirical experience, which demonstrated that sound money meant a metallic standard; that coins should contain a definite quantity of standard metal determined by law, and that all other kinds of circulating currency should be instantly redeemable in such money.[4]

THOSE WHO OPPOSE MONEY ON PRINCIPLE

Two classes of people, states von Mises, oppose the use of money, or sound money. The first are impractical moralists to whom all the processes of life appear in a monetary form; they blame money for prostitution, bribery, theft, murder, embezzlement and the entire train of crime which afflicts mankind. Even less worthy of serious attention, however, are those whose schemes of social reform would banish the monetary use of gold and silver.[5]

THE DESTRUCTION OF THE GOLD STANDARD

The gold standard did not collapse, nor was there ever any shortage of gold, as pro-inflationist propaganda would have us believe: on the contrary, it was destroyed by evil and totalitarian forces using the "whole grim apparatus of oppression and coercion . . ." by which the most solemn pledges were broken, retroactive laws promulgated, and constitutional rights openly violated; and then, after the government had used its power to accomplish these objectives by force and violence, hosts of servile writers praised the crimes committed by the state in suppressing gold, and hailed fiat currency as the dawn of a new millennium.[6]

However, they are mistaken if they believe that a return to, and the preservation of, the gold standard is economically or technically impossible.[7] It will, in due course, be restored, not only because it is desirable, but because it is mandatory if complete social and economic chaos is to be prevented. And the reasons for this are obvious and manifold.

THE GOLD STANDARD IN RELATION TO LIBERTY AND DESPOTISM

With Washington politicians and Wall Street pundits, a return to the gold standard is taboo: and the reason is obvious, because a return to this would wrench from the money-manipulators and the politicians their stranglehold on the existing system of "waste, corruption, and arbitrary government."[8]

Indeed, the excellence of the gold standard consists precisely in the fact that it removes from political control the determination of the purchasing power of the dollar. Political control of finances is possible only when governmental expenditures can be increased by issuing fiat money. The gold standard thus emerges as the indispensable instrument to maintain the constitutional guarantees of representative government.[9] Anyone who understands history knows that our Founding Fathers devised a sound monetary system as a shield to protect civil liberty against the inroads of despotism.[10]

Sound money is libertarian because it is affirmative in approving commodity-choice in the free market place; and it is negative in preventing the government from meddling with the monetary system.[11] The essential principle of sound money remains forever impregnable.[12]

The classical gold standard, then, is the only effective curb on the power of government to inflate the currency and enslave the people; without it, all other legal or constitutional safeguards can be rendered useless.[13]

The inflation of the currency is a modern form of crypto-despotism which masquerades under the name of liberalism and which, in the name of freedom, destroys all individual liberty.[14] The principal task of modern libertarians therefore, is to keep under control those who operate the government and prevent them from turning this instrument of power against those whom they have been elected to serve.[15] Unless those so entrusted can be prevented from manipulating the currency, they will become tyrants and all the marvellous achievements of western civilization and the fruits grown on the tree of liberty will be destroyed.[16]

DEFINITION OF MONEY

Von Mises defines commodity money as a medium which is itself a thing of intrinsic value, as gold or silver; fiat money is a medium simply endowed with a legal qualification; and what may be called credit money constitutes a claim against a physical or legal person.[17] "It would," he states elsewhere, "be in no way incorrect to include in our concept of money those absolutely secure and immediately convertible claims to money which we call money substitutes."[18]

THE RATIONALE OF INFLATION

Von Mises defines inflation as a monetary policy that increases the quantity of money in circulation.[19] If a country is on a metallic standard, it can change only in the direction of fiat money; but once it establishes a credit or fiat currency, the government can manipulate its quantity at will.[20] There is a widespread delusion that such an expansion increases individual income; actually, however, various portions of the population receive no more currency for some time, but are immediately compelled to pay higher prices and their true income is therefore sharply reduced[21]—as in France under the assignats.

History demonstrates that whenever governments cannot negotiate loans and dare not impose additional taxes, they resort, if possible, to the dishonest method of issuing fiat money, which then becomes their principal psychological resource and economic policy.[22]

There are various reasons why opportunists embrace the doctrines and practices of fiat money. Some believe that it actually increases wealth, for they do not realize that it reduces the value of all existing currency, and so they cry joyously: Let the State create money, and make the poor rich, and free them from the chains of capitalism![23] "When the inevitable consequences of inflation appear, they think that commodities are becoming dearer, and fail to see that money is getting cheaper."[24]

Some favor inflation so that debtors can more easily be rid of their obligations—as some of the farmers did who obtained greenbacks in 1864–65 at 35 cents on the dollar.[25]

Others admit that fiat money involves serious evils, but hold that these are outweighed by its general social benefits.[26]

Although a very small amount of inflation may pass almost unnoticed for a while,[27] the doses of this drug are certain to increase very quickly to addictive proportions. Since the semi-socialist state must fulfill its grandiose promises of universal welfare through a multiplicity of nonproductive programs and undertakings, and since it cannot secure the necessary funds by direct taxation, it invariably resorts to the issuance of more and more fiat currency,[28] which, in due course, becomes the means of deifying the state and reducing the people to robots.[29]

FIAT CURRENCY ALWAYS FAILS

Nevertheless, because no power on earth can eradicate or avoid the results of false economic practices, all monetary policies based on fiat currency are doomed to failure. There is no way to compel people to accept any kind of debased currency at face value.[30] Gold has not been dethroned; it is still the world's money, and will ever so remain, even though it now lies sequestered in the vaults of the great central banks; it can never be replaced by "the variegated products of divers government printing offices."[31]

Fiat money has failed and will always fail in the long run because it has no intrinsic value and because, sooner or later, all things must exchange at what they are worth.

FLUCTUATIONS

Von Mises is well aware that the price of gold may rise or fall when the supply is sharply increased or curtailed and, under the gold standard, this will affect all other prices.[32] However, he points out that when governments or central banks take physical possession of the entire stock—as they have done—they can manipulate the price even more, as they did in the United States after 1934, when, at $35.00 an ounce it was heavily overpriced and therefore brought immense quantities of the metal into the country. "Fluctuations in the price of gold," he observes, "are nowadays substantially dependent on the behaviour of one government, viz., that of the United States. . . ."[33] He describes how the great central banks of issue had accumulated most of the world's gold stock and how its ownership consisted, not in its physical possession, but in "foreign claims. . . ."[34]

IRVING FISHER AND THE INDEX SYSTEM

Although von Mises rejects Fisher's index system, he concedes that there are tenable methods of calculating purchasing power; however, every one of them is also totally wrong from equally tenable points of view. Under the gold standard, values are determined by the profitability of gold production, but this does not subject price levels to sudden or violent changes. The great fluctuations in the price of gold between 1850 and 1950 were due, not to the circumstances of gold production, but to the policies of governments and banks of issue.[35]

The Austrian economist, Friedrich von Wieser, long before Irving Fisher, attempted to establish a perfect monetary system based on price indexes. However, since this was also founded upon the nebulous and illegitimate fiction that other commodities—for example, loaves of bread—always retain the same value and the same utility in the objective sense, his theory led to no practical result. The use of index numbers to establish stable prices is therefore an attempt to solve the insoluble, to make the impossible possible.[36]

The basic idea of Fisher's scheme, notes von Mises, is to stabilize the currency by a commodity standard, which will not merely supplement the gold standard, but replace it entirely through an ingenious combination of the gold with the tabular standard. He wishes to retain redemption in gold, but not in units of fixed weight and fineness; only in amounts that correspond to the purchasing power of the monetary unit at the time his scheme is established.[37]

Von Mises dismisses all such tabular and index-number systems by saying that they could under no circumstances supply a measure of value comparable to that of gold; the method is crude and imperfect; changes are always occurring in the purchasing power of every commodity.* Not only would the index system be open to extreme manipulation, as is fiat money; even if it were not abused, the fluctuations in actual price levels would be far greater than under the gold standard, and would, in addition, consist of imponderables that could never supply any solid basis for computation.[38]

---

*We should note that improved methods of production can reduce the labor necessary to produce any article, and, therefore, its price drastically in a short time, as happened with wheat after the combine replaced the sickle and the mower and as occurred with radio sets, which dropped in price from $700 in 1927 to $10 in 1948. And what kind of redeemability could be offered in terms of quarts of milk, heads of cabbage, or pounds of beans? And what about sugar, which rose in price from ten cents a pound in 1973 to sixty-five cents in 1974? And how could any person engaged in free enterprise accumulate capital or an estate if such commodities were to constitute the unit of exchange value?

LORD JOHN MAYNARD KEYNES

Lord Keynes, the great proponent of full employment through the gradual and progressive expansion of the currency, receives short shrift from von Mises. Keynes had declared in 1936 that employees will resist a wage cut more vigorously than an increase in prices; therefore, the same objective may easily be achieved by simply expanding the money supply and thus reducing real wages. However, declares von Mises, even at that time Lord Keynes had already been refuted by the march of events; for the workers had learned how to evaluate the artifice of inflation; and the unions had their experts who indexed the purchasing power of wages. "The full-employment argument in favour of inflation was already passé" at the very moment when Keynes and his epigones first proclaimed it as the basic principle of progressive economics.[39]

Time was when doctrinaires declared that the shopkeeper wanted his customers to have more money so that they could spend more for goods in order to create prosperity; however, this spurious philosophy was exploded by Adam Smith and Jean-Baptiste Say. Even though the teachings of Lord Keynes are simply the revival of this expansionist nonsense, his socialistic philosophy has been adopted under the name of full employment by all governments "not entirely subject to the Soviets."[40]

THE RETURN TO THE GOLD STANDARD

The question, then, is not whether free peoples should return to the gold standard, but when, and how, this is to be done.

The first step must be to stop rampant inflation by bringing the printing presses to a standstill. Then attempts can be made to restore some kind of gold standard, as occurred in Austria in 1922.[41] It will also be mandatory that all future bank loans be based on full 100% reserves.[42]

At the same time, every one must be free to buy, sell, lend, borrow, import, export, and hold any amount of gold, whether minted or unminted, at home or abroad. This should result in a considerable influx of the metal into the United States.[43]

During the early stages of the reform, it is of the utmost importance that both the government and the Fed stay aloof from the free gold market; for, by under- or over-selling, they could manipulate its price. In 1952, von Mises estimated that the gold would exchange for $38 an ounce.[44]

An American Conversion Agency should be established with two functions only: first to sell gold to the public at whatever price is established in terms of circulating dollars; and second to buy at the same price all the gold offered it, by issuing dollars backed by a 100% gold reserve.[45]

The United States Treasury would then sell gold bullion, or newly minted coins, at legal parity for any kind of legal currency in existence before the date of the reform.[46]

Every citizen must be permitted to see gold coins changing hands, to have them in his pockets, and to spend them in anyway he may desire.

What would von Mises say concerning conversion in the present state of inflation? We believe that his solution would be the same, except that the 1975 price of gold stands at somewhere between $150 and $200 an ounce instead of $38.00. For he states that we "cannot repair the evil done by . . . deflating [the dollar]. . . . Today, people complain about inflation. If the schemes of restorers are executed, they will complain about deflation."[47] If restoration of the gold standard at $35.00 an ounce would have caused serious deflation in 1952–53, what would it be like in 1975–76?

Citations

1. von Mises, *The Theory of Money* 9
2. Greaves, *op. cit.* xii–xiii
3. von Mises, *Human Action* 471–2
4. *The Theory, op. cit.* 414–15
5. *Ib.* 92–93
6. *Ib.* 420
7. *Ib.* 448

8. *Ib.*
9. *Ib.* 416
10. *Ib.* 414
11. *Ib.*
12. *Ib.* 415
13. *Ib.* 452
14. *Ib.* 414
15. *Ib.* 413
16. *Ib.*
17. *Ib.* 61
18. *Ib.* 33
19. *Ib.* 219
20. *Ib.*
21. *Ib.* 139
22. *Ib.* 223
23. *Ib.* 219
24. *Ib.* 221
25. *Ib.* 220
26. *Ib.* 221
27. *Ib.* 431
28. *Ib.* 223
29. *Human Action* 689–90
30. The Theory, *op. cit.* 65
31. *Ib.* 420–21
32. *Ib.* 210–11
33. *Ib.* 392
34. *Ib.* 391
35. *Ib.* 17
36. *Ib.* 193–94
37. *Ib.* 401–02
38. *Ib.* 419
39. *Ib.* 425–26
40. *Ib.* 423
41. *Ib.* 391
42. *Ib.* 448
43. *Ib.*
44. *Ib.* 449
45. *Ib.* 449–50
46. *Ib.* 450
47. *Ib.* 455

D. JOHN MAYNARD KEYNES

Ironically enough, in this work we must present Lord Keynes, the principal protagonist of fiat currency, as an opponent of himself; for in 1920, when he wrote that the Carthaginian Peace imposed upon Germany at Versailles could only lead to tragedy of incomprehensible magnitude, he was a staunch proponent of sound money. Let the reader determine whether his monetary theories of 1920 were as correct and recondite as his estimate of THE PEACE, which, he warned, would "let loose such human and spiritual forces as, pushing beyond frontiers and races, will overwhelm not only you and your 'guarantees,' but your institutions and the existing order of society."[1]

Here, however, we are interested primarily in Keynes' early monetary theories. We have already reproduced a portion of a passage in which he refers to Lenin and which continues with the following elaboration: "By a continuing process of inflation, governments can confiscate, secretly and unobserved, an important part of the wealth of their citizens. By this method they not only confiscate, but they confiscate *arbitrarily;* and, while the process improverishes many, it actually enriches some. The sight of this arbitrary rearrangement of riches strikes not only at security, but at confidence in the equity of the existing distribution of wealth. Those to whom the system brings windfalls, beyond their desserts and even beyond their expectations or desires, become 'profiteers,' who are the object of hatred of the bourgeoisie, whom the inflationism has impoverished, not less than of the proletariat. As the inflation proceeds and the real value of the currency fluctuates wildly from month to month, all permanent relations between debtors and creditors, which form the ultimate foundation of capitalism, become so utterly disordered as to be almost meaningless; and the process of wealth-getting degenerates into a gamble and a lottery. . . .

"In the latter stages of the war, all of the belligerent governments practiced, from necessity or incompetence, what a Bolshevist might have done from design. Even now, when the war is over, most of them continue out of weakness the same malpractices. . . . By directing hatred against this class [the entrepreneurs], the European governments are carrying a step further the fatal process which the subtle mind of Lenin had consciously conceived. The profiteers are a consequence and not a cause of the rising prices. . . .

"The inflationism of the currency systems of Europe has proceeded to an extraordinary degree. The various belligerent governments, unable, or too timid or too shortsighted to secure from loans or taxes the resources they required, have printed notes for the balance. In Russia and Austria-Hungary the process reached a point where for the purposes of foreign trade the currency is practically valueless. The Polish mark can be bought for about three cents and the Austrian crown for less than two cents, but they cannot be sold at all. The German mark is worth less than four cents. . . ."

To some people "It appears that value is inherent in money as such, and they do not apprehend that real wealth, which this money stood for, has been dissipated once and for all." Even though currency may circulate with fair purchasing power at home for a while, it will decline at once abroad and in time will fall domestically as well.

"The note circulation in Germany is about ten times what it was before the war. The value of the mark in terms of gold is about one-eighth of its former value."[2]

We wonder what Keynes said about German inflation in 1923, when the mark fell to one to a trillion; and what would he say in 1975–76 (he died in 1946), had he lived to observe the ravages of his policies in the monetary systems of the world?

Citations

1. *The Economic Consequences of the Peace,* 36
2. *Ib.* 235–41

E.   PROFESSOR WALTER E. SPAHR

A SEA OF INCONVERTIBLE PAPER

In 1938, Walter E. Spahr of New York University published a refutation[1] of Professor Fisher's *100% Money*, in which he declares that the latter's proposal "would hurl the nation headlong into a thoroughgoing system of inconvertible paper money . . . the most effective device for defrauding innocent and helpless people . . . ever devised."[2] It would pay into circulation "at least 30 billion dollars* . . . a sea of . . . paper money from which all of Mr. Fisher's ingenious devices could not possibly rescue the nation. . . .

"History is strewn with the wreckage and records of suffering caused by 'ingenious devices' to issue and 'control' the consequences flowing from inconvertible money. These efforts to create wealth out of paper, to make something out of nothing, are a species of black magic, and they have always failed."[3]

GOVERNMENT BONDS AS A 100% RESERVE

Under Fisher's plan, there would, of course, be no metallic reserves against the United States Notes to be issued by his Currency Commission. The reserves would be government bonds in the possession of the Commission. In other words, one kind of paper would be substituted for another.[4] The "assets of the banks—the promises of others to pay on demand—would be converted into promises of the government to pay on demand, although these promises . . . are made . . . with the full

*The Federal Reserve note circulation in 1935-36 totalled about $3 billion (1935 *SA*, 222).

knowledge that it could not . . . redeem these notes. . . . Thus the Fisher Plan . . . rests upon the doctrine that it is wise and proper for the government to enter into agreements that it cannot fulfill."[5]

BONDS VS. CURRENCY

Professor Spahr points out that the conversion of interest-bearing government bonds into currency involves a basic confusion concerning their functions: for currency is wholly different from evidences of debt which, since they bear interest and are payable only at date of maturity, are placed in strongboxes, while the owners collect their interest. Under Fisher's plan, the government would, in effect, wipe out the national debt with printing press money, which would have expanded the currency in 1938 by about 1,000%, with catastrophic effects upon prices.[6]

What Fisher proposes, then, declares Spahr, is a fraudulent scheme used by various nations in the past, "a dishonest and immoral government and banking device. . . ."[7]

THE PROBLEM OF RESERVES

"The fact that our various economic instrumentalities are designed to carry an average or certain expected load, but not all that could, in fact, and perhaps even legally be thrown upon them, is one of the notable characteristics of our economic system. It means economy of our resources. . . ." A 100% reserve of gold is unnecessary and would involve a great waste of actual wealth.[8] Furthermore, Fisher's proposed 100% reserve is nothing but "a fire escape made of paper."[9]

FRACTIONAL RESERVES

Professor Fisher declares that when a bank lends $10 million on the basis of a $1 million reserve, it has performed a miracle; but Professor Spahr replies that this is not the case at all:

it has simply used its own credit to guarantee the integrity of demand deposits; and since people use the money thus made available for useful activity, there is no serious danger of inflation.[10]

NO WELL-MANAGED PAPER CURRENCY

"It should be emphasized," declares Professor Spahr, "that there has never been a permanently well-managed inconvertible paper currency, just as there has never been a permanent suspension of specie payments. . . ."[11]

"The most poorly 'managed' currencies in the world have been those severed from gold. All the currencies that have not in time been reanchored in gold or silver at a fixed ratio, have become unmanageable. . . . There is not one iota of evidence in monetary history to justify the . . . assertions of the advocates of a 'managed' inconvertible paper currency that such a system can succeed or that we need not and will not return in due time to the gold standard. . . .[12] The French had an aphorism—after the printing press, the guillotine."[13]

REGULATING THE VALUE OF MONEY

Professor Spahr notes—in 1938—that there was then an active group, both within and outside of Congress, who wished to place the issuance and the retirement of an inconvertible currency in the hands of some government agency so that its supply could be controlled and manipulated—i.e., inflated.[14] Among these, Professor Fisher had become the leader and prophet. These fiat-money proponents declared that the constitutional power of Congress to regulate the value of money means that it may determine its value on the basis of index numbers. However, that "clause has never had, and does not have, this meaning. It refers to the power of Congress to fix the weight and fineness of the standard monetary unit and of other coin, and the character and denominations of our various kinds of money. If Professor Fisher will consult the case of *Juilliard v.*

Greenman and of *Knox v. Lee,* he will find that the meaning of this was fully examined and expounded by the United States Supreme Court."[15]

Citations

1. Spahr, *The Fallacies of Professor Irving Fisher's 100% Money Proposal*
2. *Ib.* 3
3. *Ib.* 4
4. *Ib.* 7
5. *Ib.* 12–13
6. *Ib.* 13
7. *Ib.* 14
8. *Ib.* 15
9. *Ib.*
10. *Ib.* 19–20
11. *Ib.* 34
12. *Ib.* 35–36
13. *Ib.* 37
14. *Ib.*
15. *Ib.*

F. HENRY HAZLITT

REFUTATION OF KEYNES

Henry Hazlitt, the syndicated conservative columnist, published *The Failure of the New Economics* in 1959, which analyzes page by page the propositions set forth in Lord Keynes' *General Theory of Employment, Interest, and Money*, described as the "most influential book of the present era, both in theory and economic policy. . . ."[1] but which, we are told, contains "an incredible number of fallacies, inconsistencies, shifting definitions, and usages of words and plain errors of fact."[2]

The Keynesian economic system is condemned because it holds that unemployment is to be relieved by deficit spending, euphemistically called "government investment,"[3] and by an artifical reduction in interest rates which can be accomplished only through the issuance of printing-press money, i.e., deliberate inflation.[4]

Keynes' remedy for unemployment emerges, then, as a process of perpetual inflation; and his system is nothing more nor less than a reversion in more complicated form to the practices advocated by currency cranks[5] in all ages from John Law to Silvio Gesell.*

Hazlitt quotes approvingly an article by Professor Jacob Viner published in 1936 in the *Quarterly Journal of Economics:* "Keynes' reasoning points . . . to the superiority of inflationary remedies for unemployment. . . . In a world organized with Keynes' specifications, there would be a constant race between

---

*Gesell was a German industrialist and economist (1862–1930) who wrote a book called *Die Verstaatlichung des Geldes—The Nationalization of the Currency*—in which he advocated the use of stamped vouchers as the medium of exchange.

the printing press and the business agents of the trade unions,*
with the problem of unemployment largely solved if the printing
press could maintain a constant lead. . . ."[6]

ON INFLATION AND THE GOLD STANDARD

In 1963, Hazlitt published a book entitled *What You
Should Know about Inflation,* in which he defines this
phenomenon simply as an increase in credit and the money
supply. Again and again, he emphasizes that inflation and fiat
currency are the instruments universally employed by
governments, whenever they can, to control and rob their
people, destroy their savings, continue in a course of deficit
spending, and finally end in bankruptcy and repudiation. There
is no way to avoid this situation except by a return to the gold
standard.[7]

Fiat money means slavery, and a currency redeemable in
specie means freedom, together with a thrifty and responsible
government.[8]

"The monetary managers," declares Hazlitt, "are fond of
telling us that they have substituted a 'responsible monetary
management' for the gold standard. But there is no historic
record of responsible paper-money management. Here and there
it is possible to point to brief periods of 'stabilization' of paper
money. But such periods have always been precarious and
short-lived. The record taken as a whole is one of hyperinflation,
devaluation, and monetary chaos. And as for any integrity in
paper-money management, we need merely recall the record of
Sir Stafford Cripps, who, in the two-year period preceding his
devaluation of the pound sterling on September 18, 1949,
publicly denied any such possibility no fewer than a dozen times.

---

*In the Twenties, union plumbers did an ample day's work for $10.00. In June,
1974, the plumbers in Arizona rejected an offer of $14.00 an hour, or $112.00 a
day. Yet even at this fantastic wage—in the face of government taxes and
constant inflation—they are little better off than they were fifty years before.
Contemplate, then, the conditions of those millions who are on fixed incomes,
which, in many cases, are only slightly higher than they were in the Twenties.

"This is what happens under monetary management without the discipline of the gold standard. The gold standard not only helps to ensure good policy and good faith; its own continuance or resumption requires good policy and good faith. . . . The gold standard is not important as an isolated gadget but only as an integral part of the whole economic system. Just as 'managed' paper money goes with a statist economy in which the citizen is always at the mercy of bureaucratic caprice, so the gold standard is an integral part of a free-enterprise economy under which governments respect private property, economize in spending, balance their budgets, keep their promises, and above all refuse to connive in inflation—in the overexpansion of money or credit.

"How, then, does one halt inflation? . . .

"1—Start balancing the budget.

"2—Stop using the banking system either to buy and peg government bonds at fixed prices, or as a dumping ground for huge new issues of short-term government securities.

"3—Insist that the Federal Reserve Banks impose discount rates that would penalize borrowing by member banks rather than make it profitable.

"4—Restore the legal reserve requirements of the Federal Reserve Banks . . . to 40 percent. . . ."9

There are some, says Hazlitt, who would prefer to re-establish the gold dollar at $35.00 an ounce. This, however, would involve serious economic dislocations; and he offers the "following time schedule of gold resumption . . . for purposes of illustration:

"1—The Administration will immediately announce its intention to return to a full gold standard by a series of steps dated in advance. The Federal Reserve Banks and the Treasury will temporarily suspend all sales or purchases in gold . . . a free market in gold will be permitted.

"2—After watching this market, and meanwhile preventing any further inflation, the government, within a period of not more than a year, will announce the dollar-gold ratio at which convertibility will take place.

"3—On and after Convertibility Day, and for the following six months, any holder of dollars will be permitted to convert them into gold bars, but at a moderate discount.

"4—Six months after Convertibility Day, the country will return to a full gold-bullion standard.

"5—One year later still . . . the country will return to a full gold-coin standard, by minting gold coins and permitting free conversion.

"A full gold-coin standard is desirable because a gold-bullion standard is merely a rich man's standard. A relatively poor man should be just as able to protect himself against inflation, to the extent of his dollar holdings, as a rich man. The reason for returning to a full gold-coin standard in several stages is to prevent too sudden a drain on gold reserves before confidence has been re-established. We achieved this end after the Civil War by delaying actual resumption for four years after passage of the Resumption Act [in 1875]. A program like the foregoing would provide a faster schedule."[10]

Citations

1. Hazlitt, *The Failure of the New Economics* 1
2. *Ib.* 7
3. *Ib.* 421
4. *Ib.* 422
5. *Ib.* 434
6. *Ib.* 425
7. Hazlitt, *What You Should Know About Inflation,* 195
8. *Ib.* 207–8
9. *Ib.* 214–16
10. *Ib.* 223–24

G.   ELGIN EARL GROSECLOSE

SOUND MONEY, THE BASIS OF INDUSTRY

Elgin E. Groseclose is the author of several books dealing with the monetary question, of which perhaps the most important is his *Money and Man*,[1] which appeared first under the title *Money, the Human Conflict* in 1935.[2] "Money," declares the author, "has made possible the division of labor . . . has, in short, created the vast and complicated structure of modern economic society."[3]

THE STORY OF SOLON AND ATHENS

The author's interest in money centers primarily on its historical roles. In 594 B.C., Solon, the Athenian sage, "shook off the burdens" by emancipating all those who had become slaves because of debt, abrogating all agricultural and personal loans, reducing the content of the drachma by 27%, and stabilizing the coinage at that level. By means of these drastic reforms, he inaugurated a social, political, and economic revolution which still amazes historians. Thus freed from debt and slavery at a single stroke, the citizens of Athens became free men and created the most glorious culture of all time. "Athens built a commercial system that dominated the Mediterranean" for centuries[4] because, as they proved themselves the clearest thinkers in history, they solved their monetary problem.

THE GOLDEN AGE OF ROME

When the Roman Empire embarked on its Golden Age, it had three principal coins which maintained their stability for generations: the copper sestertius; the silver denarius (similar to the Greek drachma); and the imperial, golden aureus, approximately equal to an English sovereign (about $5.00 when America was under the gold standard).[5]

MONETARY DEBASEMENT AND DECLINE

However, during the two centuries following Caesar Augustus, the empire gradually fell into decay, and the coinage was progressively debased. Toward the close of the third century, A.D., the debasement became so flagrant that the public lost all faith in money; good coins were hidden and inferior ones circulated, with the result that prices rose into an inflationary crisis so devastating that the Empire fell into literal anarchy, because the exchange of goods, except by barter, became virtually impossible. To remedy this situation, the desperate Diocletian issued his celebrated decree in 301 A.D. setting the prices of all goods and services from a pound of wool to a lawyer's fee. In an attempt to stave off total collapse, a vast bureaucracy was created to enforce the law and a total police state was established—all of which merely exacerbated the fearful conditions already rampant on every hand.[6] After the Fall of Rome, the kings of Europe followed her example with even more terrible results.[7] More than a thousand years elapsed during which the splendid civilizations of Greece and Rome were submerged in a state of universal anarchy and barbarism.*

JOHN LAW AND THE LOUISIANA BUBBLE

Groseclose describes the theories of John Law and the destruction wreaked by them upon France, after the Regent, the

---

*In 277 B.C., the Roman denarius had 66 grains of pure silver. By the reign of Emperor Severus in 200 A.D., its weight had shrunk to 26 grains, of which only 50% was silver. Even this, however, looked like hard money just a few years later. By 215 the denarius had sunk so low in weight and quality that it was really no more than a copper penny. Despite a series of price-control regulations—some of which carried the death penalty—the massive increase in Rome's money supply during this period and the decades following, used to finance progressive social welfare programs, caused such inflation that well-to-do families were forced onto the public dole.

Duke of Orleans, fell victim of his siren song. Law, born in Edinburgh, was the son of a goldsmith, who theorized that the circulating currency should be based, not on metal, but upon properties such as land, canals, etc. He proposed a form of money which would possess no intrinsic value and the quantity of which would be fixed by the state; gold and silver would be relegated forever to industrial uses or to the scrap heap.[8] Promising that he would make France rich beyond her wildest dreams, simply by issuing legal tender based on the land in Louisiana, he obtained a charter for a private bank on May 2, 1716, the notes of which were made legal tender the following October. In 1718, this Banque Générale was converted into a State Bank, which financed the Louisiana Bubble with a capital of 100,000,000 livres. Law then proposed the conversion (actually, the liquidation) of the national debt of $1.5 billion livres by selling shares in the Louisiana Company which would pay dividends of 3% and which rose in price from 500 to 5,000 livres per share in 1719. The printing presses were working overtime.[9]

Law's Bank issued 2 billion livres, which soon became worthless and plunged France into conditions so chaotic that civilized life came virtually to an end.[10] As in ancient Rome, exchanges of goods could take place only in the most primitive manner. In October, 1720, the system collapsed completely, the notes of the Bank were outlawed as currency, and all new contracts had to be negotiated and discharged in gold and silver. Law, who had been the financial, and, in a sense, the political dictator of France for two years, fled the country to save his life.[11]

"For the first time in history," observes Groseclose, "western civilization was presented with an experiment in paper money, pure and simple. . . ." For the first time, an attempt was made on a national scale to operate a "managed currency."[12]

HOW MUCH GOLD?

Groseclose states that of the estimated 2 billion ounces (63,000 tons) of gold produced since the discovery of America, approximately 60% now lies in the vaults of the great central banks; at $35 an ounce, this hoard alone is now worth $42 billion; at $200, $240 billion.[13]

A PROPOSAL FOR CONVERSION TO GOLD

Groseclose has a definite proposal for re-establishing the gold standard. He recommends (as of 1967) that gold units be issued, based on a valuation of $150 an ounce, and be used to validate all the circulating currency with a full gold reserve, instead of being used to support a new pyramid of credit.[14]

Since the Gold Reserve Act of 1934 vested all this metal in the Treasury, says Groseclose, the extinction of all credit money and its replacement with a new, intrinsic, and wholly metallic currency is now practicable. The first step would be to place all the impounded gold into circulation by making all federal payments in gold or gold certificates at $150 an ounce.[15]

The second step would consist in contracting the deposit credits used in banks in making loans by requiring them to hold all deposits of gold and gold certificates in separate accounts, which would then be 100% liquid.[16]

The third step would be the withdrawal of the checking privilege from all old accounts; checks could then be made out only against the new ones covered by gold certificates or by metal actually in the vault. "Checkbook currency" would thus represent gold stores in a warehouse.[17]

The effect of this would be that as existing bank loans are terminated, the old accounts would disappear, and all current checking accounts would be offset in equal amounts of cash and would, in fact, be nothing more nor less than drafts on gold in storage.[18]

Citations

1. Now published by Friedrich Unger
2. Published by the University of Oklahoma Press
3. Groseclose, *Money and Man*, 3–4

4. *Ib.* 15–16, 18
5. *Ib.* 32
6. Groseclose, *The Decay of Money*, 4; *Money and Man*, 43–44
7. *Money and Man*, 66
8. *Ib.* 141
9. *Ib.* 125–35
10. *Ib.* 141–42
11. *Ib.* 144
12. *Ib.*
13. *Ib.* 210, 269
14. *Ib.* 274
15. *Ib.* 274–75
16. *Ib.* 275
17. *Ib.*
18. *Ib.* 276

H. PAUL BAKEWELL

GENERAL PROPOSALS

Paul Bakewell, who died in 1972, wrote two books in which he explained (1) the desirability of the gold standard and (2) his practical suggestions for returning to it. His *Inflation in the United States,* 1958, and *13 Curious Errors About Money,* 1962, both published by the Caxton Printers of Caldwell, Idaho, are considered classics by many serious students of monetary problems. He proposes that a national, nonpartisan commission be established for the purpose of recommending legislation to Congress, or, if necessary, amendments to the Constitution which would:

"a) Require Congress to 'fix' a permanent metallic standard of value;

"b) Require Congress to coin money and regulate the value of all coins by measuring the value of their pure metal against that fixed standard;

"c) Limit legal tender to coin of full value or to currency which the government must redeem upon demand in coins of full value.

"The amendments suggested, if adopted, would restore the system of coined money, which was intended by the Constitution, and under which this nation prospered. They would prevent a recurrence of the existing situation. They would abolish the system of managed, but irredeemable paper currency, which has brought the greatest inflation the United States has ever had.

"The suggested amendment should have the support of every citizen. It would protect the value of savings, insurance policies, pensions, and social security benefits. It would protect the people and the government from the ravages caused by inflation. Most of all, it would protect the workingman."[1]

In another passage, Mr. Bakewell spells out what he believes to be the ultimate remedy for the inflation and social destruction now threatening the nation:

"1. The establishment of a metallic standard of value consisting of gold, because gold is the universally recognized standard;

"2. Means for the preservation and protection of the uniformity and purity of that standard of value;

"3. The requirement that the value of all other coined money shall be regulated by that standard;

"4. The ultimate return to the coinage of gold and the right of the people to own gold as money;

"5. Laws which limit legal tender to gold coins of full weight or to paper currency which itself is redeemable in such gold coins upon demand;

"6. The restoration of gold coin as our basic banking asset and as the reserves of our banking system;

"7. The prohibition of the issuance of paper currency against government bonds and the prohibitions against the use of government bonds as the basis for the expansion of bank credit.

"Those remedies are essential to prevent inflation. The adoption of all of them would make it impossible for our government to cause a currency inflation. But the existing inflation is here, and the practical problem is to get rid of it and return to a sound monetary policy without wrecking our economy or bringing about the destruction of our social order. The only possible end of continued and continuing inflation is disaster. . . .

"The seven requirements specified are the exact requirements which formerly governed our money and our currency. They insured sound money under which our citizens achieved the highest standard of living in the most prosperous nation in the world."[2]

SPECIFIC PROPOSALS FOR RETURNING TO THE GOLD STANDARD

Bakewell suggests that the conversion methods employed by Germany and France could, in principle, be utilized in the United States to re-establish the gold standard here. In 1923, Germany replaced all the marks then in circulation at a ratio of 1 trillion to 1; and in 1948, under Adenauer, at the rate of 10 for 1. French francs were replaced under De Gaulle at the rate of 100 to 1. This, however, occasioned little loss to anyone in either country; for all debts contracted before the dates of conversion, were payable in full with the previously circulating marks or francs, or their equivalents.[3] (We are not, of course, referring to the wild inflation of 1923, which wrought extreme havoc.)

Writing in 1962, when the American dollar was worth approximately half of its foreign redemption value, Bakewell stated:

"Reducing the face value of our domestic currency by 50 per cent and making that currency redeemable in gold at its face value would protect the value of our currency, as measured by gold.

"The Commission [which would be set up under Bakewell's proposal] might find a way to propose that after a specified date:

"a) All of our paper currency held in the United States should be called in and exchanged for a new currency having a face value 50 per cent less than the currency surrendered, but such new currency would be redeemable in gold upon demand at the rate of 15-5/21 grains of gold [our dollar, as then declared] for each $1.00 face amount of such currency. Thus, for each $100 . . . of irredeemable currency, the American holder would receive $50 of new currency redeemable in gold.

"b) All domestic obligations contracted before the specified date, which promised payment in our existing form of currency, should be discharged upon payment of 50 per cent of their face value in the new currency.

"c) All wages, salaries and fixed rates should be paid at 50 per cent of their former amount in the new currency.

"d) All domestic obligations contracted after the specified date be discharged by payment of the specified amount of such new currency.

"That course would apply to all within the United States. Every citizen would have the property he previously held; his assets and liabilities would be the same, but would be expressed in terms of the new paper currency. Since that currency would be redeemable in gold, his assets and liabilities would be expressed in terms of gold and not in terms of an irredeemable currency.

"The internal economy of the nation should quickly adjust itself to the new medium of exchange, and such adjustment would be reflected in new prices based upon gold. By that course, the government could make our currency in the hands of American citizens as good as gold. The course would affect the nominal value of our currency only within the United States." It would not, the author maintains, affect or conflict with any provision of our International Monetary Agreement.[4]

That Bakewell was a keen student of monetary problems is reflected in the fact that he declared in 1962 that "We cannot continue the absurdity of maintaining a gold standard for international transactions and a paper currency standard for domestic transactions."[5]

We note that since the American dollar has fallen far below the purchasing power it had in 1962, the implementation of Bakewell's proposal would require the replacement of perhaps four or five Federal Reserve dollars in 1976 with one dollar of the new currency. This, however, would not, as he points out, cause any loss or gain of serious consequences to anyone, since all debts incurred prior to the exchange would be payable either with the same number of the old dollars or with a smaller number of new ones, which, however, would possess proportionately greater purchasing power and be redeemable in gold. The effect of this would be to reduce the number of dollars in circulation from about $75 billion to about $18 billion; and with $11.4 billion of gold in the Treasury, we could then have an ample reserve of about 65%, which, with proper management, could soon be increased significantly and perhaps doubled in a few years.

Citations

1. Bakewell, *13 Curious Errors about Money,* 160
2. Bakewell, *Inflation in the United States,* 43–44
3. *13 Curious, op. cit.* 167–68
4. *Ib.* 169–70
5. *Ib.* 159

I. THE AMERICAN INSTITUTE FOR ECONOMIC
RESEARCH

THE STABILITY OF REDEEMABLE CURRENCY

One of the most important proponents of the gold standard is the highly respected American Institute for Economic Research, located at Great Barrington, Massachusetts, which has a staff of more than seventy-five independent scholars and scientists. Among its various publications is a 1963 pamphlet called *Why Gold?*, which states that "Gold continues to be a highly desirable commodity and the basic form of money throughout the world. It is the world's money, because it is a universally acceptable medium of exchange and it serves as a stable measure and store of value."[1]

The statement elaborates that if a redeemable currency were restored, the wiser and more farsighted of the nation's citizens could and would demand gold and thus force Treasury and bank officials to act in accordance with monetary responsibility. The publication declares:

"Although all money-credit systems require some control . . . the automatic features of the gold standard give early warning of . . . unsound procedures. . . . Because it minimizes the excuse for controls, the gold standard is especially disliked by those who seek to enmesh the economy in a network of socialist restrictions. . . . Throughout the course of history, governments relieved of fulfilling their promises to redeem currency on demand sooner or later have taken advantage of such an invitation to reckless irresponsibility.

"The fixed amount of gold in each dollar" and its "exchange value . . . has remained remarkably stable for generations. Changes in prices based on gold usually have been gradual, rather than seriously disruptive. . . ."

THE UNIVERSAL DESIRABILITY OF GOLD

"Gold is universally accepted as a medium of exchange. Even when practically all nations of the world have been 'off the gold standard', as far as domestic redeemability was concerned, they have sought gold; and the people of the world, whenever there was widespread fear of monetary depreciation, have done likewise. Gold is universally recognized as a valuable substance that does not deteriorate in storage. The fact that a currency is convertible into gold should secure for that currency virtually the same value in exchange and acceptability as gold itself. Such was the Nation's experience for the several decades during which the United States adhered to the full gold standard. Moreover, history shows that experiments with managed paper-money standards, tried by many of the principal nations of the world in the past 250 years, inevitably failed."[2]

PROSPERITY UNDER THE GOLD STANDARD

The Institute offers a detailed exposition of what happened in the United States to industrial production and the general price level as long as the gold standard continued: "In 1879, fourteen years after the end of the Civil War, the United States returned to the gold standard. For the decade of the 1870s, the average level of commodity prices measured by one comprehensive index was 117.5. For the three successive five-year periods beginning with 1880–84, the average levels of commodity prices measured by the same index were 101, 84, and 78. The decline was almost continuous, and by the end of the fifteen-year period following 1879, prices were down 40 per cent from the average price level for the 1870s.

"During the same period, industrial production increased at the most rapid rate for the most prolonged period in the Nation's history. Specifically, if the average physical volume of manufactured products for the 1870s be considered the base or 100-percent level, the average index numbers for each of the next three successive five-year periods were 158, 196, and 245. . . . These developments show how groundless were the widespread fears . . . that resumption of the gold standard would be calamitous and that a prolonged fall of prices must inevitably be accompanied by industrial stagnation."[3]

We find, therefore, that with complete freedom for enterprise under the gold standard, increasing efficiency in manufacturing brought lower prices in the market place, together with higher wages and increasing general prosperity and living standards.

GOLD STANDARD GIVES THE PEOPLE CONTROL

The Institute thus summarizes its case for the gold standard: "A fully redeemable currency would restore to the people some degree of control over unsound banking and spendthrift government. Since the departure from the gold standard in 1933, the people of the United States have lost, in large part, their control over the public purse. The full gold standard would restore that control and help prevent the large losses that continuing inflation causes. It would help to preserve the system of free enterprise and free markets that has made the Nation the leading industrial power of the world. . . ."[4]

METHODS OF RETURNING TO
THE GOLD STANDARD

"Some devaluationists," observes the Institute, "would prefer to see established what they call a 'free market' for gold" in which "everyone would be a.lowed to exchange currency for gold and gold for currency at whatever 'price' those who offered the gold and those who sought to acquire it might agree upon." In this manner, the free market would determine "the appropriate weight of the new gold dollar. The standard dollar then would be fixed permanently at whatever fraction of an ounce of gold was indicated."[5] The Institute points out, however, that under this plan, "none of the government's vast stock of gold would be allowed to come on the market and thus serve as a restraint upon what could otherwise be a substantial increase in the 'price' of gold."[6]

In addition to the preceding, the Institute suggests and seems to favor the following solution:

"Once inflationary purchasing media have been placed in circulation . . . sound money-credit relationships may be restored . . . by means of devaluation, that is, reducing the gold weight of the monetary unit so much that the increase in the number of (smaller) gold dollars equals or exceeds what had been the inflationary part of total purchasing media. . . .

"In order to give a gold backing to all of what is now inflationary purchasing media, a devaluation would have to transform the present gold stock from the 16 billion monetary units [as of 1963], of which it now consists, to about 90 billion smaller monetary units. It would have to reduce the weight of the dollar from the present 1/35 of an ounce of gold to about 1/190 of an ounce, that is, the 'price' of gold would have to be raised from $35 to about $190 an ounce. Each present gold dollar would have to be made into about five-and-a-half new (devalued) gold dollars. The new dollar would have a gold content equivalent to the amount of gold now represented by about 18 cents."[7]

If, then, such a monetary reform were to be instituted in 1975 or 1976, gold would be priced at perhaps $200 an ounce and the existing Federal Reserve gold stock could be minted into about $55 billion of coin; and if all Federal Reserve notes now in circulation were to be redeemed at face value, dollar for dollar, in new United States Treasury currency, we would have a gold reserve of about 65 or 70%—which would be ample under all ordinary circumstances.

Citations

1. *Why Gold?* 12
2. *Ib.* 40-41
3. *Ib.* 47
4. *Ib.* 48
5. *Ib.* 85
6. *Ib.* 85-6
7. *Ib.* 86

J. ROBERT L. FAUCETT

Mr. Faucett is a retired lawyer who has spent years in the careful study of monetary problems and what should be done about them. The following is from a letter he wrote to Mr. Peter Cook, of the Monetary Science Institute, already cited in the previous chapter.

April 16, 1974

Dear Mr. Cook:

I find nothing in the Constitution which grants power to Congress to create and operate a banking system [such as you propose]; and . . . the idea that Congress should have the right to create bank credit out of nothing, seems to me to be immoral and repugnant to common sense.

I cannot, therefore, find any fault with the Liberty Amendment just because it would explicitly prohibit the U.S. government from doing what it does not have authority to do anyway. I see no way to put an end to the burgeoning bureaucracy, unless we take government out of business of all kinds, including banking. If government attempts to operate our banking system, it will inevitably be done with men whose lives have been devoted to private deposit and loan banking, and we may very well find that money manipulators will operate behind a government shield.

No person or institution should enjoy the right to create out of nothing, a medium of exchange which can be used to purchase something of value. Government might assert this right, backed by its power of coercion; but it would not be morally right or just. . . . No government can be trusted with the power to create legal tender currency, not redeemable in specie, even if it were constitutional to do so—which it is not. History reveals no government which did not abuse such powers to create money (or money substitute) out of nothing. . . . Government bureaucrats cannot be trusted with such powers, any more than we can trust those who now create money substitutes (bank credit) out of nothing. . . .

Forget Benjamin Franklin and his scrip, to which he allegedly attributed the success of the colonies and their industrial and agricultural growth, prior to the time that English banks tried to force them to borrow their money from such bankers. Scrip might work as a temporary measure, in a local area for limited purposes, but in the long run it would not be satisfactory as a means whereby holders could use it as a store of wealth, while trying to accumulate capital for use in promoting private enterprise. Nonconvertible currency is no better than scrip. Mr. Voorhis is a fine man and wishes to get this nation out of debt, but he does not believe that U. S. currency must be redeemable in gold or silver in order to be sound money (another way of saying "constitutional money"). But he has not been able to define our unit of value, the dollar, so it could be put into a currency statute and make sense. I have found no one else who can do that either, although it should be self-evident that we must choose some commodity in which we can define the dollar, by weight and fineness. Gold and silver are not perfect commodities for that purpose, but I know of no better commodities—do you?

People who pretend that they know what a dollar is, when they cannot define it, are dreamers. If you told me that you know what a pound is, but could not define it scientifically, should I *believe you?*

Sincerely yours,
Robert L. Faucett

K.   THE CONSTITUTIONAL ALLIANCE

The Constitutional Alliance of Lansing, Michigan, published a pamphlet in 1969 called *Deflation or Gold Standard,* from which the following material is taken. The author was Professor Hans F. Sennholz, Chairman of the Department of Economics at Grove City College, Pennsylvania, who holds two Ph.D.s, has written hundreds of articles on monetary subjects, and is a member of various organizations, including the Economists National Committee on Monetary Policy.

WHY THE GOLD STANDARD?

The "gold standard," declares Dr. Sennholz, "is a monetary system in which gold is proper money and all paper moneys are merely substitutes that are payable in gold. Under the gold standard, the U.S. dollar is a piece of gold of a certain weight and fineness.

"The gold standard is as old as civilization. Throughout the ages, it emerged again and again because man needed a dependable medium of exchange. And gold provided such a medium" because "it was the most marketable good that gradually gained universal employment—and this became money. . . . The ancient Chinese used gold coins 3,000 years ago. The merchants of ancient Greece made payments in gold and silver over 2,500 years ago." However, during the Middle Ages, when culture dropped to the lowest level of human subsistence and when the great majority died in infancy, gold gradually disappeared.

"When trade and production expanded during the 18th and 19th centuries, the gold standard re-emerged," and became the basis of industry and prosperity—a development which occurred independently of government. "In fact, the gold standard needs neither rules nor regulations; no legislation or government control, merely the individual freedom to own gold," to buy, sell, use, and exchange it without restraint or government regulation of any kind.

GOVERNMENT VS. THE GOLD STANDARD

We must understand and recognize that the congenital nature of all government is to become a tyranny by destroying individual freedom, an objective which it achieves largely through control over the money supply; and herein we find the basic reason why every government seeks to replace the gold standard with bimetallism or with fiat currency. However, it has been proved over and over that a bimetallic standard is inoperable, for, under Gresham's Law, the inferior form of legal tender will always drive the other out of circulation. In the United States, for example, when gold was minted at a ratio of 15 to 1 between 1792 and 1834, it disappeared because it was overpriced; under the Act of 1834, its ratio was placed at 16 to 1, by which it was slightly underpriced, and therefore gradually drove silver into disuse. Only one metal can serve as a standard of value, and others can be used only as tokens or as commodities, subject to a price determined by the standard unit.

Gold did not become the standard of value by legislation, but by inexorable economic law. When Great Britain became the leader in industry, trade, and finance, it did so through the operation of the gold standard, which other countries, in imitation, were forced to adopt. However, since this confers freedom upon individuals and enterprise, governments by their very nature always oppose it. "In recent decades," therefore, most of them "have worked fervently . . . to sabotage and destroy the gold standard" and have "been so successful that it is now practically extinct. Governments have seized complete control over the monetary systems" by establishing "the fiat standard. . . ."

VARIATIONS OF THE GOLD STANDARD

The gold standard exists in three forms, but only that in which this metal is minted into coins and thus made available to all citizens is the true one. "It is immaterial that some notes were endowed with legal tender power. . . . As long as they were redeemable on demand, they represented definite quantities of the metal, gold."

In order to restrict individual freedom and gain control over the monetary supply, governments substituted the gold-bullion standard, under which the circulation of gold was restricted and the government managed the bullion. Gold coins were melted into bars and accumulated in the vaults of the central banks. The national currency was then no longer redeemable in gold coin, but only in large gold bars. Several European countries reverted to this expedient during the 1920s.

Following this, the gold-exchange standard was established, in which governments held the reserves of their countries in foreign claims to gold; and thus the world's supply of the metal was gathered into the vaults of a few great central banks.

THE FED AS THE WORLD'S BANKER

During the 1960s, the American Fed became the "ultimate reserve bank of the world," because it continued to exchange gold for its own reserve notes held by foreign central banks at $35 an ounce. The inevitable result was that "the U.S. dollar gradually fell from its position of predominance. Several monetary crises . . . greatly depleted the American stock of gold. . . . Therefore, in March, 1965, most governments joined the U.S. in halting gold redemption. . . . Thus ended the gold exchange standard. The gates were flung wide open for inflation."

THE TRAGEDY OF FIAT CURRENCY

The tragedy that ensued was the direct result of government control over the money supply through the establishment of fiat currency. "The gold-coin standard means sound money; it makes the value of money independent of government . . ., protects the monetary system from the influence of government. . . . As the quantity of gold in existence is utterly independent of the wishes and manipulations of government officials, parties, and pressure groups . . ., it is a social institution that is controlled by inexorable economic law."

Since no government or anyone else can produce or obtain gold without labor or its equivalent, its value is independent of politics; but fiat money can be produced without effort or limit. All governments by instinct hate and fear the gold standard, for it makes the manipulation of the monetary system, as well as excessive expenditures for political purposes, impossible. In other words, it binds down the politician with the chains of the Constitution.

THE GOLD STANDARD INDEPENDENT OF GOVERNMENT

"The international gold standard evolved without intergovernmental treaties or institutions. No one had to make the gold standard work as an international system. . . . The gold standard united the world as international payments ceased to be a problem. It facilitated 'international trade and finance, thereby promoting a world-wide division of labor. . . . But above all, the gold standard encouraged exportation of capital from the industrial countries to the backward areas."

THE GOLD STANDARD PREVENTS INFLATION

The gold standard makes inflation through credit expansion impossible. When banks need only government securities to create loans by fractional reserve banking, there is scarcely any limit to the possible resulting inflation. Every scheme ever attempted to create prosperity by emitting cheap or irredeemable currency has inevitably ended in disaster. "The gold-coin standard cannot be manipulated by government and, therefore, presents an insurmountable obstacle to all attempts at credit expansion and regulation through monetary policy. . . ."

HOW GOVERNMENTS MUTILATE AND DESTROY THE GOLD STANDARD

"The gold standard never failed—it was mutilated and finally abolished. It springs eternally from freedom—but succumbs to laws and regulations. Its implacable enemy is government in search of revenue."

And the reason for this is not far to seek: individuals work and produce in order to make a living; governments, on the other hand, expropriate the wealth of their subjects in order to meet their evergrowing and extravagant budgets, and by "inflation, which is the creation of new money by the authorities" as a "convenient source of revenue." For this reason it is absolutely certain that whenever the government or any agency erected by it is permitted to manage the money supply, inflation will be inevitable, just as it has done in every nation which has abandoned the gold standard.

Inflation "shifts wealth and income . . . reduces the standards of living of people with fixed incomes, in particular the aged and handicapped. And it diminishes the value of savings bonds and savings accounts, mortgages, and insurance policies and other savings . . . it . . . breeds a political and economic radicalism that tends to destroy our private property order."

As a result of government monetary manipulations in the United States, the purchasing power of the dollar, according to official government statistics, dropped from 100 to 37 cents between 1933 and 1969; according to other authoritative computations, it fell to 16 cents.

THE ENEMIES OF THE GOLD STANDARD

First and foremost among the enemies of the gold standard are governments, individually and collectively, because they seek forever the power to manipulate the currency and the money supply and to increase their revenues through taxation and the issuance of fiat money. Since the pressure to do this is irresistible, the classical economists have always sought to inculcate confidence in the monetary policies of government and its agencies. For example, David Ricardo declared: "In a free country, with an enlightened legislature, the power of issuing paper money . . . might be safely lodged in the hands of commissioners appointed for that special purpose, and they might be made totally independent of the control of the ministers."

Other ardent opponents of the gold standard are "the nationalists of all countries," for they favor "autarchy in all matters" and "resent their monetary dependence on gold. The fiat standard is their system." When the United States finally repudiated its solemn promises to redeem its currency held by foreigners, the native nationalists achieved their ultimate triumph: they no longer had to purchase foreign obligations of $66 billion with $10 billions of gold, and there remained no vestige of restraint upon unlimited inflation.

Perhaps the most implacable enemies of the gold standard are the professional proponents of unlimited welfare: to them federal spending and easy money constitute the panacea for all social and economic ills. Since they find it impossible to operate as they wish on the taxes that can be levied, they pressure the federal government into deficit spending, financed with new printing press money which fires still further the furnaces of inflation.

The Keynesians oppose the gold standard because they favor credit expansion as a means to full employment and economic growth. They declare that newly created credit can lower interest rates, give employment, increase real wages, and foster economic growth, all of which require more money than is possible under the gold standard. Another reason the Keynesians need more fiat money is that they would outlaw all private investment.

Among all the enemies of the gold standard, however, the most consistent and determined are the socialists and the communists, together with their "liberal" allies of all stripes who advocate large and bureaucratic government. For, according to Professor Sennholz, "Their very *raison d'être* is government control and direction of all phases of economic life. How can they tolerate the gold standard, which springs from individual freedom and private property? Gold coins are a medium of exchange—but there is no free exchange in a command economy."

Wherever, therefore, you find anyone proposing fiat money or a managed currency, you may be certain that you are dealing with a socialist, or someone who has been duped by clever propaganda expounded by exponents of regimentation and expropriation.

A POPULAR FALLACY

One of the most popular fallacies is that there is not enough gold to support an adequate supply of redeemable currency. How, it is asked, can the $10 billion in gold held by the U.S. Treasury redeem $42.7 billion in paper dollars, or $150 billion of demand deposits held by banks?

"The answer is simple. The fiat money now in the cash holdings of the people must stay in circulation . . . side by side with gold. . . ." The problem will solve itself once people are permitted to own, buy, sell, mint, and exchange gold for other products or reserve notes without any interference from government.

When the Gold Reserve Act of 1934 was passed, the basis

was laid for all the monetary woes that have since descended upon us, and that now threaten to destroy us utterly. In order to break the chains of economic and political slavery that have been laid upon us, we must restore the gold standard.

HOW TO EFFECT THE RESTORATION

To accomplish this, four steps will be necessary:

(1) "The first objective must be *the freedom to trade and hold gold.* Everyone must be free to buy and sell, to lend and to borrow, to import and to export any quantity of gold, to hold it at home or abroad, whether minted or unminted. There must be no government interference . . . no regulation or controls, no dictation that would sabotage the gold markets. . . ." Americans lost "this freedom 'temporarily' in 1933 when the Roosevelt Administration seized all private gold holdings.

(2) "The next objective must be *the individual freedom to use gold in all economic exchanges* . . . without the interaction of government money. . . .

"At this point, we have arrived at the 'parallel standard'. . . . The Federal Reserve System could continue its operations, its inflation and credit expansion, and the U.S. Treasury could receive its taxes and make payments in Federal Reserve money. All contracts stated in U.S. dollars would have to be met in U.S. dollars, but contracts in ounces and grains of gold would have to be met in gold. Government money and gold would be circulating side by side. . . .

(3) "The third objective . . . would be *the individual freedom to mint coins.* . . . As these coins would not be endowed with 'legal tender,' no one would be obliged to accept them in payment of debt. . . .

(4) "The fourth and final phase is not really vital for the restoration of the gold standard. An enlightened government may at this time decide to make its own money freely convertible into gold."

SUMMARY

The author notes that this circuitous route for a return to the gold standard is not the only one possible; for he is well aware of the proposals of Ludwig von Mises, whom he calls "the great dean of monetary theory, who would establish the gold standard without this circuitousness" by an almost immediate conversion which we explain in our discussion under Percy L. Greaves, Jr.

Professor Sennholz then concludes his monograph with these words: "Step by step, the federal government has assumed control over our monetary system. It has thus captured a potent source of revenue and a vital command post over the economic lives of its people. This is why every friend of freedom is dedicated to the restoration of free money, which is also sound money. It is the gold standard."

L.   PERCY L. GREAVES

Percy L. Greaves, Jr., a student and disciple of Ludwig von Mises, and a scholar in his own right who has devoted a lifetime to the monetary problems of society, declares in his recent book, *Understanding the Dollar Crisis,* published by Western Islands in 1973: "Permitting politicians to manipulate the quantity of money permits them to affect indirectly the value of every market transaction. . . . Increasing the quantity of money does not increase the quantity of goods people wish to buy. It helps some at the expense of others.

"If men are to remain free and if Western civilization is to continue, people must regain the right to limit the political expansion of the quantity of money and/or credit. We must *never* again permit politicians to print money or get their hands on the money we put in banks and think it is always there. A free market economy cannot permanently operate on a politically manipulated paper-money standard. Free men need a market-selected money. Under present conditions, this means a gold standard."[1]

Following the principles and proposals previously enunciated by his master, Ludwig von Mises, Greaves declares: "Two things must be done instantly. One is to stop the artificial increase in the quantity of money, and the other is to take the government out of the gold market. Then we should permit a free market in gold. After a period of time, the free market in gold will stabilize, at some ratio, the monetary unit to gold. Then that ratio should be adopted into law, and that ratio should be defended from then on out, with all of the paper monetary units convertible into gold upon demand. The paper money would then be interchangeable with the agreed legal quantity of gold."[2]

Discussing the nature of money, Greaves makes the following observations: "Money is the most important commodity in a market economy. . . ." Its "role . . . is to make trade easier . . . it leaves more time for production and helps to boost the number of transactions which are expected to increase the satisfaction of each participant." In the earlier days, exchanges took the form of barter. "So, before barter became so involved, men decided to exchange something they had for something that was in more popular demand, something acceptable to others. . . . The most marketable commodity for the early Romans was cattle. The Latin word for money is *pecunia,* which comes from *pecus* . . . cattle. At times it has been shells. It has been beads. It has been furs. The Aztecs used cocoa beans and cotton handkerchiefs. In World War II, United States troops used cigarettes. . . .

"Over the years, it was found that the intermediate, more marketable, more acceptable commodity had to be one that didn't spoil, that was easily recognized, that could be divided or combined without loss of value, and that had a high value in small quantities, making it easy to transport without great expense.

"Over the years, the media of exchange gradually narrowed down to the metals. At first copper was used. Then came other metals, and with their use people developed a market system of prices in terms of the locally selected medium of exchange. . . .

". . . by the nineteenth century, civilized nations had narrowed down their moneys to the precious metals—gold and silver."[3]

Citations

1. Greaves, *Understanding the Dollar Crisis,* 167
2. *Ib.* 168–69
3. *Ib.* 141–48

M.   HARRY BROWNE

THE SUPERIORITY OF GOLD

In his 1974 bestseller, *You Can Profit from a Monetary Crisis,* Mr. Browne maintains that only currency redeemable in gold, or, to a lesser extent, in silver, is worthy of reliance. Any money not backed by, or exchangeable for, specie, is doomed to disaster;[1] as a result of thousands of years of experience, it is recognized as the safest medium of exchange;[2] the value of gold rests upon its durability, compactness, divisibility, convenience in handling, consistency of quality, desirability simply as a commodity, and its comparative rarity, since there are less than 100,000 tons of it in existence.[3] Whenever governments have attempted to dethrone gold, their currencies have collapsed; they can pass laws *ad infinitum,* but they can never compel people to exchange something of value for something else which is devoid thereof.[4]

Inflation is caused by the issuance of fiat money;[5] as prices go higher and higher, the economy at last collapses; and, as in Germany in 1923, million-mark notes are at last not worth a small copper. Finally, in desperation, governments are forced to reintroduce a currency redeemable in gold, and then the nation, following its harrowing ordeal, slowly fights its way back to solvency and perhaps even to prosperity.[6] "A durable money commodity is the lifeblood of civilization—making possible the specialization of labor, the ability of one person to employ another, the opportunity to accumulate long-term savings."[7] The destruction of the currency entails the virtual return to savagery, or at least to barbarism.

Mr. Browne points out that bimetallic standard units of currency are impossible, because the cheaper metal will always drive the other out of circulation.[8] He notes that the Lincoln greenbacks were doomed because they were fiat currency and, as such, represented nothing of intrinsic value.[9]

Again and again, the author emphasizes "that gold will reign supreme long after most paper currencies have been turned to ashes." Governments always love to pay their expenses, extend their power, increase their budgets, create seeming prosperity, and perpetuate themselves in power by the easy expedient of printing fiat money; the longer they try to ignore gold, however, the more intolerable becomes the situation they create, and the more their currencies depreciate. It is useless to tell governments not to issue fiat money; for once they have embarked on this treacherous course, politicians know no other solution than to create more of the disease of which the patient is already dying. However, the impossible cannot be achieved; and, sooner or later, the bankrupt nation must restore gold to its immemorial position in order to avoid universal starvation, complete social chaos, and the destruction of violent revolution.[10]

"Gold and silver," declares Mr. Browne, "are the only real monies with universal acceptance in the world today. And gold is more honored than silver, as it has been through the ages."[11]

"Sooner or later," therefore, "gold will be the measuring standard for all currencies. To maintain its value, a currency has to be convertible into gold. And if a government has inflated its currency to where convertibility isn't possible, there are only two ways it can remedy the situation"—(1) to deflate, or (2) to lower the gold content of the official unit of value to what it will buy in the market place.[12]

CONVERSION INTO SWISS FRANCS

Since Mr. Browne believes that the U.S. dollar will continue to decline in value until it falls far below its 1974–75 level, he suggests that Americans convert their money into Swiss francs and keep them in Swiss banks because the currency of that country has one of the strongest gold reserves in the world and is not likely to lose its value.

Mr. Browne does not venture to predict precisely how soon our own currency will collapse: but sooner or later it must do so unless conversion to gold precedes this catastrophe.[13]

PRACTICAL PROPOSALS

The author believes that the following specific steps should be taken forthwith:

(1) The dollar should be devalued at least 75%, which would create a gold redemption price of $160 an ounce, and give us a gold reserve of about $40 billion. However, a redemption rate of $300 would be much firmer, and would create a gold reserve of about $75 billion.

(2) The various world currencies should then be permitted to float and find their own value in the market place.

(3) Although a severe and perhaps devastating depression is inevitable, its extent, duration, and agony will be determined largely by whether or not the government cuts its budget and permits the General Market to bring back recovery and prosperity as soon as possible after 1974–75.

(4) All government controls must be terminated.

(5) The government must stop printing fiat money; otherwise runaway inflation will be inevitable, with a subsequent crisis that will terminate only through massive devaluation, the restoration of convertibility for foreigners, drastic cuts in federal budgets, and a stabilization of the money supply.

As long-term requirements, the following will be mandatory:

(1) The dollar must be devalued to $400 an ounce and all U.S. citizens must be permitted to convert their Federal Reserve notes at will into gold.

(2) The government must withdraw entirely from the General Market, leaving its operation to automatic economic law.

(3) All government economic controls, as, for example, over wages, labor laws, investments, etc., etc., must be terminated.

(4) Federal budgets must be drastically reduced, and all future budgets must be met from current taxation; and a 100% reserve for all circulating currency must be maintained to guarantee immediate redeemability.

(5) The Federal Reserve System must be abolished and all government regulation of private banking must be terminated.[14]

SUMMARY

Three principal theses dominate Mr. Browne's message: (1) that gold only is real money and that no currency can long remain stable without convertibility into this metal; (2) that the General Market must be the determinant of economic life—and government must stay out of it; and (3) that inflation will continue in the United States until convertibility is re-established. In the meantime, the wise American will convert his money into Swiss francs, keep them in Swiss banks, or, as a second choice, in the currency of some other country which has a strong, gold-backed monetary system.

Citations

1. Browne, *You Can Profit from a Monetary Crisis,* 4
2. *Ib.* 41
3. *Ib.* 42
4. *Ib.* 43
5. *Ib.* 51
6. *Ib.* 68
7. *Ib.* 70
8. *Ib.* 84
9. *Ib.* 103
10. *Ib.* 212
11. *Ib.* 234
12. *Ib.* 218
13. *Ib.* 212-18
14. *Ib.* 125-27

CHAPTER X

Summary of Gold and Fiat Pros and Cons

A. FOR A MANAGED CURRENCY

ARGUMENTS AGAINST THE GOLD STANDARD

The principal arguments of those opposing a return to the gold standard may be placed under three general headings: (1) there is simply not enough of the metal in the world to serve as a basis or a reserve for the redemption of all the currency in circulation; (2) it can be shipped by financiers from one country to another at will in order to collapse any monetary system they may wish to destroy; and (3) the commodity price of gold fluctuates so much from one period to another that it can never serve as a dependable yardstick for a stable unit of currency.

ARGUMENTS FOR FIAT CURRENCY

The proponents of government fiat currency maintain (1) that in the United States only the federal government has power under the Constitution to issue any kind of money; (2) that coining (or minting) money and regulating the value thereof is identical to emitting notes not redeemable in specie; (3) that a stable dollar can easily be established and maintained by controlling the amount of currency in circulation or by using a tabular or commodity index to determine its purchasing power; (4) that any excess currency in circulation, which might otherwise cause inflation, can quickly be recaptured through taxation; (5) that the integrity of the dollar can be guaranteed by the power of taxation vested in the federal government; (6) that its value should and can be determined, not by sterile gold, but by the credit of the nation and the productive capacity of its citizens; (7) that there is no essential difference between an interest-bearing bond issued by the government and a noninterest-bearing note emitted by the same authority; (8) that the federal government can, without danger of inflation, meet all its expenses and pay the cost of vast welfare programs by issuing its own notes; (9) that the resumption of this power by the Treasury would free the nation from the clutches of the greedy financiers who have enslaved us, and (10) that a monetary system operated by the government and free from the bonds of redeemability could and would confer prosperity and happiness forever upon our citizens.

There are, of course, variations and additions to these arguments; but, in the main, these constitute the basic positions of such outstanding fiat proponents as Fisher, Voorhis, and Keynes.

B.   FOR THE GOLD STANDARD

ANSWERING THE FIAT PROPONENTS

Since the advocates of a managed currency rarely present elaborate arguments in support of their proposals, we could do little more than repeat them; however, since those who believe in redeemability have written many detailed treatises explaining their views, we find it necessary to summarize them at some length, which we do in the following pages, in *seriatim.*

WHY IS STERILE GOLD SO COVETED?

If gold, as the proponents of fiat money declare, is a sterile commodity of little real value, why do all people desire it so avidly, and why, particularly, do all communist, socialist, and other authoritarian governments insist on monopolizing every ounce of the metal?

The answer, as many scholars have pointed out, is that the monopoly possession of gold confers upon bankers and unlimited governments the power to manipulate the currency, control the people, and reduce their citizens to political and economic peonage. On the other hand, a redeemable currency and the freedom to produce, own, buy, sell, import, or export gold confers political and economic freedom upon the people. It also guarantees a stable currency and makes it impossible for the government to squander untold sums of money in wasteful projects and in the support of a vast and self-perpetuating bureaucracy.

FIAT CURRENCY A SOCIALIST INSTRUMENT

All proponents of managed currencies, like Franklin D. Roosevelt, have proclaimed their desire to establish a stable dollar. However, when we examine their proposals we find that, almost without exception, they want fiat currencies so that the government can issue great quantities of this for welfare programs of every kind. In other words, virtually all proponents of managed currencies support socialistic programs and profess to believe that, by some kind of magic, government can create wealth by stamping pieces of paper with certain mystic symbols, such as $10 or $10,000.

THE WORLD'S GOLD STOCK

Since we have been told a thousand times that the stock of gold in the world is insufficient to supply an adequate reserve for its currency, let us see how much of it there is in the "free" world, which, of course, excludes Russia, China, and other Communist nations.

Groseclose estimated in 1935 that 2 billion ounces had then been produced since the discovery of America; but this did not include the gold produced before 1500 or after 1935. In 1940, the gold production in the United States alone was more than 6 million, and world production 42.3 million ounces.[1] Since then, this has ranged between 40 and 50 million ounces annually.[2] Since 1940, therefore, it has totalled about 1.25 billion ounces, or 40,000 tons, worth about $256 billion at $200 an ounce.

After the production of gold in the United States was limited to a by-product of other mining operations following 1953, it fell from 6 million ounces in 1940 to 1.4 million in 1970. However, with a return to a free market, domestic production should soon surpass all previous records; with at least 100,000 tons or 3.2 billion ounces, worth more than $100 billion at $35 an ounce and $600 billion at $200, lying underground in the territory of the United States, there should in the course of a few years be an ample supply to give us a 100% gold reserve for our currency.

At all events, an estimate of 150,000 tons, or 4.8 billion ounces, as the present total world stock of gold, seems quite conservative. If each car carried forty tons, it would require a train with 3,750 flattops and 75 miles in length to transport all of this metal at once. At $200 an ounce, its value is $960 billion.

We should note also that world production has been increasing steadily from 32.7 million ounces in 1950 to an average of nearly 50 million in the Seventies. This means that total gold reserves are growing at the rate of about 2,000 tons a year (in addition to potential increases from American sources), which, at $200 an ounce, would have a value of $12.8 billion. In one decade, therefore, the world's gold reserve may be expected to increase by $128 billion; and in 75 years from 150,000 to 300,000 tons, worth about $1.9 trillion—amply sufficient to serve as a solid base for all the currencies in the world.

Let us assume that the population of the free world stands at 2 billion: we will then have a per capita gold supply in 1975—again at $200 an ounce—of $480, which should increase to $700 by the year 2,000. The per capita circulation in the United States in 1840 was $4.99; in 1900, $27.35; in 1950, $179.03;[3] in 1960, $177; and in 1972, $317.[4]

The present gold stock in the free world is therefore at the present time ample to create a 100% reserve for all the currency in circulation; and since history has demonstrated for centuries that a 40% reserve, or even less, is sufficient for a solid currency, we conclude that a full gold standard is practical and entirely possible throughout the free world with a per capita currency of $1,200, whereas even in the United States in 1972, the actual amount was only slightly more than one-fourth of that; and it was certainly far less in the other countries of the world.

The gold reserves held by the Fed decreased from about 800 million ounces in 1952 to about 275 million in 1974. But even this fearfully depleted reserve at $200 an ounce is worth $50 billion and could serve as a 75% reserve against all the Federal Reserve notes now in print.*

*As of Dec. 31, 1973, FR notes in print totalled $65,470,861,000 (*60th Annual Report* of Fed, 273).

HOW MUCH GOLD IS NECESSARY
FOR REDEEMABILITY?

Proponents of fiat currency sometimes argue that no gold stock could ever be sufficient for redeemability, since money—according to their definition—includes not only currency, but also bonds, checkbook credits, deposits in savings and loan associations, etc. This position, however, is in total error; for checkbook deposits are not currency, but only the means of transferring credits from one account to another; nor are bonds, redeemable only at maturity. The only kind of money that ever needs to be redeemed in specie on demand consists of circulating notes, which promise such redemption on their face.

We have been asked seriously to explain what would happen if every person holding a bond, a check, a commercial acceptance, a token coin, a bank passbook, or a certificate of deposit were to demand cash or gold at the same moment; the answer is of course that they could not be paid, even if there were a 400 or 500% gold reserve for the entire circulating currency; for to satisfy such a demand might require more than a trillion dollars. An equally good counterquestion, however, is this: if the money were paid, what would people do with it and why would they want it? The answer is also that the money would not be paid on bonds, for example, because it is not due until they mature. Nor could they take cash for their checks because they must be used to meet current obligations. And no one but an idiot would mortgage his property for money to be concealed in a safety box or buried under the floor of the basement, because there it would continue to decline in value—at least under present conditions; and in the meantime the interest on the loan would soon consume the principal and bring the loss of the pledged property.

There are, of course, misers who stash money in tin cans and other esoteric hiding places, or carry it around on their persons; but such hoards, especially of gold, invite thieves and murderers; they are sterile because they are completely unproductive; they are expensive to store in safety, and, under normal conditions, account for only an insignificant portion of the national currency. It is only when people lose confidence in the circulating medium that they remove substantial amounts of gold or silver from circulation in the expectation that this metal can shortly be resold at a substantial profit.

We should note that in the past the gold reserve has often been far greater than necessary to guarantee redeemability for all circulating notes; this, however, posed no problem at the time: for both the gold and the redeemable notes simply lay dormant in the Treasury awaiting the needs of the people and of business for their release.

The question then arises: can a 40% or even a 25% specie reserve be sufficient to guarantee redeemability for a currency? The answer is that so long as the public has confidence in the government which issues the money, such a reserve is ample, for the simple reason that very few will desire gold in preference to redeemable currency, or, better, some form of revenue-producing investment.

So long, therefore, as people can at any time obtain gold for their notes, it is highly unlikely that even 1% of them will do so. This fact has been established by the universal experience of mankind—in fact, it was precisely this which first brought circulating notes and marginal reserve banking into existence.

Professor James L. Laughlin, who may be called the uncle of the Federal Reserve System, declared that "The fear of a scarcity of money is purely fictitious, because if immediate redemption of the media of exchange [in gold] is always preserved,* there will always be perfect elasticity of the currency. . . . Hence, in a properly constituted monetary system, there can never be a place for a 'managed currency,' since that means the currency is intentionally issued as a means of controlling prices, and not to provide a legitimate medium of exchange."[5]

*A comparatively small amount of redeemable currency is ample because, first, almost 95% or even 99% of all transactions are consummated by means of checks or credit cards; and, second, because currency, whether in the form of specie or in notes redeemable in gold, will never be hoarded, since, in themselves, they are completely sterile, and will therefore be spent or invested quickly, and thus returned to the banks or the Treasury—that is, by all normal individuals.

HOW MUCH CURRENCY IS NECESSARY?

In our economic system, where the great bulk of all transactions consists of credit transfers by means of cards and checks, a comparatively small amount of currency is sufficient; and the total necessary is declining progressively. For example, in 1973, all the reserve banks in the United States received and counted only $56.8 billion of reserve notes and $14.4 billion in coin; and since the units of which this consisted were undoubtedly received and counted several times during the year, it is unlikely that the total coin and notes in actual circulation exceeded $15 or $20 billion, which would seem to indicate that most of the $78 billion of Federal Reserve notes in print were held by foreigners and were without relevance to the American economy.

However, the same banks handled $3,845,234,479,000 in checks—which exceeded by more than 5,000% all currency received. In other words, for every $200 consummated by cash transactions, those by check totalled $10,000. And this does not include payments by credit cards, or take into consideration the fact that each Federal Reserve note may have been counted several times in the banks.

But even this fantastic total fades into insignificance when compared to the $23,479,745,588,000,[6] which represents the total transfers of funds and which means that for every dollar of currency in circulation, fund transfers totalled about $300.00, or about ten times the total value of all real and personal property in the United States.

Since there is no need for the redeemability of anything except circulating notes, we would say that 100 million ounces of gold at $200 an ounce would create a reserve of 100% for all the circulating notes required by the American economy.

THE MANIPULATION OF THE GOLD SUPPLY

The second principal argument of those who advocate a managed currency is that the financiers have in the past and will in the future manipulate any gold reserve used for redeemability.

Those who support the gold standard declare, on the contrary, that the very reason banks and governments desire a fiat money is precisely because under such a system they can manipulate the gold at will. Whatever manipulation occurred in the United States between 1913 and 1934 was due largely to the existence of the Fed, and could not have happened under a constitutional money system. Even so, the extent of this at that time was comparatively insignificant and had no influence whatever upon the value of United States money, nor did it make it necessary or desirable to establish a fiat monetary system. At no time between 1929 and 1935 was there any deficiency of gold in the United States Treasury or the Fed.

Let us examine the record.

During the Twenties, as during the years following 1879, the country enjoyed a period of great expansion, tremendous activity in every economic field, under the gold standard. Yet the price index, which had risen from 35 in 1915 to 60.9 in 1920 because of the wartime inflation, fell to 53 in 1922, and continued to decline thereafter to 52.5 in 1925, 51.3 in 1929, and 50.0 in 1930; and this in spite of the fact that wages had risen and general living standards were everywhere enhanced. The reason for these developments was the fact that the exchange value of all commodities was measured and determined by a fixed monetary unit, i.e., the gold dollar; as industry became more efficient, prices declined by inexorable economic law; neither the bankers nor the government could manipulate the currency or the price of goods and services.

It is interesting to note that the gold reserve remained virtually constant through this period and that the supply of Federal Reserve notes in circulation declined sharply from $3,065 million in 1920, to $1,849 in 1924, and to $1,693 in 1929, which marked the point of highest prosperity. With a stable dollar, the amount of currency automatically declines, and the gold reserve increases proportionately. Whereas in 1920, the Federal Reserve notes in circulation exceeded the gold reserve, this relationship underwent a dramatic alteration with the resumption of peacetime economy. As early as 1922, there was enough gold in the United States Treasury to redeem every Federal Reserve note and still leave $1,646 million of the metal intact; by 1930, the gold was sufficient to redeem every Fed note in circulation three times and still leave $1,329 million of the gold in the Treasury.

It is true that there were other notes in existence, such as the $346,681,000 of greenbacks, about $800 million in National Bank Notes, and other smaller issues, most of which, however, had been withdrawn from circulation. But even if we add all of these, there was enough gold in the Treasury for total redemption and for a residue which varied from $911 million in 1924 to $1,625 million in 1930.

It is certainly worth noting, furthermore, that not only did we have prosperity without inflation or deficit spending: on the contrary, between 1920 and 1930, the national debt, created under Wilson, declined from a high of $24,299,321,000 to $16,185,310,000—a reduction of $8,114 million.

Even though the depression dragged on following the stock market crash of October, 1929, the gold reserve continued to increase until September, 1931. However, between that date and June, 1932, it fell by $1,040 million;* this was due to conversion by Americans of their currency into gold and to withdrawals by foreign financiers. This development resulted from the decision of the Fed to liquidate the possessions of productive American, middle-class citizens, who had simply

---

*Friedman and Schwarz declare, *Monetary History of the United States* 315–16: "The climax for the foreign difficulties came on September 12, 1931, when, after runs on sterling precipitated by France and the Netherlands, Britain abandoned the gold standard. Anticipating such action on the part of the United States, central banks and private holders in a number of countries—notably France, Belgium, Switzerland, Sweden, and the Netherlands—converted substantial amounts of their dollar assets in the New York money market to gold between September 16 and October 28. . . . From September 16 to September 30, the gold stock declined by $275 million, from then to the end of October by an additional $450 million. These losses about offset the net influx during the two preceding years and brought the gold stock back to its average level during 1929. . . . Currency was being withdrawn internally by depositors justifiably fearful for the maintenance of the gold standard."

become too prosperous and independent during the gold-standard years of the Twenties.

Then, in March, 1933, Roosevelt closed the banks and forbade the conversion of Fed notes into gold; and on January 30, 1934, the Gold Reserve Act was passed, which wrote finis on the free American economy, and made it possible for the international financiers to manipulate our gold supply at will, and deflate or inflate the currency without limit.

Roosevelt said that he increased the price of gold in order to raise the domestic price level and he promised a dollar that would remain stable for generations to come. In this, as in almost everything else, he proved to be an infinite deceiver; the fact is that he did simply whatever the financiers, his masters, decreed should be done, once the gold standard was removed.

The devastation wreaked upon the American people by the Great Depression almost defies description. Cities, which had been beehives of activity, became economic cemeteries. Factory workers, if employed at all, sometimes brought home weekly paychecks of less than $2.00. Except for a few federally financed and highly uneconomic projects, scarcely any construction whatever took place between 1930 and 1945. Virtually every home, apartment house, store, shopping center, office building, theater, and plot of vacant land was seized or foreclosed for nonpayment of taxes or failure to meet contract or mortgage obligations. The Federal Reserve Board had decreed that virtually all loans be called and that no credit be extended, which caused an almost universal liquidation of the assets belonging to ordinary and productive citizens.

With the passage of the Gold Reserve Act, the country entered upon what Dr. Sennholz calls the Gold-Bullion Standard, under which all coins are melted into bars, then used to transfer large quantities of the metal from one central bank to another. Obviously, Roosevelt had no intention of raising prices or permitting any return of prosperity—for this was not what the bankers desired at that time.

Instead, they decreed that the Depression must continue so that almost all assets owned by the people could be expropriated; second, they wanted them to suffer so long and so bitterly that they would at last accept even a terrible war as the only possible means of obtaining work; and, third, they intended to sell their overpriced gold to the American Fed.

We note, first, that the price index which had gradually decreased from 53 to 50 during the Twenties, plummeted to 40.3 in 1933, and remained at approximately that level until 1941. Had Americans been permitted to own, buy, sell, and exchange gold at will, all prices would have risen; but, since this was forbidden, its price had no relevance in the domestic market.

Note that between 1933 and 1940, the gold stock increased from $4,322 to $22,040 million. Since less than $1 billion of this came from domestic mines, we know that more than $16 billion came from foreign sources. Here, then, was the greatest instance of gold manipulation engineered by the international financiers that had ever taken place in history. They sold their overpriced metal to the American Fed at a profit of at least $7 billion, and possibly as much as $10 billion.

What happened in the Thirties, however, was only a prelude to the crimes perpetrated after 1940, when Fed notes totalled only $5,482 million and could have been redeemed four times over in gold with a residue still remaining. It was, therefore, possible to increase the note circulation during the war to $25 billion, and to place more than $115 billion of government bonds with the Fed and the commercial banks by 1945,* a total of $140 billion, which was more than half of the national debt at the close of the war.

We should understand that probably the principal reason why Roosevelt conspired for years to drag this nation into the holocaust of WW II was to enable his masters to obtain many tens of billions of dollars of government bonds for nothing, on which they would collect interest in perpetuity from the

---

*In 1930, the Fed banks held $531 million in federal securities; in 1945, $24,262 million; in 1930, the commercial banks held $4,977 million; in 1945, $90,800 million—which was 41% of the total, obtained by them through mere bookkeeping entry. (Cf. 1956 *SA* 382.)

taxpayers, and which—most important of all—they would use for the creation of credit in their fractional banking system. Without such reserves, the Fed becomes practically inoperable. With a huge federal debt, the profits of the bankers soar into the stratosphere.

Meanwhile, the Roosevelt administration continued its war on the little people by causing the confiscation of the income property of some seven million small landlords through a program of ferocious rent control which lasted for ten years and made it impossible for the owners to meet their taxes, mortgage payments, and other enormously increased expenses from the depression incomes enforced against them. And thousands of small business people who were able to survive the war years were shortly thereafter attacked by the Internal Revenue Service and destroyed by the use of unknown, or simply invented traps in the Code, and by an enforcement thereof which surpassed in cruelty and mendacity anything ever known even under fascist regimes, and comparable only to the monstrous crimes of the Inquisition or to the Stalinist regime in Russia.

During and after the war, prices rose rapidly domestically; and gold, in due course, at $35 an ounce, became increasingly underpriced. And now what Dr. Sennholz calls the second false gold standard was put into operation. The central banks of Europe—owned by the same clique of international financiers who were in control of our Fed—no longer moved gold bullion from place to place; they simply earmarked it for foreign ownership. In 1925, of the $4,360 million of the metal owned by the Treasury, only $22 million was earmarked to foreign ownership; by 1930, this declined to $8.8 million. However, by 1945, this amount had increased to $4,293 million and in 1955 to $6,941 million. In 1972, it had reached the astronomical total of about $18 billion, which, having been purchased at $35 an ounce, will yield a neat profit of about $85 billion. All of this vast hoard of gold ingots lies in the vaults of the New York branch of the Fed; it does not belong to the American people or to the United States Treasury; it does not even belong to the Fed—it is owned by, and presumably stored without charge to, the credit of unknown foreign investors, who, under Section 895 of our generous Internal Revenue Code, will be immune, not only to taxation on their profits from the sale thereof, but even from the embarrassment of disclosure. In short, no one, except a few insiders, will ever be permitted to learn who has robbed the American people of more than $80 billion by manipulating our gold supply under our fiat system of currency.

All through the Twenties, the total money stock remained at about $8.4 billion—which included the gold reserve itself, all kinds of notes, and every denomination of coin. The money in circulation averaged about $4.6 billion, which was ample for all purposes. Had the gold standard continued, there is no reason whatever to believe that the per capita money supply would have required any increase at all in order to maintain a sufficient means of exchange for prosperity.

Frightful as was the theft of our gold, this was not the worst effect resulting from the abolition of the gold standard. Obligations to foreigners, which did not even exist before WW II, increased from $11.9 billion in 1955 to $65.9 billion in 1972, which was then 6.5 times the existing gold reserve, and therefore forced our government to repudiate the currency held by foreigners unilaterally in 1973, just as the same action had been taken domestically, without the slightest necessity, in 1934. The floodgates for uncontrolled inflation were thus thrown wide open and the position of the United States in the world suffered the greatest defeat it had ever known.

This was simply an additional result of monetary manipulation, made possible by the abandonment of the gold standard. Most of these obligations were the indirect consequence of domestic inflation, which drove our manufactures out of the world markets and pressured our industrial capital to move into foreign countries where it has been used to build factories of all kinds. This has caused millions of Americans to lose their jobs and has intensified the imbalance of international payments.

In order to meet the crisis—as the gold reserve continued to melt away—the Fed and the government in desperation printed and issued more and more billions of fiat currency. In

1925, the gold reserve constituted 54.1% of the total money stock, including all circulating coin and the gold itself; in 1934, it was 57.6%; in 1940, 77.3%; after 1955, however, the ratio declined inexorably, year after year. At that time, the money stock totalled $53.3 billion, and the gold reserve was 40.8%; in 1972, this total had increased to $78.6 billion, and the gold reserve—even after devaluation—had dropped to $10.4 billion, or 13.2%.

Since, under a fiat currency, politicians can think of no means of maintaining employment and prosperity except through inflation, the money supply was increased by almost $70 billion, or 700% in the forty years following 1933. In the meantime, the price index rose from 39.6 to 129.8 in 1972; in 1974, this had risen to about 150 or more and there seems to be no foreseeable prospect except destruction, revolution, or drastic reform of our monetary system. What we must envision is nothing less than the virtual death of the American dollar.

However, should the gold reserve be returned to its proper owner—the United States Treasury—it will be impossible for the international financiers to manipulate it for their own benefit by removing it from one country to another in order to collapse any money system they might wish to destroy. With the abolition of the Fed, which operates in tandem with the international banking fraternity, laws will certainly be passed providing that the greater portion of our gold stock shall be minted into coins, prohibiting their export, or the use of gold bullion for any purpose except the settlement of international trade balances. Furthermore, with the enactment of such laws, these should never again be unfavorable; and by encouraging the domestic mining of gold, there should be a constant increase in the Treasury reserve. As long as prudent laws are enforced regarding the use of gold in foreign transactions, there will never be any domestic shortage of the metal.

HOW IS REDEEMABLE CURRENCY PAID INTO CIRCULATION?

We are sometimes asked how the Treasury pays redeemable currency into circulation. Actually, nothing could be simpler: when mines produce gold or silver, these may be delivered to federal mints, where they are transformed into coins or bars of bullion. The Treasury pays for the metals with notes which pass into general circulation and which state on their face that they are redeemable in the specie they represent.

Between 1934 and 1960, the Treasury minted and placed in circulation some 2 billion silver dollars. Since the Fed now has on hand enough gold to mint about $55 billion of that metal at $200 an ounce, it could do so, and then exchange nearly all Federal Reserve notes now in print for new United States currency redeemable in gold.

Should 20 million ounces of new gold be delivered to the Treasury, it could pay for this with $4 billion in gold certificates, which would go into immediate circulation. Actually, since history demonstrates that a 40% reserve is ample, the Treasury could safely issue $10 billion in new currency, based on 20 million ounces of gold; and, as American mines increased their production, the number of such notes could, of course, also be increased.

There are some who seem to believe that an excess of gold in the Treasury beyond what is necessary for business and exchange would cause inflation. However, this is not true;* for any superfluity would be retained in the mints or the Treasury; its value is not determined in the least by its quantity, but only by its cost of production and replacement. However, should large new lodes suddenly be discovered, its commodity value and price would decline and all other prices would increase under the gold standard, as they did between 1897 and 1914. However, under conditions similar to those existing between 1879 and 1897, and again between 1922 and 1930, under the full gold standard, prices would fall during periods of great prosperity and business expansion, regardless of the quantity of available gold.

---

*For example, in 1940 the Fed had more than five times the amount of gold necessary for full redeemability; but this did not cause prices to rise.

PRICE FLUCTUATIONS OF COMMODITY GOLD

The third basic argument against the gold standard, advanced especially by Professor Fisher, is that its commodity price fluctuates to such an extent that it cannot serve as a base for a stable dollar.

It is true that the value of gold, like that of any other commodity, is affected by its current cost of production: there have been periods when unusually large amounts have been discovered, and when, therefore, its replacement cost has declined temporarily.* However, history records few such bonanzas; and even these have exercised comparatively little influence on its price, since this is measured primarily by its rarity, availability over a long period and the total stock existing in the world.

When the price of all commodities rises in terms of fiat currency, this does not mean that gold or other products of labor are worth more, but only that the medium of exchange has deteriorated. The indisputable fact is that there is nothing else on earth which can compare with gold as a commodity that can be stored; which is neither too rare nor too plentiful; which can be minted into coin, and which can be used par excellence as the perfect basis for a stable unit of monetary value. Since the demands for the metal in industry are not heavy, its availability as a reserve for money is greatly enhanced. The world's supply therefore increases constantly. Because of its rarity and quality, it is precious; it is virtually indestructible, it can assume a thousand shapes, and be retransmuted into any previous form.

*We have noted how Professor Fisher was disturbed over the fall of prices between 1879 and 1897 and their increase between 1897 and 1914. Friedman and Schwarz note, *op. cit.* 136–37: "Prices in the United States rose between 40 and 50 per cent from 1897 to 1914. . . . The proximate cause of the world price rise was clearly the tremendous outpouring of gold after 1890 that resulted from discoveries in South Africa, Alaska, and Colorado, and from the development of improved methods of mining and refining," particularly the use of cyanide.

Over a period of fifty years, there was an important price cycle which saw the index fall from 100 in 1873 to 71 in 1894, or 39 points; and then return to 100 in 1914. In other words, at the end of the half century, prices stood at exactly the same level as at the beginning (*Historical Statistics, op. cit.* 231).

We can only say that gold is far more stable than any other commodity as a general measure of value; and that fiat currency is no measure at all.

NO CONGRESSIONAL SOLUTION UNDER FIAT MONEY

History demonstrates that neither Congress nor anybody authorized by it can ever be trusted to maintain a stable, fiat dollar. It is far easier for the legislature—especially at the federal level, far removed from local restraints—to enact budgets that require deficit spending than it is to restrain or reject the multifarious and powerful pressures for enormous waste. The members of Congress love, above all else, their power to give away money: for that is the road to self-perpetuation in office. The voice of the taxpayer—working himself into exhaustion in order to pay government levies—is only a whisper on the distant wind, but the roar of those demanding gratuities and enormous profits at government expense are like the thunder of many Niagaras in the politician's ear. Furthermore, those who receive such gifts are the very ones who supply the votes and the campaign funds which mean re-election—the aureate vision of the congressman.

When Francis Bacon, the Lord Verulam, the English writer and philosopher who was also an eminent judge, was charged with accepting bribes, his defense was that since he accepted gifts from both sides, the course of justice was not disturbed. In the good old days, the members of the English parliament, when preparing to vote on any important issue, sold their votes openly and in public view to agents who set up their tables within the legislative chamber itself. Today, bribery in America is not quite so blatant, but it is nevertheless almost as pervasive and decisive. Neither the Congress nor the judiciary represents the interests of the electorate, but of powerful forces which operate behind the scenes. They will give us Watergates, but they will not discuss the unconstitutionality of the Fed, the crimes committed by the Internal Revenue Service, or the enormous waste perpetrated by the Federal government.

Anyone who hopes, therefore, to stem inflation by appealing to Congress or to any agency established by it for redress, is indulging in daydreams. Neither Congress nor the Executive will ever voluntarily renounce or even curb their power to spend money so long as the income tax can be administered and so long as we have a "managed currency." Politicians and judges are persuaded that more votes are to be gained by giving away money than are lost by extracting it from the taxpayers or creating it by issuing fiat money.

For example, the Congress in debating the 1975 budget wavered between a figure of $295 and $305 billion, an increase of about $30 billion over the enormous amount of the previous year—a total so fantastic that it staggers the imagination. Even so, we read that the 1974 session had before it 450 bills which would have required a budget of $871 billion[7] and which, if enacted, could rise to $1 trillion, almost enough to consume the entire national income. The bureaucracy itself is now costing the taxpayers more than fifty times as much as it cost to operate the federal government in the Twenties.

Seemingly much encouraged by the excesses and the deficits of fiscal 1975, Congress determined that it would spend at least $350 billion—and perhaps $375 billion—in fiscal 1976, with a deficit of perhaps $75 billion and a result debt approaching $600 billion.

The fact is that the government has a deep vested interest in a fiat currency and inflation; for these confer upon it an unbridled power to spend, control, and perpetuate itself. Inflation is one of the most productive sources of the revenue it must have to perpetrate its offenses against the people; for, as prices and incomes rise, it collects an ever-increasing ratio of personal incomes in the form of taxes. For example, the family that earned $4,000 in 1925 paid no tax; but a comparable living standard in 1975, based on an income of $20,000, pays a federal income tax of about $3,000 and perhaps $5,000 in other taxes.

Labor hierarchies and banking oligarchies, in alliance with government bureaucrats, also claim their pounds of flesh: the former create perpetual careers for themselves by negotiating increased wages to compensate for inflation; and the latter now collect 12% instead of 6% on loans triple or quadruple the size necessary to finance homes in the Twenties.

Except for a very few, the members of Congress are the creatures of bribery, corruption, venality, and spendthrift waste—they are the servants of special interests and pressure groups; they are, in effect, the enemies of those who elect them to office and pay their salaries and munificent emoluments. The same is true of the federal judges who receive extremely generous compensation and are endowed with powers so awesome to protect their privileged positions that they constitute a major threat to our nation. Wherever the Constitution interferes with the purposes of judges and congressmen, they ignore it as if it did not exist.

The same powers that engineered the passage of the Federal Reserve Act will persuade or compel the members of Congress—on pain of political suicide—to do their bidding in the future, as they have in the past. And this will apply to any body of men placed in a position of power with regard to money, unless kept in leash by economic law; for they would be subject to every kind of influence and bribery that make the members of Congress the servants of the same evil forces. However, neither the bankers, nor Congress, nor any body of men, nor any force on earth can produce enough gold to make it worthless, or even to reduce its enduring value; but with the fiat dollar, we must expect that unit to purchase less and less in the market place as prices rise, year after year, month after month, in endless and dreary succession.

Well aware of these eternal truths, Jefferson declared that, since it is the nature of all government to destroy the liberties of its citizens, a revolution might be necessary every nineteen or twenty years; and he laid it down as an everlasting principle that must be observed in order to avoid tyranny that "In questions of power, then, let no more be heard of confidence in man, but let us bind him down from mischief by the chains of the Constitution."

CAN FIAT MONEY BE CONSTITUTIONAL?

Since the Constitution does not specifically prohibit the federal government from issuing fiat money, some have maintained that ART. I, Sec. 10, Par. 1 does not apply to the United States Treasury, but only to the states. However, while interpreting the Fourteenth Amendment in 1954, the Supreme Court declared: "In view of our decision that the Constitution prohibits the states from maintaining racially segregated public schools, it would be unthinkable that the same law would impose a lesser duty on the Federal government." (347 U.S.400.) This can only mean that the 14th Amendment not only makes the provisions of the Constitution applicable to the respective states—it also makes strictures placed upon them equally applicable to the central government. Pursuant to this decision, therefore, neither a state nor the federal government can make anything but gold and silver a legal tender for the payment of debts.

This fact has been acknowledged by the highest authority, at least insofar as our international obligations are concerned. When Roosevelt declared the dollar debased by more than 40% on January 31, 1934, the Philippine government had funds on deposit in the United States. The change in the value of the American dollar did not reduce this obligation; for on May 20, 1959, Congress authorized payment of $34,836,751 in gold dollars of pre-1933 weight and fineness. In another act, Congress admitted that our debts to the Panamanian government must be met in dollars of the same weight in standard gold as had existed when the treaty was executed.[8]

When it came to our own citizens, however, Congress decided to disregard the Constitution. We can only say that when the Supreme Court declared, on February 18, 1935, that domestic obligations need not be met in dollars of the same kind that existed when the contracts were signed, it violated and abrogated one of the basic provisions of the American Constitution; for this declares (ART. I, Sec. 10, Par. 1) that "No State shall . . . pass any . . . law impairing the Obligations of Contracts . . ." a restriction that applies with equal force to the central government and to every American citizen or corporation.

The Constitution states also that Congress shall have power "to coin Money, regulate the Value thereof, and of foreign Coin. . . ." Since to coin is, according to *Webster's Collegiate Dictionary,* "to make coins by stamping, convert metal into coins; mint," we know that this provision has nothing to do with any other process; however, by extension, this power, as we have shown elsewhere, includes the emission of currency so long as it is redeemable in coin. This power and mandate to mint money and regulate its value is conferred upon the federal legislature only; no one else may determine the weight and quality of metal in the monetary unit—which is the meaning of regulating the value thereof. This function may no more be delegated by Congress to anyone else than it may farm out the task of assessing and collecting taxes, or of declaring and waging war. Then, in ART. I, Sec. 10, Par. 1, the Constitution declares: "No State . . . shall make any Thing but gold and silver coin a Tender in Payment of debts. . . ."

Since it is inconceivable that two different kinds of legal tender could exist under the Constitution; since the states cannot make anything but gold and silver legal tender for the payment of debts, and since only the federal government can coin money and regulate the value thereof, it follows categorically that should the latter issue fiat money, this could not be authorized as legal tender for use in any state—a totally impossible situation.

It is a basic concept in all jurisprudence that the Supreme Court may not legislate, nor may it amend the Constitution—its function is only to interpret; however, it has a duty to strike down any law passed by Congress if it is in distinct violation of the Constitution. The high court itself has declared: "An unconstitutional law is not a law; it confers no rights; it imposes no duties; it affords no protection; it creates no offices; it is, in legal contemplation, as inoperative as though it had never been passed."⁹

On the question of redeemability, the Supreme Court has spoken in the most explicit terms. In *Bronson vs. Rhodes,* 74 U.S. 229, 247, 19 L. Ed. 141, it declared that "Lawful money of the United States" could be "only gold and silver coin, or that which by law is made its equivalent, so as to be exchangeable therefor at par and on demand, and does not include a currency which, though nominally exchangeable for coin at its face value, is not redeemable on demand."

INFLATION AND DEPRESSION AT ONCE

There are many who wonder why it is possible to have galloping inflation, unprecedented interest rates and growing depression at the same time. The answer, once we understand the operation of the Fed, is simple enough: since that body supplies almost unlimited funds for wasteful spending to the government which indulges, in addition, in a vast program of deficit spending; and when it reduced the reserve requirement in November, 1972, from 17 to 10, erosive inflation became inevitable. On the other hand, by manipulating interest rates through the FOMC, the Fed was able to increase them to confiscatory levels and fill the coffers of the financiers with untold billions, while destroying the buying power of the producer-consumers and making it virtually impossible for small business to survive. The crucial reason for the tight money and depression conditions of 1974–75 is the fact that the Fed increased reserve requirements to 18, thus reducing the lending power of the banks by almost 45% and compelling them to call loans totalling many billions.

THE DEVALUED GOLD DOLLAR

It is obvious that we cannot return to a 25- or even a 12-grain gold dollar: any attempt to do so would throw our economy into chaos, since all debts recently incurred would then be payable in currency worth several times the consideration on which they are based. For example, a home carrying a recently incurred mortgage of $25,000 would be required to repay the equivalent of perhaps $125,000 in terms of 1975 dollars.

We cannot undo the tragic events of forty years of mismanaged currency; but we can prevent the further erosion of the dollar, which, at the present rate of decline, could fall to a value of less than five cents in the foreseeable future. It is still possible to save this nation from the fate that has befallen every other which has embarked on the perilous pathways of monetary irresponsibility.

In short, we can still have a redeemable currency simply by obeying the constitutional mandates concerning money established by our Founding Fathers. We can do this by either of two principal methods: (1) by continuing the gold dollar at its present official status of 12.322 grains of gold, which can be done by exchanging approximately five Federal Reserve notes for one new United States dollar;* or (2) by issuing new notes redeemable in about two-and-a-half grains of gold exchangeable, dollar for dollar, for existing Federal Reserve notes. The new currency would, of course, be redeemable in gold upon demand; the new dollar would consist of whatever quantity and quality of metal that Congress might determine under its power to coin money and regulate the value thereof.

THE ULTIMATE EXPLOITATION

And so we conclude with Jefferson, von Mises, Bakewell, Greaves, the American Institute of Economic Research, and many others, that even as the gold standard gave us modern industry, economic freedom, and universal prosperity, so has its abolition brought misery and economic dislocation to our people, while making the international financiers the masters and virtual owners of the world, a situation which finds concrete

---

*If this solution were adopted, previously existing debts would be payable in a smaller number of dollars—possibly at the rate of 1 to 5.

expression and demonstration in the fact that the productive portion of the American people are now paying at least 50% of their earnings in direct and indirect taxes, and another 13–15% in interest—leaving them only about 35% of the wealth they create for the support of their own families. Never before in the history of mankind has legal robbery been perpetrated on a comparable scale.

It is true that American ingenuity has increased the productive capacity of our nation to a point where all useful citizens could be enjoying a much-increased and well-earned improvement in all living conditions. Are we going to admit that Marx was right when he declared that no system based on exploitation will ever permit its productive people an income larger than just enough to sustain a minimum standard of consumption—with nothing left over for the creation of an estate?

Like Solon of Athens in 594 B.C., we are dedicated to the proposition that this injustice must end; and we offer the contents of this book as our contribution toward the accomplishment of this objective.

Citations

1. 1956 *SA* 748, 749
2. 1973 *ib.* 666
3. 1956 *ib.* 430
4. 1973 *ib.* 456
5. Laughlin, *op. cit.* 222
6. 1973 *Annual Report* of Fed. 286
7. Arizona *Republic* of April 13, 1974
8. *13 Curious Errors, op. cit.* 27
9. *Norton vs. Shelly County*, 118 U.S. 442

PARTIAL BIBLIOGRAPHY

Adams, Silas Walter, *The Legalized Crime of Banking,* private publication, 1958

——*The United States Treasury System,* private, 1959

——*A Debtless Nation,* private, 1959

Allen, Gary, *None Dare Call It Conspiracy,* Concord, 1972

Anderson, Tom, *Silence is Not Golden—It's Yellow,* Western Islands, 1973

Annual Report, Board of Governors of the Federal Reserve System, published annually.

Bakewell, Paul, *Inflation in the United States,* Caxton, 1962

——*13 Curious Errors about Money,* Caxton, 1962

Beard, Charles, *Rise of American Civilization,* Macmillan, 1930

Beter, Peter, *The Conspiracy against the Dollar,* Braziller, 1973

Brittanica, Encyclopaedia, 1929 Edition

Browne, Harry, *How I Found Freedom in an Unfree World,* Macmillan, 1973

——*You Can Profit from the Monetary Crisis,* Macmillan, 1974

Chodorov, Frank, *The Income Tax: Root of All Evil,* Devin-Adair, 1954

Coogan, Gertrude, *The Money Creators,* Omni, 1971

Cook, Peter, *The Magic of Reserve Banking,* Monetary Science Institute, 1972

——*Capitalism Unmasked,* 1973

——*Constitutional Money,* 1973

Cooley, Marvin, *The Big Bluff,* private publication.

Dall, Curtis B., *My Exploited Father-in-Law,* Liberty Lobby, 1963

Diogenes, *The April Game,* Playboy Press, 1973

Dobslaw, William R., *Stay Tuned for the Next Depression,* private, 1973

Dwinnell, Olive Cushing, *The Story of Our Money,* Forum, 1946

Elsom, John R., *Lightning Over the Treasury Building,* Omni, 1961

Emry, Sheldon, *America without Debt, Crime, or War,* Lord's Covenant Church, 1970

Federal Reserve Act, The, Board of Governors of the Fed, 1971

Federal Reserve Structure and the Development of Monetary Policy, House Committee on Banking and Currency, 1971

Federal Reserve System, The, Its Purposes and Functions, Board of Governors of the Fed, éditions of 1939 and 1963

Federalist Papers, The, Everyman, 1910

Ferm, Jack S., and Schmitz, John Noel, *Money and Taxes,* Omni, 1973

Field, A. L., *All These Things,* Omni, 1963

Fisher, Irving, *The Instability of Gold,* Alexander Hamilton Institute, 1912

——*Stabilizing the Dollar,* Macmillan, 1920, 1925

——*The Money Illusion,* Adelphi, 1929

——*100% Money,* Adelphi, 1935

Franklin, Benjamin, *Memoirs,* Everyman, 1910

Friedman, Milton, and Schwarz, Anna Jacobson, *A Monetary*

History of the United States, 1867–1960, Princeton University Press, 1963

Glass, Carter, *Adventures in Constructive Finance,* Doubleday, 1927

Greaves, Percy L., Jr., *Understanding the Dollar Crisis,* Western Islands, 1973

Grem, June, *Karl Marx, Capitalist,* Enterprise Publications, 1972

Groseclose, Elgin Earl, *Money and Man,* Univ. of Oklahoma Press, 1934; Frederick Unger, 1967

——*Money, the Human Conflict,* Univ. of Oklahoma Press, 1935

——*The Decay of Money,* Institute for Monetary Research, 1962

——*Fifty Years of Managed Money,* Macmillan, 1965

Grubak, Olive and Jan, *The Guernsey Experiment,* Omni, 1969

Hazlitt, Henry, *The Failure of the New Economics,* Nostrand, 1959

——*What You Should Know about Inflation,* Conservative Book Club, 1963

Historical Statistics of the United States, 1789–1945, U.S. Department of Commerce, 1949

Holdridge, Herbert C., *How to Gain Freedom from Slavery,* Holdridge Foundation, 1961

Hoover, Herbert, *Memoirs,* 3 Vols., Macmillan, 1951–52

House, Edward Mandell, *The Intimate Papers,* 4 Vols., Houghton–Mifflin, 1926

Jefferson, Thomas, *The Writings of,* 4 Vols., Grey and Brown, 1930

——*The Writings of,* 7 Vols., H. W. Derby, 1861

——*The Writings of,* 20 Vols., Library Edition, Jefferson Memorial Association, 1903

——*Basic Writings,* Willey Book Co., 1944

Johnson, Brian, *The Politics of Money,* McGraw-Hill, 1970

Kenan, H.S., *The Federal Reserve Bank,* Noontide, 1967

Keynes, John Maynard, *The Economic Consequences of the Peace,* Harcourt, Brace, 1920

——*A Treatise on Money,* Macmillan, 1930

——*The General Theory of Employment, Interest, and Money,* Harcourt, Brace, 1936

——*The Collected Writings,* 14 Vols., Macmillan, different dates.

Kitson, Arthur, *The Fraudulent Standard,* Omni, 1972

Krefetz, Gerald, *The Dying Dollar,* Playboy Press, 1972

Laughlin, J. Lawrence, *The Federal Reserve Act, Its Origin and Problems,* Macmillan, 1933

Lerner, Abba P. *Flation,* Quadrangle, 1972

Lindbergh, Charles A. Jr., *The Wartime Journals,* Harcourt, Brace, Jovanovich, 1970

Lindbergh, Charles A., Sr., *Banking and Currency and the Money Trust,* Omni, 1971

——*Your Country at War,* Omni, 1971

——*The Economic Pinch,* Omni, 1968

Lundberg, Ferdinand, *America's Sixty Families,* Vanguard Press, 1937

——*The Rich and the Super-Rich,* Lyle Stuart, 1968

McFadden, Louis, T., *Collective Speeches,* Omni, 1970

McGeer, G. G., *The Conquest of Poverty,* Omni, 1967

Machiavelli, Nicolo, *The Prince,* Everyman edition, 1916

Meek, Paul, *Open Market Operations,* New York Federal Reserve Bank, 1969

Money Facts, House Committee on Banking and Currency, 1964

Mullins, Eustace, *The Federal Reserve Conspiracy,* Omni, 1971

Norburn, Charles S. and Russell L., *Mankind's Greatest Step,* Vantage, 1971

Owen, Robert L., *The Federal Reserve Act,* Century Co., 1919

Peterson, Merrill, *The Jefferson Image and the American Mind,* Oxford University Press, 1963

Poperin, Joan van, *The Unfinished Business—Abolish the Federal Reserve,* private publication.

Popp, Dr. Edward E., *Money, Bona Fide or Non-Bona Fide,* Wisconsin Education Fund, 1970

Preston, Robert L., *How to Prepare for the Coming Crash,* Hawkes, 1972

——*Wake-Up America,* Hawkes, 1972

Primer on Money, A, House Committee on Banking and Currency, 1964

Rhodesia and World Report, May, 1974

Sennholz, Hans F., *Deflation or Gold Standard,* The Constitutional Alliance of Lansing, Mich., 1969

Snow, John Howland, *The Case of Tyler Kent,* Long House, 1965

Snyder, Leslie, *Why Gold?,* Exposition Press, 1973

Solzhenitsyn, Alexandr I., *The Gulag Archipelago,* Harper and Row, 1973

Spahr, Walter E., *The Fallacies of Professor Irving Fisher's 100% Money Proposal,* Farrar and Rinehart, 1938

Statistical Abstract, United States Department of Commerce, published annually.

Stern, Philip M., *The Rape of the Taxpayer,* Vintage, 1974

Stone, Willis E., *Where the Money Went,* Fact Sheet, 1971

Tansill, Charles Callan, *Back Door to War,* Henry Regnery, 1952

Theobald, Rear Adm. R. A., *The Final Secret of Pearl Harbor,* Devin-Adair, 1954

Van Doren, Carl, *Benjamin Franklin,* Viking Press, 1935

Vennard, W. B., *Conquest or Consent,* Forum, 1965

von Mises, Ludwig, *The Theory of Money,* first published in Austria in 1912; translated into English and published in England in 1923; published by Yale University Press, 1953

——*Human Action,* Yale University Press, 1963

Voorhis, Jerry, *Out of Debt, Out of Danger,* Devin-Adair, 1943

——*The Strange Case of Richard Milhous Nixon,* Popular Library, 1972

Warburg, Paul Moritz, *The Federal Reserve System,* 2 Vols., Macmillan, 1930

Why Gold? The American Institute for Economic Research, 1963.

Willis, Dr. Henry Parker, *The Federal Reserve System,* Ronald Press, 1923

INDEX